TO:

_____

FROM:

_____

DATE:

_____

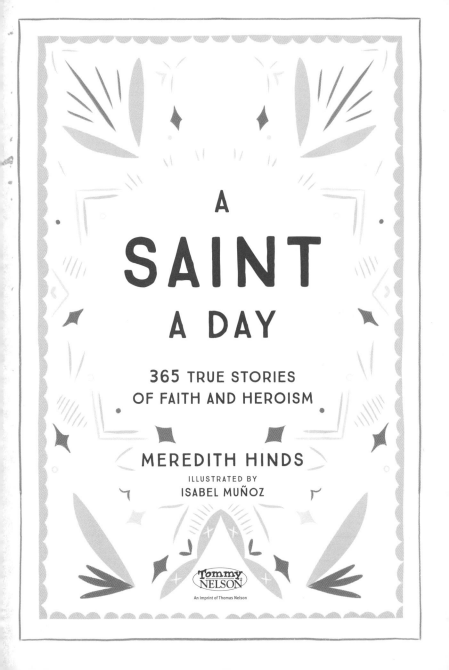

A SAINT A DAY

365 TRUE STORIES OF FAITH AND HEROISM

MEREDITH HINDS

ILLUSTRATED BY
ISABEL MUÑOZ

Tommy
NELSON

An Imprint of Thomas Nelson

CONTENTS

INTRODUCTION

The word *saint* refers to all Christians, but this book focuses on Saints with a capital S—those who have been officially recognized by the Catholic Church. To be recognized as a Saint, a few things must happen. First, when a righteous person dies, witnesses provide evidence to the Catholic Church of the person's love for Jesus. The person's letters, diaries, and books are studied. If the Church believes there is evidence to prove he or she lived a holy life, the person is declared a "Servant of God." Then, as more evidence is presented, he or she becomes known as "Venerable," then "Blessed," and finally as "Saint." For clarity, anyone in this book who is in this process is noted as being "on track to become a Saint."

Saints may have multiple names, dates, and locations associated with their life. These devotions use only one name to refer to each Saint, include each Saint's approximate lifespan, and mention only the locations relevant to the devotion. Locations are presented as they were known during the Saint's lifetime. A modern name of their location is included if applicable. Many, but not all, devotions are ordered by the Saints' feast days. The devotion dates that do not match the feast days are marked with an asterisk by the devotion date (e.g., January 3*).

The life of each Saint inspires us to love Jesus the way that each Saint loved Him. All Saints loved Jesus with everything they had. As you read their stories, remember this: all people (including you!) are called to give Jesus *everything*.

MARY, MOTHER OF GOD

FIRST CENTURY • GALILEE (MODERN-DAY ISRAEL)

HERE AM I

Mary said, "Here am I, the servant of the Lord; let it be with me according to your word." Then the angel departed from her.

LUKE 1:38

Mary was amazed at what she was seeing and hearing. First, an angel named Gabriel appeared right in front of her. Next, Gabriel told her that she would have a baby. Then Gabriel said that her baby would be the Savior of the world. Mary's jaw dropped. How could any of this be true? She wasn't even married! Gabriel finished his greeting by telling Mary that her cousin, who was old enough to be her grandmother, was pregnant with a baby too, even though she was too old to have children. *Well,* Mary thought, *if anyone can do the impossible, it's God!* Mary said to Gabriel, "Here am I, the servant of the Lord." She was saying to God, "Yes! Yes to all of the impossible things You want to do through me!"

> MARY WAS LIKELY VERY YOUNG WHEN SHE HAD JESUS, POSSIBLY AS YOUNG AS FOURTEEN.

Jesus, help me say yes to You, just like Your mother, Mary.

SAINT BASIL THE GREAT

329–379 • CAPPADOCIA (MODERN-DAY TURKEY)

NOTHING WOULD CHANGE HIS MIND

For I am convinced that neither death, nor life, nor angels, nor rulers, nor things present, nor things to come, nor powers, nor height, nor depth, nor anything else in all creation, will be able to separate us from the love of God in Christ Jesus our Lord.

ROMANS 8:38–39

Basil worked in the Church, teaching about Jesus. During Basil's life, some leaders and teachers began to teach a terrible lie: they taught that Jesus was not fully God. Maybe Jesus was like God, these false teachers argued, but He certainly wasn't God. Basil knew the truth: Jesus *was* and *is* fully God. Basil stood up to these teachers and proudly said Jesus is God, but they were angry and threatened to kill him. Calmly, Basil told these false teachers that they could take his possessions, his home, and his life. All he wanted was God. False teachers could do nothing to change his mind.

SAINT BASIL THE GREAT'S OLDER SISTER, SAINT MACRINA THE YOUNGER, ENCOURAGED HIM TO LEAVE HIS LAW CAREER BEHIND AND DEDICATE HIS LIFE TO JESUS.

Jesus, help me to be like Saint Basil the Great, defending the truth about You.

SAINT TELESPHORUS

UNKNOWN–136 • ROMAN EMPIRE (MODERN-DAY ITALY)

GLORY TO GOD

Glory to God in the highest heaven, and on earth
peace among those whom he favors!

LUKE 2:14

During Christmas services, people gather in churches to sing about the miracle of Jesus' birth. On Easter Sunday, churches all over the world are full of people celebrating Jesus' resurrection. How long have Christians been singing about His birth and celebrating His resurrection? For almost two thousand years! Telesphorus, who served as a pope, established traditions less than a hundred years after Jesus died, rose, and returned to heaven. Telesphorus told people to sing the same beautiful words that the angels had sung to the shepherds that Christmas night: *Gloria in excelsis Deo*, which means "Glory to God in the highest!" He offered Sunday as the day to celebrate Jesus' resurrection. With these celebrations, Telesphorus reminded Christians of the beautiful truths of Jesus' birth, death, and resurrection.

> SAINT TELESPHORUS WAS THE EIGHTH ROMAN BISHOP TO SUCCEED SAINT PETER THE APOSTLE, THE FIRST LEADER OF THE CHURCH.

*Jesus, I will remember Your birth and resurrection with
song and celebration, just as Saint Telesphorus did.*

SAINT ELIZABETH ANN SETON

1774–1821 · THE UNITED STATES

LOVE IS STRONGER

The sting of death is sin, and the power of sin is the law. But thanks be to God, who gives us the victory through our Lord Jesus Christ.

1 CORINTHIANS 15:56–57

While she was still a young wife and mother, Elizabeth Ann Seton lost her husband to a terrible disease called tuberculosis. Her children were fatherless, and she was without a husband. Her sorrow was overwhelming, but it did not consume her. She turned to Jesus. With His strength, Elizabeth Ann Seton started helping people who were hurting in the same way her family was hurting. She created a community for women who did not have husbands or families. This community of women helped build and run orphanages, which are homes for children who have no parents. In Elizabeth's life, the love and hope of Jesus was stronger than the sting of death.

> SAINT ELIZABETH ANN SETON WAS THE FIRST AMERICAN-BORN PERSON TO BE CALLED A SAINT.

> *Jesus, help me turn to You when life is hard, just as Saint Elizabeth Ann Seton did. Show me how to keep helping others, even when I am sad.*

JANUARY 5

SAINT JOHN NEUMANN

1811–1860 • BOHEMIA (MODERN-DAY CZECHIA) AND THE UNITED STATES

GO FROM YOUR COUNTRY

Now the LORD said to Abram, "Go from your country and your kindred and your father's house to the land that I will show you."

GENESIS 12:1

John Neumann was born in Eastern Europe. As John grew up, he heard the stories of people who had left his country to go to America. In America, they were called immigrants. These immigrants were often poor and homesick. They needed the care and support of someone who understood their country and their history. After he became a priest, John left everything he knew to go to America to help the immigrants. He built schools, orphanages, churches, and hospitals. John had left his own home to go to a strange place and help other people feel at home there.

WHENEVER SAINT JOHN NEUMANN WAS TOLD THAT POOR PEOPLE USED THE MONEY HE GAVE THEM FOR FUN INSTEAD OF FOOD, HE WAS NEVER BOTHERED. HE JUST SAID, "I GAVE THE MONEY TO GOD!"

Jesus, help me love people who are far away from their homes.

SAINT ANDRÉ BESSETTE

1845–1937 · CANADA

PRAY WITHOUT CEASING

Rejoice always, pray without ceasing, give thanks in all circumstances; for this is the will of God in Christ Jesus for you.

1 THESSALONIANS 5:16–18

André Bessette knew what it was like to need prayers. He had been sick since he was born, and both his parents died by the time he was twelve years old. André was so frail that it was difficult for him to find work. But he always found time for prayer. He joined a religious community, performing the tasks he could while keeping up his good attitude and staying devoted to prayer. Soon, sick and hurting people started coming to him from all around the world to ask for his prayers. André always told them that he was not able to heal them and pointed them toward prayer instead. André spent as many as eight hours a day talking to people who asked for his help! Many of these people were healed by God.

SAINT ANDRÉ BESSETTE WAS SO WEAK WHEN HE WAS BORN THAT HIS PARENTS WERE AFRAID HE WOULD DIE. BUT HE LIVED TO BE NINETY-ONE YEARS OLD.

Jesus, I know that You hear me when I pray. Help me to love prayer, just as Saint André Bessette did.

SAINT RAYMOND OF PEÑAFORT

1175–1275 • SPAIN AND ITALY

GOD'S ORDER

God is a God not of disorder but of peace.

1 CORINTHIANS 14:33

Imagine opening a board game and reading the instructions. Then, just before the first turn of the game, another set of instructions falls out of the same box. These instructions are about the same game but have completely different rules! How confusing. That confusion is what Saint Raymond of Peñafort encountered but on a much bigger scale. Raymond was passionate about learning the law and history of the Catholic Church. But Raymond had a problem: some of the laws conflicted with each other! The bishop asked Raymond to solve this problem. Saint Raymond was able to dedicate his mind to the task. He read through the laws and brought order to them, working with other priests as he went. After Raymond finished his work, everyone could read the same set of rules and laws.

> SAINT RAYMOND OF PEÑAFORT LIVED AT THE SAME TIME AS SAINT THOMAS AQUINAS AND WROTE LETTERS TO HIM (JAN. 28).

*God, You love order, and Your order brings me
peace. Help me understand Your ways.*

SAINT ANGELA OF FOLIGNO

1248–1309 • ITALY

MORE THAN GOLD

*Truly I love your commandments more
than gold, more than fine gold.*

PSALM 119:127

Angela loved money, beautiful clothes, and large houses. This was a problem. Not because money, clothes, and houses are bad, but because Angela loved these things more than she loved God. If someone gave Angela a choice between God's love and more gold, she would walk away with the gold. After many years of living this way, Angela realized how sad her life really was. It looked good from the outside, but on the inside, she felt miserable. During the second half of her life, Angela chose God over wealth. She even wrote a book that helped others understand Him and His love, which is greater than all the wealth in the world.

> SAINT ANGELA OF FOLIGNO WAS SO FULL OF WISDOM THAT PEOPLE CALLED HER THE "TEACHER OF THEOLOGIANS." (A THEOLOGIAN IS AN EXPERT ON RELIGION AND GOD.)

*Jesus, I want to love You more than I love
anything else. Help me value You more than
things, just as Saint Angela of Foligno did.*

SAINT ADRIAN OF CANTERBURY

UNKNOWN–710 • AFRICA, ITALY, FRANCE, AND ENGLAND

WAIT FOR THE LORD

Wait for the LORD; be strong, and let your heart
take courage; wait for the LORD!

PSALM 27:14

Adventure awaited Adrian. Pope Vitalian told Adrian to move from his home in Italy all the way to England. When he arrived, Adrian would help lead the church, build new churches, and teach people about Jesus. There was only one problem. During his trip, a powerful mayor in France learned of Adrian and was convinced that he was a spy. The mayor thought that Adrian was up to no good, and he put Adrian in prison. Instead of becoming angry and blaming the mayor, Adrian waited. His patience paid off. After two whole years, the mayor realized that Adrian wasn't a spy after all and allowed him to leave and begin his work.

> SAINT ADRIAN OF CANTERBURY WAS BORN IN AFRICA BUT SPENT THIRTY-NINE YEARS IN ENGLAND.

Jesus, it's hard to wait. Please help me be patient like Saint Adrian of Canterbury. I know my future is in Your hands.

JANUARY 10

SAINT GREGORY OF NYSSA

335–395 • CAPPADOCIA (MODERN-DAY TURKEY)

TAKEN CAPTIVE

"Blessed are you when people revile you and persecute you and utter all kinds of evil against you falsely on my account."

MATTHEW 5:11

A few hundred years after Jesus died, Gregory served as a bishop in Nyssa. He taught people, built churches, and solved problems. Unfortunately, some people were jealous of Gregory's important role as bishop because they had hoped to be picked for the office themselves. They made up lies about Gregory, then captured him and treated him terribly. He escaped his captors but then had to wander from place to place to keep from being captured again. Finally, the envious people in his town lost their power, and Gregory returned to his church to serve the people again.

> SAINT GREGORY OF NYSSA WROTE A BOOK CALLED *THE LIFE OF MOSES,* WHICH TAUGHT IMPORTANT CHRISTIAN LESSONS BASED ON MOSES' LIFE.

Jesus, if others say bad things about me, help me remember what You say about me.

BLESSED WILLIAM CARTER

1548–1584 • ENGLAND

SPEAK THE TRUTH

Speak the truth to one another.

ZECHARIAH 8:16

William promised himself that he would write the truth about Jesus, even when he was told to stop writing it—or else. "If you write about Jesus that way and publish it," the authorities warned, "we will put you in prison. We might even execute you!" William didn't care what they said. He kept writing anyway. One night they broke into his house and found what they called evidence of his guilt—garments for priests and more books that affirmed what William believed. He spent a year and a half in prison for these crimes and was eventually condemned to die. William's devotion to God and the truth encouraged other Christians to keep the faith.

> BLESSED WILLIAM CARTER WORKED AS A PRINTER, A JOB THAT HE HELD FROM A YOUNG AGE.

Jesus, help me speak nothing but the truth about You, no matter the cost.

BLESSED WILLIAM CARTER IS ON TRACK TO BECOME A SAINT.

SAINT MARGUERITE BOURGEOYS

1620–1700 · FRANCE AND CANADA

QUICK TO SERVE

"For the Son of Man came not to be served but to serve, and to give his life a ransom for many."

MARK 10:45

At twenty years old, Marguerite loved God so much that she dedicated herself to serving others for His glory. She said she would go anywhere for Him, and her chance to prove it came when she was invited to move from France to Canada. She moved all the way across an ocean to serve God! In this new world, she built schools and helped families. As she traveled around the new colony to help anyone in need, Marguerite often thought of the way Jesus' mother, Mary, went quickly to see Elizabeth, her cousin. Marguerite wanted to be just as quick to believe and serve God as Mary was.

SAINT MARGUERITE BOURGEOYS HELPED MANY YOUNG PEOPLE FIND HUSBANDS AND WIVES IN THE NEW CANADIAN COLONY, SO THEY NICKNAMED HER THE "MOTHER OF THE COLONY."

Jesus, I want to be quick to serve You, just like Saint Marguerite Bourgeoys.

JANUARY 13

SAINT HILARY OF POITIERS

315–368 • GAUL (MODERN-DAY FRANCE)

THE TRUTH

Jesus said to him, "I am the way, and the truth, and the life."

JOHN 14:6

Hilary loved to read. He read everything he could find, looking for answers to some big questions: Who are we? Why are we here? Who is God? One day he read copies of the Old Testament and the Gospels and found the answers to his questions. Hilary read that Jesus is the Savior of the world—and Hilary believed this immediately. The truth was so good that Hilary needed to sing about it! He wrote some of the first hymns of the Western world, based on the beautiful truths he read in the stories of Moses and of Jesus, as a way to spread the gospel around the globe.

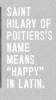

SAINT HILARY OF POITIERS'S NAME MEANS "HAPPY" IN LATIN.

Jesus, You are the Truth. I know more about You by reading Your Word, the Bible. Help me read Your Word and love it, just as Saint Hilary of Poitiers did.

SAINT GREGORY NAZIANZEN

329–390 • CAPPADOCIA (MODERN-DAY TURKEY)

THREE IN ONE

"Go therefore and make disciples of all nations, baptizing them in the name of the Father and of the Son and of the Holy Spirit."

MATTHEW 28:19

God gave Gregory the gift of teaching—and he was amazing at it. Gregory explained confusing truths about God in ways that people understood. After hearing Gregory teach, people walked away saying, "Oh! That's what God meant all along!" Gregory taught people many wonderful truths, including the truth about the Trinity. God is one God but three persons—God the Father, God the Son, and God the Holy Spirit. Gregory had enemies who couldn't believe this truth. They wanted Gregory to stop teaching, but he didn't give up. He taught the truth about our great God, the one God in three persons, for his whole life.

ONE EASTER, SAINT GREGORY NAZIANZEN'S ENEMIES CAME AND ATTACKED HIM, RIGHT IN THE MIDDLE OF THE CHURCH SERVICE! HE WAS WOUNDED, BUT HE LIVED.

Jesus, teach me the truth about the Trinity. I want to know You more.

SAINT PAUL THE HERMIT

228–341 • EGYPT

BREAD FROM HEAVEN

When the Israelites saw it, they said to one another, "What is it?" For they did not know what it was. Moses said to them, "It is the bread that the LORD has given you to eat."

EXODUS 16:15

When he was young, Paul escaped from people who wanted him dead. Why did they want him dead? Because Paul was a Christian. Christians were hated so much during Paul's lifetime that people often brought them before leaders who hated them and had them killed. Many Christians had to run away—far away—to survive. Paul ran all the way to the desert. As the story goes, God provided for Paul, giving him enough food and water to survive. He drank water from a nearby stream, and a raven brought him a loaf of bread each day. In all of his time alone, Paul prayed constantly to God.

> EVENTUALLY, SAINT ANTHONY OF EGYPT (JAN. 17) FOUND SAINT PAUL THE HERMIT, AND THE TWO INSTANTLY BECAME FRIENDS.

Jesus, You are in control. Help me have faith that You will provide for all my needs, even on days when I'm alone and afraid.

SAINT BERARD

UNKNOWN–1220 • ITALY AND MOROCCO

COURAGE LIVES ON

My flesh and my heart may fail, but God is the
strength of my heart and my portion forever.

PSALM 73:26

Berard and his friends chose a dangerous mission. They left their homes in Italy to go preach in lands where the truth about Jesus was both unfamiliar and unwelcome. Everywhere Berard and his friends went, they were treated badly, and their message was not accepted. But they didn't give up. When they eventually went to Morocco, they were killed by a leader who had had enough of their preaching. As far as they knew, no one came to know Jesus as a result of their mission. Not even one person! This sounds like a terrible failure, but did they really fail? Their courage inspired people back home in Italy and beyond, who would later do amazing things for God.

> SAINT ANTHONY OF PADUA (JUNE 13) WAS INSPIRED BY SAINT BERARD AND HIS COMPANIONS TO GIVE HIS LIFE FOR THE GOOD NEWS.

Jesus, help me remember that You have the whole story in mind. What looks like failure may be a new beginning. Give me the courage to share the good news like Saint Berard.

SAINT ANTHONY OF EGYPT

251–356 • EGYPT

QUIET TIME

I waited patiently for the LORD; he inclined to me and heard my cry.

PSALM 40:1

Anthony lived in the desert. There were almost no people, hardly any buildings, and very few ways to get food. So why live there? Anthony wanted to know God and see God. Anthony left all of life's distractions behind him, and in the silence of the desert, God's answers were clear to Anthony. Anthony wasn't concerned about finding the best-tasting food or doing the most fun activity, so he concentrated on hearing God's voice. God revealed to Anthony that Christians are fighting a battle against the devil. Christians find strength by getting rid of distractions and turning to God, just as Saint Anthony did.

WE KNOW ABOUT SAINT ANTHONY OF EGYPT'S LIFE BECAUSE SAINT ATHANASIUS (MAY 2) WROTE A BOOK ABOUT HIM.

Jesus, help me turn to You instead of distractions.

SERVANT OF GOD MOTHER MARY LANGE

1784–1882 • THE UNITED STATES

ASK FOR THE IMPOSSIBLE

Do not worry about anything, but in everything by prayer and supplication with thanksgiving let your requests be made known to God.

PHILIPPIANS 4:6

Mary Lange met other people's needs—even when the needs were great. Mary lived during the 1800s in America. In many places, White children could go to school, and Black children couldn't. Mary saw this pattern across her city, and Mary, who was Black, wanted Black children to be able to attend school too. She wanted to give them that education herself. But in the 1800s, Black people didn't usually become priests or teachers. But Mary trusted that God would make a way for her. Mary spent her life, her work, and her prayers on creating a school that welcomed Black students and teachers. God made Mary's impossible school possible.

> IN ADDITION TO STARTING A SCHOOL, SERVANT OF GOD MOTHER MARY LANGE ESTABLISHED AN ORPHANAGE AND A WIDOW'S HOME.

Jesus, remind me to ask You for the impossible,
just like Servant of God Mother Mary Lange.

SERVANT OF GOD MOTHER MARY LANGE IS ON TRACK TO BECOME A SAINT.

JANUARY 19*

SAINT FABIAN

UNKNOWN–250 • ROMAN EMPIRE (MODERN-DAY ITALY)

SIGN OF THE DOVE

The LORD said to Samuel, . . . "The LORD does not see as mortals see; they look on the outward appearance, but the LORD looks on the heart."

1 SAMUEL 16:7

In the year 236, the Church in Rome needed a new leader, or pope. Priests and bishops gathered to choose the new leader. Many important people insisted that they should be chosen. "I have land!" one would say. "I have money!" said another. Fabian came to the meeting, but he was not important. He came to help choose a leader, not to become one. But as the story goes, a beautiful white dove flew down and landed on Fabian's head during the middle of the argument. Everyone stopped talking and stared, then chose him as the new pope. Fabian must have thought, *Me? I'm not important! I don't have money or power to give!* But God doesn't need our power and our money. God works wonders through people who give their hearts to Him.

WHEN A CRUEL NEW ROMAN EMPEROR, DECIUS, STARTED PERSECUTING CHRISTIANS, SAINT FABIAN HAD THE COURAGE TO SPEAK OUT AGAINST HIM.

Jesus, You see my heart. Give me a heart full of love for You.

JANUARY 20

SAINT SEBASTIAN

256–288 • ROMAN EMPIRE (MODERN-DAY ITALY)

THE ULTIMATE SACRIFICE

"For those who want to save their life will lose it, and those who lose
their life for my sake, and for the sake of the gospel, will save it."

MARK 8:35

A thousand years after he died, artists still painted pictures of
Sebastian. These paintings showed a young man pierced by many
arrows. The paintings are beautiful, but the truth is that historians don't
really know how Sebastian died. But they do know
Sebastian was a martyr: a person killed for believing that Jesus is the Savior of the world. Many of
the saints in this book are also martyrs, just like
Sebastian. Dying for God can be a beautiful act
of service to Him, even more beautiful than paintings and songs. All the martyrs in history imitate

> BECAUSE OF THE
> STORY ABOUT THE
> ARROWS, SAINT
> SEBASTIAN IS THE
> PATRON SAINT
> OF ARCHERS
> AND ATHLETES.

Jesus, who gave His life for us on the cross as a sacrifice to God. As
the story goes, Sebastian lived through the attack with the arrows. He
kept on telling others about Jesus. Later, he died for his faith in Jesus.

*Jesus, Your story is so amazing. Thank You
for the courage of the martyrs.*

SAINT AGNES OF ROME

291–304 • ROMAN EMPIRE (MODERN-DAY ITALY)

ONLY JESUS

They rejoiced that they were considered worthy to
suffer dishonor for the sake of the name.

ACTS 5:41

Imagine a beautiful girl trapped in a dark and terrible prison. Is she crying and scared? Is she shaking with cold and fear? No, she's happy! Agnes was happy in prison; she glowed with joy! Why? Because of her love for Jesus. Agnes grew up in a wealthy home, and she could have had anything she wanted. But she didn't want wealth and marriage; she wanted only to serve and to love her Savior. Many men proposed to Agnes, but she always refused them, even though they promised a life of comfort and ease. "I only want Jesus," Agnes would tell them. These men became angry and reported her faith to the government, and Agnes was imprisoned and killed. Agnes died calmly and peacefully, knowing that she was headed for heaven.

IN PAINTINGS OF SAINT AGNES OF ROME, SHE'S OFTEN SHOWN HOLDING A LAMB.

*Jesus, I want to love You more than I love anyone
in this world, just as Saint Agnes of Rome did.*

SAINT VINCENT OF ZARAGOSSA

UNKNOWN-304 · SPAIN

SO MUCH COURAGE

With the LORD on my side I do not fear. What can mortals do to me?

PSALM 118:6

Vincent lived in a time and place where Christianity was illegal. Christians were hunted by the leaders of their cities, and they often had to hide for their safety. Vincent was captured and tortured. His jailers told him that the torture would stop if Vincent said that Jesus wasn't real. But Vincent never said anything against Jesus. The emperor who ordered that Vincent be tortured backed down. Then the emperor said that if Vincent would give up only the sacred writings about Jesus, the torture would stop. Vincent could simply say that writings about Jesus were not true. Again, Vincent said no. Because these sacred writings were defended by Christians like Vincent such a long time ago, we still have them today!

> SAINT VINCENT OF ZARAGOSSA SHOWED SO MUCH COURAGE IN THE FACE OF TORTURE THAT HIS JAILER CONVERTED TO CHRISTIANITY.

Jesus, help me stand up for You and Your Word,
just like Saint Vincent of Zaragossa.

JANUARY 23

SAINT MARIANNE COPE

1838–1918 · GERMANY AND THE UNITED STATES

MISSION OF MERCY

As he entered a village, ten lepers approached him. Keeping their distance, they called out, saying, "Jesus, Master, have mercy on us!"

LUKE 17:12–13

God called Marianne to a place that no one else wanted to go—a place where the people suffered from a terrible disease that made their bodies weak and gave their skin sores. In the Gospels, Jesus and His disciples called this disease leprosy, and the same disease is now known as Hansen's disease. Where were people suffering from Hansen's disease? Hawaii! Hawaii sounds like paradise, but Marianne headed to Hawaii for a mission of mercy, not for a vacation. She cared for desperately sick people whom no one else wanted to touch. She worked with people who suffered from Hansen's disease for more than thirty years. Marianne's story sounds like she lived a thousand years ago, but Marianne died just over a hundred years ago.

> SAINT MARIANNE COPE NEVER CAUGHT HANSEN'S DISEASE, MOST LIKELY BECAUSE HER PROCEDURES FOCUSED ON CLEANLINESS AND SAFETY.

Jesus, thank You for Saint Marianne Cope's courage.
Give me the courage and mercy to be kind to
the people no one else wants to be around.

SAINT PAUL

FIRST CENTURY · SYRIA

BLINDING LIGHT

He asked, "Who are you, Lord?" The reply came,
"I am Jesus, whom you are persecuting."

ACTS 9:5

Paul hated followers of Jesus. Those people, Paul said, took the truth and twisted it. Those people claimed that the Savior of the world was a carpenter from an unimportant city. *The Savior is supposed to be a king, not a carpenter*, Paul thought. Paul knew that Christians believed this man, Jesus, had died and risen and returned to heaven. *The Savior isn't supposed to die*, Paul thought. *He is supposed to conquer the world.* Paul wanted anyone who loved and followed Jesus to be killed. He did some of that work himself. One day, on his way to find more followers of Jesus, Paul was blinded by a bright light from heaven.

> SAINT PAUL WROTE MUCH OF THE NEW TESTAMENT IN THE FORM OF LETTERS TO CHURCHES HE HELPED BUILD.

It was Jesus Himself calling Paul into His service. From that day forward, Paul believed the impossible—the carpenter from nowhere was the Messiah.

*Jesus, help me see the light and know the truth,
just as You helped Saint Paul believe!*

SAINT FRANCIS DE SALES

1567–1622 · FRANCE

A CALM AND GENTLE WORD

A soft answer turns away wrath, but a harsh word stirs up anger.

PROVERBS 15:1

Francis knew that loud arguments and big speeches convinced no one—they just made people angry. He lived during a time of great division among the followers of Jesus in France. What was the right way to worship God? People fought and argued over this question, going so far as to steal books and destroy churches! Instead of arguing, Francis invited people into his home, where he talked to them. Calmly and gently, he explained his thoughts. He wrote down his views and published them so that people could read the words for themselves and think over them calmly. He led people to agreement, not by forcing them or scaring them but by inviting them into conversations.

SAINT FRANCIS DE SALES'S WRITINGS SPREAD ALL OVER FRANCE. EVEN PEOPLE IN PRISON DISCUSSED THEM TOGETHER.

Jesus, help me speak calmly and gently,
even when my feelings are strong.

SAINTS TIMOTHY AND TITUS

FIRST CENTURY • LYSTRA (MODERN-DAY TURKEY) (TIMOTHY)
FIRST CENTURY • GREECE (TITUS)

BETTER TOGETHER

*Though one might prevail against another, two will
withstand one. A threefold cord is not quickly broken.*

ECCLESIASTES 4:12

God gave Paul a huge task. He sent Paul to share the news about Jesus with the Gentiles—that is, anyone who wasn't Jewish. Paul couldn't do it alone. Timothy and Titus, both of whom were Gentiles, became two of Paul's trustworthy companions.

In Paul's letters, he wrote about Timothy and Titus, thanking God for them and putting whole churches in their care. Timothy and Titus visited and encouraged churches, even though they were threatened by people who hated Jesus. Together, Timothy, Titus, and Paul spread the word about Jesus around the world.

> THE NEW TESTAMENT BOOKS 1 AND 2 TIMOTHY AND TITUS WERE LETTERS WRITTEN FROM SAINT PAUL TO SAINTS TIMOTHY AND TITUS, RESPECTIVELY.

*Jesus, three can accomplish more than one
person can alone! Please show me whom I am
supposed to team up with to serve You.*

SAINT ANGELA MERICI

1474–1540 • ITALY

NEED TO SERVE

In all this I have given you an example that by such work we must support the weak, remembering the words of the Lord Jesus, for he himself said, "It is more blessed to give than to receive."

ACTS 20:35

When Angela returned to her hometown, she didn't like what she saw. Angela had been orphaned ten years before and had grown up in her uncle's house, where she enjoyed reading, learning, and growing in her faith. When Angela came back to her town as an adult, she saw that the young girls of her town were just left to themselves throughout the day. These girls needed direction and the opportunity to read and to pray together. They needed an excellent teacher. So Angela decided to do something about it. She took the girls into her care, opening their eyes to the truths in the gospel and in the world.

SAINT ANGELA MERICI TOLD HER STUDENTS THAT THEY HAD A NEED TO SERVE THE POOR. ACCORDING TO ANGELA, THEIR NEED TO SERVE WAS MORE DESPERATE THAN A STARVING PERSON'S NEED FOR FOOD.

Jesus, help me see needs in my community and meet them, just as Saint Angela Merici did. Help me know that one of my own needs is to meet the needs of others!

SAINT THOMAS AQUINAS

1225–1274 • FRANCE AND ITALY

SEEK THE LORD

Now set your mind and heart to seek the LORD your God.

1 CHRONICLES 22:19

Thomas was curious. One of his favorite questions to ask at school was "What is God?" He asked his teachers over and over. Turns out, Thomas would dedicate his life to answering the question he started asking as a young boy. Over the course of his life, he wrote almost sixty books. One of those books, a book with many volumes, is called the *Summa Theologica*—a masterpiece of thoughtful and complete responses to very difficult questions about God, the universe, and life as a Christian. Thomas argued that all knowledge, whether gained by faith or by reason, ultimately comes from God. Christians remember Thomas as one of the greatest thinkers of all time. He gave his whole mind to answering questions—all for the glory of God.

ONE OF SAINT THOMAS AQUINAS'S TEACHERS WAS SAINT ALBERT THE GREAT (NOV. 15).

Jesus, I want to ask good questions for Your glory. Help me work hard for You.

SERVANT OF GOD BROTHER JUNIPER

UNKNOWN–1258 • ITALY

CLOTHED WITH RIGHTEOUSNESS

Let your priests be clothed with righteousness,
and let your faithful shout for joy.

PSALM 132:9

When Brother Juniper looked at his clothing, he didn't think, *I like this color* or *I would love to have three more of these.* He just thought about people who needed help and the ways he could give his clothing away! On many days Brother Juniper left his church and returned without a coat. When the priest in charge of Brother Juniper asked where his coat was, Brother Juniper simply replied, "I gave it away." This happened so frequently that the priest told Brother Juniper that he needed to start keeping his cloaks and tunics, but Juniper still didn't prevent anyone from just taking them! Even though he didn't bother to keep track of his cloaks, he knew he was clothed with righteousness.

> SERVANT OF GOD BROTHER JUNIPER WOULD GIVE ALMOST ANYTHING AWAY, EVEN THINGS THAT THE OTHER PRIESTS CONSIDERED VERY IMPORTANT!

Jesus, I want to give freely to people who need my help, just as Servant of God Brother Juniper did.

**SERVANT OF GOD BROTHER JUNIPER IS
ON TRACK TO BECOME A SAINT.**

BLESSED MARY ANGELA TRUSZKOWSKA

1825–1899 • POLAND

WANTING TO HELP

Religion that is pure and undefiled before God, the Father,
is this: to care for orphans and widows in their distress.

JAMES 1:27

On the way to her church, Mary Angela passed a child dressed in rags. She knew that the child had no home and no one to teach him about Jesus. Mary Angela loved this child and the other children like him. She went to church every day to pray for them. One day it occurred to her that Jesus had provided someone to teach these children and give them a home: Mary Angela herself! The next day she reached her hand out and asked the children to come to her home. She took them to church and taught them about Jesus. Mary Angela gathered other women who wanted to help children in need, and they became the Felician Sisters, women who cared for children without homes and other people in need.

> BLESSED MARY ANGELA TRUSZKOWSKA WAS OFTEN SICK, AND BECAUSE OF THIS, SHE TOOK SPECIAL CARE OF OTHERS WHO SUFFERED FROM SICKNESS.

Jesus, I want to help people just as Blessed Mary Angela Truszkowska did. Help me give to those in need.

BLESSED MARY ANGELA TRUSZKOWSKA IS ON TRACK TO BECOME A SAINT.

SAINT JOHN BOSCO

1815–1888 · ITALY

ALL CHILDREN

Jesus said, "Let the little children come to me, and do not stop them; for it is to such as these that the kingdom of heaven belongs."

MATTHEW 19:14

A crowd of wonderstruck boys gathered in a circle around a young boy named John. He performed for the little crowd. He juggled, he sang, and he amazed them with magic tricks. The performer led up to his grand finale: words from the priest on Sunday, repeated for his audience. Only a few months before, the same group of boys bullied John. Now they hung on his every word. John told his mother that he was going to be a priest who gave time and attention to the littlest of churchgoers—including the unruly boys! John's dream came true. He became a priest who cared for all children—boys and girls, rich and poor, well behaved and otherwise.

> SAINT JOHN BOSCO RAN A SCHOOL THAT INCLUDED A CARPENTRY WORKSHOP AND A SHOEMAKING SHOP.

Jesus, You love all children. Help me care for the other children around me, no matter who they are or how they act.

SAINT BRIGID OF IRELAND

451–525 • IRELAND

FOR THE LORD

Whatever your task, put yourselves into it, as done for the Lord and not for your masters, since you know that from the Lord you will receive the inheritance as your reward; you serve the Lord Christ.

COLOSSIANS 3:23–24

The beauty of the oak tree took Brigid's breath away. *Under this tree*, she thought, *I will build a house that is used for God's glory.* But years before this, Brigid was faced with a difficult decision. Brigid's father, an Irish chieftain, wanted her to marry a chieftain who worshipped false gods. But Brigid knew she was called to worship and serve Jesus only. She convinced her father that she would never marry and focused on ways to work for the Lord. Eventually Brigid built a house under the oak tree, just as she'd planned. She created a place where women lived, worked, and prayed together. The beautiful place that was built due to Brigid's determination was called Cill-Dara, which means "the church of the oak."

> SO MANY MEN ASKED TO MARRY SAINT BRIGID OF IRELAND THAT SHE PRAYED FOR HER GOOD LOOKS TO GO AWAY.

Jesus, I want to do all the work for Your glory.
I don't want to serve anyone else.

SAINT SIMEON

FIRST CENTURY · JUDEA (MODERN-DAY ISRAEL)

PROMISE KEPT

*My eyes have seen your salvation, which you have prepared
in the presence of all peoples, a light for revelation to
the Gentiles and for glory to your people Israel.*

LUKE 2:30–32

Simeon waited for the Lord. The Holy Spirit told Simeon that he would not die until he had seen the coming Savior with his own eyes. In the temple day after day, Simeon prayed for the Savior and waited to see Him. Then one day, a very old Simeon saw a woman and a man walking into the temple. They were holding a baby, and suddenly, Simeon knew. This baby was the promised Savior. Simeon was so full of joy that he started to sing. He took the new baby in his arms and sang over Him. God did what He had promised. He showed Simeon His Son, the Savior of the world.

> SAINT SIMEON TOLD MARY (JAN. 1) THAT HER SON WOULD CHANGE THE WORLD—AND THAT SHE WOULD HAVE TO SUFFER, TOO, BUT FOR A GLORIOUS ENDING.

*Jesus, You keep Your promises. I want to believe
You, just as Saint Simeon believed You.*

FEBRUARY 3

SAINT BLAISE

UNKNOWN–316 • CAPPADOCIA (MODERN-DAY TURKEY)

FAITH OVER LIFE

"Those who find their life will lose it, and those
who lose their life for my sake will find it."

MATTHEW 10:39

For a time, the Roman Empire had made Christianity illegal. In the year 311, those laws were repealed, or taken away. People could worship Christ without the threat of being killed—at least, they were supposed to be able to! But changes in the law take time.

Many enemies of Christ and of Christians still hunted down Christians and tried to kill them. Blaise, who was a bishop, had to flee for his life. Eventually some of these enemies found Blaise and gave him a choice. They told Blaise that he could offer sacrifices to their idols or lose his life. Blaise chose to lose his life instead of his faith in Jesus.

AS THE STORY GOES, SAINT BLAISE ONCE PRAYED FOR A CHILD WHO HAD A FISH BONE STUCK IN HIS THROAT, AND THE BONE CAME OUT. THIS IS WHY SAINT BLAISE IS THE PATRON OF THROAT AILMENTS.

*Jesus, even when laws change, You never do. Help
me choose You over everything—even life.*

SAINT JOSEPH OF LEONESSA

1556–1612 • ITALY

FAST AND PRAY

We fasted and petitioned our God for this,
and he listened to our entreaty.

EZRA 8:23

Joseph was used to giving things up. No, he didn't give up when his work became difficult. Joseph practiced fasting. He gave up things like delicious foods or comforts so he could focus on prayer, on God, and on doing good things for others. He once fasted for an entire year! Fasting works like this: a person could give up all of her desserts for a week. Each time she wanted to have dessert, she would remember that she'd given them up, then she would pray instead of having dessert. These reminders, or fasting, help Christians remember to pray. It worked for Joseph!

> SAINT JOSEPH OF LEONESSA GREW FRESH VEGETABLES IN HIS GARDEN SO HE COULD GIVE THEM AWAY TO THE POOR.

Jesus, help me grow in my relationship
with You by fasting and prayer.

BLESSED ELIZABETH CANORI MORA

1774–1825 • ITALY

FAITHFUL LOVE

Love is patient; love is kind.

1 CORINTHIANS 13:4

When Elizabeth married, she imagined a beautiful future for herself and her husband, Christopher. She hoped they would have many children and a wonderful life together. And they promised to love each other for their whole lives. Unfortunately, Christopher didn't pay much attention to the promise. He spent their money unwisely, running up large debts. He spoke to her unkindly and spent his time with other people, leaving her lonely. But Elizabeth never stopped praying for Christopher. She gave her whole heart to Jesus and begged Him to be merciful to her husband, even though he had treated her so badly. After Elizabeth died, Christopher dedicated his life to Christ and became a priest.

> BLESSED ELIZABETH CANORI MORA WAS WILLING TO SELL HER WEDDING DRESS AND RINGS TO PAY FOR CHRISTOPHER'S DEBTS.

Jesus, You can change anyone's heart. Help me love people even when they act in ways that are not loving to me.

BLESSED ELIZABETH CANORI MORA IS ON TRACK TO BECOME A SAINT.

SAINT PAUL MIKI

1564–1597 • JAPAN

COURAGE TO FORGIVE

Jesus said, "Father, forgive them; for they do not know what they are doing."

LUKE 23:34

Paul's family was from Japan, and most people in their country were Buddhists during their lifetime. But they converted to Christianity from Buddhism after talking with Christian missionaries, and Paul was baptized when he was just five years old. He studied for more than ten years to become a priest when the Japanese emperor began persecuting, or mistreating, these new Christians in Japan. Christianity was outlawed, and anyone who was a Christian could be killed. Paul and twenty-five others who believed in Jesus were sentenced to die on crosses, just as Jesus had died. Paul announced to the crowd who had gathered to watch his friends die that he forgave them. He hoped they would all come to know Jesus.

SAINT PAUL MIKI STUDIED BUDDHISM SO HE WOULD BE ABLE TO ANSWER THE QUESTIONS BUDDHISTS HAD ABOUT CHRISTIANITY.

Jesus, give me the courage to forgive people who have hurt me.

SAINT COLETTE

1381–1447 · FRANCE

EMPTY HOUSE

Taking the five loaves and the two fish, he looked up to heaven, and blessed and broke the loaves, and gave them to the disciples, and the disciples gave them to the crowds. And all ate and were filled.

MATTHEW 14:19–20

C olette stood in an almost empty house. It was hardly ever used. But Colette knew that the empty building was an opportunity for God to work miracles. Colette hoped that one day the building would be full of women, serving, working, and praying together. Colette knew that God could take almost nothing and multiply it, just as He multiplied the loaves and fish when Jesus fed the five thousand (Matthew 14:13–21). God could start with just her—one faithful woman. Colette was one of the Poor Clares. The Poor

> SAINT COLETTE AND THE OTHER SISTERS WENT EVERYWHERE BAREFOOT.

Clares is an order, or religious group, that Saint Clare of Assisi started. Colette reached out to other women in her city, sharing her hope for that empty house. Soon the house was full, and the news of their faith spread across Europe.

Jesus, take my efforts and multiply them into miracles,
just as You did for Saint Colette and the Poor Clares.

SAINT JOSEPHINE BAKHITA

1869–1947 • SUDAN AND ITALY

THE SMALL SILVER CROSS

He himself bore our sins in his body on the cross, so
that, free from sins, we might live for righteousness;
by his wounds you have been healed.

1 PETER 2:24

Josephine held the crucifix and saw the scars on Christ's body. On this silver cross, she saw a man who had suffered like she had suffered.

She was born in Sudan, and she became a slave when she was only a child. She endured horrible torture and had many scars. She was sold to owners who were from Italy. These owners gave her to another family but left her a gift—the small silver cross. Then Josephine started going to church.

SAINT JOSEPHINE BAKHITA HELPED OTHERS BY COOKING AND SEWING FOR THEM.

When her owner wanted to take her back to Sudan, she said she would not go. A court declared that Josephine was free. She became a nun, serving others and praying always. Josephine was free in two ways—she was free from slavery and free in Christ.

Jesus, thank You for the cross.

FEBRUARY 9*

SAINT JEROME EMILIANI

1486–1537 • ITALY

A NEW PERSON

Clothe yourselves with the new self, created according to the likeness of God in true righteousness and holiness.

EPHESIANS 4:24

Jerome fought as a soldier, but he wasn't a good person. Jerome didn't think he needed anybody but himself, and he wasn't going to go out of his way to help anyone else. He was selfish and cruel—until he wound up in prison. Jerome was captured in the middle of a battle. While he was in prison, he had lots of time to think and pray. In the darkness of the prison, he suddenly knew that he needed God. When Jerome was released from prison, his life was completely different. Jerome dedicated his life to educating the young and caring for the sick. The man who had never cared for anyone else started giving away everything he owned! He was a completely new person.

> SAINT JEROME EMILIANI WAS THE MAYOR OF HIS CITY WHILE HE STUDIED TO BECOME A PRIEST.

Jesus, You can make anyone a new person. Help me be selfless, just like Saint Jerome Emiliani.

SAINT SCHOLASTICA

480–543 • ITALY

FAMILY TIME

How very good and pleasant it is when kindred live together in unity!

PSALM 133:1

Scholastica loved her brother, Benedict, but they almost never saw each other. Both Scholastica and Benedict dedicated their lives to Jesus. Scholastica lived with a community of religious women, and Benedict lived with a community of religious men. They were so busy studying, serving, and praying that they hardly ever sat and talked. Once, on one of the few days they were together, Benedict needed to leave earlier than Scholastica expected. The thought of Benedict leaving made Scholastica so sad that she prayed that God would make it impossible for Benedict to leave. Then a huge storm swept across the sky. Benedict had to stay through the night and into the next morning, spending more time with his sister.

SAINT SCHOLASTICA AND SAINT BENEDICT (JULY 11) WERE TWINS!

Jesus, thank You for time with my family. Help us spend our time loving one another and praying together.

43

SAINT GREGORY II

669–731 • ITALY

GOD'S KINGDOM FIRST

He said to them, "Give therefore to the emperor the things that
are the emperor's, and to God the things that are God's."

MATTHEW 22:21

The Christians who lived during Gregory's life had to make a difficult choice. The emperor of their country told them, "Don't look at
any pictures of Jesus, and certainly don't hang up
any crosses! That's wrong! Get rid of those pictures, | PART OF SAINT
especially the crosses!" What were the Christians | GREGORY II'S
| WORK WAS TO
supposed to do? They loved their paintings and | HELP REBUILD
crosses. The art reminded them to pray and thank | THE WALLS OF
God for Jesus' sacrifice. Gregory, who became a | HIS CITY, ROME.
pope, wrote letters and sent them to Christians all over the country.
He wrote that God's kingdom is the most important kingdom, and God
is the most important King. He said that loyalty to one's country comes
after loyalty to God's kingdom. So the Christians kept their beautiful
art and continued to honor God and His kingdom above all else.

Jesus, help me love my country well
but to love You most of all.

FEBRUARY 12*

SAINT APOLLONIA

UNKNOWN–249 • EGYPT

GENUINE FAITH

So that the genuineness of your faith—being more precious than gold that, though perishable, is tested by fire—may be found to result in praise and glory and honor when Jesus Christ is revealed.

1 PETER 1:7

Apollonia loved Jesus, and she had for a long time. Apollonia was old enough to be a grandmother. She was a leader in her church and helped lead people to Jesus. One day the ruler of her city of Alexandria decided that Christianity was illegal. The ruler ordered his soldiers to kill Christians immediately, so Christians began fleeing the city. Apollonia was caught by an angry mob who beat her, knocking out all her teeth. The mob told Apollonia to say false things about Jesus, to say that He was terrible and that He wasn't God at all, or they would throw her in a fire they had lit. Apollonia threw herself into the fire, becoming a martyr, because she would rather die than curse her God.

PAINTINGS OF SAINT APOLLONIA OFTEN SHOW HER HOLDING A GOLDEN TOOTH TO REPRESENT LOSING ALL HER TEETH.

Jesus, I want to have genuine faith like Saint Apollonia, unwilling to say anything against You.

BLESSED JORDAN OF SAXONY

1190–1237 · GERMANY

ASK FOR WISDOM

If any of you is lacking in wisdom, ask God, who gives to all generously and ungrudgingly, and it will be given you.

JAMES 1:5

Jordan traveled across many countries. He met people, visited churches, and saw beautiful landscapes. Finally, at the end of his travels, he met the emperor who ruled over all the places Jordan had seen. Jordan was ready to give an account of what he had seen in order to help the emperor become a better ruler. But the emperor wasn't interested in what Jordan had to say at all! Jordan asked him why, and the proud emperor said that he already knew all he needed to know. Jordan couldn't believe it. "Jesus was God, and even Jesus asked questions of His disciples!" Jordan exclaimed. "You should try to be more like Him." After saying this, Jordan left! He knew that we must continually seek God's wisdom.

ONLY A FEW YEARS AFTER BLESSED JORDAN OF SAXONY'S SHORT CONVERSATION WITH THE EMPEROR, THE POPE INSISTED THAT THE EMPEROR NEEDED TO LEAVE THE CHURCH.

*Jesus, show me when I need to ask for wisdom,
and help me learn with humility.*

BLESSED JORDAN OF SAXONY IS ON TRACK TO BECOME A SAINT.

SAINT VALENTINE

UNKNOWN · ITALY

LOVE YOU FOREVER

"No one has greater love than this, to lay
down one's life for one's friends."

JOHN 15:13

On February 14, Valentine's Day is celebrated around the world. People give each other love notes or "valentines." So did Saint Valentine write love notes? No! In fact, there wasn't just one Saint Valentine—there were *three*. Each Valentine was a martyr who gave up his life for Christ. Not much else is known about these three men, but this is certain: all three Saint Valentines loved Jesus more than they loved their own lives. Their love wasn't about candy or love notes—it was about the true Savior of the world.

ABOUT A THOUSAND YEARS AFTER THE SAINT VALENTINES DIED, SOMEONE NOTICED THAT FEBRUARY 14, THE DAY PEOPLE CELEBRATED THE FEAST OF ONE OF THE VALENTINES, WAS AROUND THE TIME BIRDS WOULD FIND THEIR MATES. THAT'S WHY THE DAY CELEBRATES LOVE.

Jesus, show me how to love those around me.

SAINT CLAUDE DE LA COLOMBIÈRE

1641–1682 • FRANCE AND ENGLAND

AN ENCOURAGING WORD

Therefore encourage one another and build up
each other, as indeed you are doing.

1 THESSALONIANS 5:11

Claude wondered at the beauty of his friend Margaret Mary Alacoque's words. Claude became convinced with each sentence Margaret Mary (Oct. 16) spoke: God had revealed Himself to her. Claude told her as much. He said God gave her a beautiful truth that should be shared with others. Margaret Mary didn't know if she was important enough to share what she heard from God. "Write it down," Claude begged her. "We all need to hear these beautiful truths." Margaret Mary did, and her words encouraged Christians all over the world. Claude helped her share a gift God gave her with everyone else.

> SAINT CLAUDE DE LA COLOMBIÈRE WAS FALSELY ACCUSED OF TRYING TO KILL THE KING OF ENGLAND.

*Jesus, help me encourage my friends. I want to be
joyful when someone else has a great idea.*

SAINT GILBERT OF SEMPRINGHAM

1083–1189 • ENGLAND

STRONG HEART

Who am I, and what is my people, that we should be able to make this freewill offering? For all things come from you, and of your own have we given you.

1 CHRONICLES 29:14

Gilbert coughed and sneezed. He was often sick and unable to do the things that the other children could do. In fact, his body stayed sick and weak as an adult too. If he was able to live through his sickness, he wouldn't become a knight, like many of the other boys from wealthy families. What could he do? Gilbert grew up thinking about that question. He would never fight in battles, but he was given beautiful lands and houses by his parents. Gilbert did something extraordinary— something that needed the strength of his heart, not the strength of his body. He decided to give his land back to God. The beautiful houses became churches and houses of prayer.

SAINT GILBERT OF SEMPRINGHAM OFTEN REFUSED POWERFUL JOBS, THINKING THAT THEY MIGHT GIVE HIM THE CHANCE TO DO WRONG.

Jesus, strengthen my heart so that I can give back to You the good things that I get.

SEVEN FOUNDERS OF THE SERVITE ORDER

THIRTEENTH CENTURY · ITALY

ALL WE NEED

"For where two or three are gathered in my name, I am there among them."

MATTHEW 18:20

Seven men gathered in prayer. They asked God big questions: How should we live? What should we do? How should we pray? They believed that Mary, the mother of God, appeared to them in a vision, showing them what to do next. They needed to live away from the world and keep praying and keep listening. During their time away from the world, they came up with some strict rules to live by, things they decided not to have or do. Why? These seven men weren't saying that God is harsh and strict. The rules were a lesson for others, and the lesson was this: Jesus is all that anyone needs! The Seven Founders were joined by many people who devoted themselves to prayer.

THE SERVITES GREW IN NUMBER AND EVENTUALLY SPREAD AS FAR AS INDIA.

Jesus, remind my friends and me that all we need is You. Help us remember Your life and talk about You.

BLESSED JOHN OF FIESOLE

1387–1455 • ITALY

MASTERPIECE

We have gifts that differ according to the grace given to us.

ROMANS 12:6

John loved prayer, but he also loved to paint. Fortunately for John, he found a way to do both at the same time! John created masterpieces that showed scenes from the Gospels and other stories from the Bible. John used bold, beautiful colors. He wanted anyone who saw his paintings to be struck by their beauty and their meaning. Another painter named Michelangelo once said that John's paintings were so beautiful that John must have seen heaven! Whether or not John had seen heaven, his paintings made people want to know and love God more.

ONE OF BLESSED JOHN OF FIESOLE'S MOST FAMOUS PAINTINGS IS OF THE TIME THE ANGEL GABRIEL VISITED MARY, THE MOTHER OF GOD (JAN. 1).

Jesus, Blessed John of Fiesole created his art for You. I want to use the gifts You've given me to create beauty for You too!

BLESSED JOHN OF FIESOLE IS ON TRACK TO BECOME A SAINT.

FEBRUARY 19

SAINT CONRAD OF PIACENZA

1290–1351 • ITALY

THE TRUTH

"You will know the truth, and the truth will make you free."

JOHN 8:32

One day Conrad went hunting, one of his favorite hobbies. He asked the people on his hunting trip to start a fire to scare some animals out of the nearby brush. Because the wind was strong that day, the fire went out of control, and fields and houses burned up. A man who happened to be nearby was accused of starting the fire. Conrad watched in horror as the innocent man was led to his death. His hands were bound, and his head hung down. Conrad's heart beat faster and faster. He knew he should be in that innocent man's place. Conrad could have gotten away with everything, but he just couldn't stay silent. He ran toward the accused man and told the executioners the truth, and the innocent man was set free.

> SAINT CONRAD OF PIACENZA, WHO HAD BEEN WEALTHY, HAD TO SELL EVERYTHING HE OWNED TO PAY FOR THE DAMAGES, INCLUDING HIS OWN HOUSE.

Jesus, help me tell the truth, even when it will cost me.

SAINT PETER DAMIAN

1007–1072 • ITALY

PEACEMAKER

"Blessed are the peacemakers, for they
will be called children of God."

MATTHEW 5:9

Peter heard angry shouts from the cathedral, and he made up his mind—this fight couldn't continue; his church at Milan needed to be united. A large crowd had gathered in front of the beautiful church, and people yelled at each other about the actions of their church leaders. If Peter didn't stop this, it would turn into a riot. He ran into the middle of the crowd and started talking loudly enough for everyone to hear him. As Peter told them what needed to be done, the loud voices started to quiet down. Finally, the crowd parted, and people left. They knew, just as Peter knew, that the church had to be united and have peace.

SAINT PETER DAMIAN SPENT MUCH OF HIS LIFE AS A HERMIT, OR A PERSON WHO LIVES ALONE AND PRAYS.

*Jesus, You are the Prince of Peace. Make me
a peacemaker, like Saint Peter Damian.*

SAINT JACINTA MARTO

1910–1920 • PORTUGAL

PRAYER WARRIOR

Out of the mouths of babes and infants you have founded a bulwark
because of your foes, to silence the enemy and the avenger.

PSALM 8:2

W hen Jacinta was just a little girl, she worked with her brother
Francisco and her cousin Lucia, tending the sheep that their family owned. One day, while all three children were out in the pasture with the sheep, they believed that they saw Mary, the mother of God, who had a special message for them. They believed that Mary told them their prayers—yes, the prayers of children—could change the world. God wants the world to know that prayer truly matters. Prayer can lead the world to salvation. So when she was less than ten years old, Jacinta, along with Francisco and Lucia, led a crowd of seventy thousand people in prayer, knowing that God would hear them.

THE SIBLINGS LATER TOLD OTHERS THAT SAINT JACINTA MARTO COULD SEE AND HEAR THE VISION OF MARY, WHILE SAINT FRANCISCO MARTO COULD ONLY SEE HER.

*Jesus, You will forgive the sins of anyone who asks. Help me
remember to pray for everyone who doesn't know You.*

SAINT FRANCISCO MARTO

1908–1919 • PORTUGAL

SHEPHERD BOY

He is the atoning sacrifice for our sins, and not for ours
only but also for the sins of the whole world.

1 JOHN 2:2

Francisco didn't think he was very important. He didn't have money
or clothing or a beautiful and large home. All he had was his family,
his work as a shepherd, and his faith. But Jesus often gives wonderful
treasures to people who don't have much, and He gave Francisco great
faith! After Francisco and his sister Jacinta (Feb.
21) and his cousin Lucia believed that they saw
Mary, the mother of God, Francisco spent much
of his time alone, praying to Jesus. Francisco
believed that the time he gave to Jesus was special to Him. Francisco knew that even though he
didn't have much, he did have time and prayer,
and he gave that to Jesus.

SAINT FRANCISCO
MARTO IS
CONSIDERED
A SPECIAL
PROTECTOR, OR
PATRON SAINT, TO
ANYONE WHO IS
MOCKED FOR THEIR
DEDICATION TO GOD.

*Jesus, help me use my time to serve You and pray
for others. I ask that You give mercy to all the
people who have not given their lives to You.*

SAINT POLYCARP

69–155 • SMYRNA (MODERN-DAY TURKEY)

HE BELIEVED

Therefore, my brothers and sisters, whom I love and long for, my
joy and crown, stand firm in the Lord in this way, my beloved.

PHILIPPIANS 4:1

Polycarp believed the stories of the apostles. He believed that Jesus had died and risen from the grave and that Jesus had performed miracles. Polycarp believed that Jesus was the son of a carpenter, and he believed that Jesus was God. During Polycarp's life, some people weren't too sure about these beliefs. "Jesus was important," they would say, "but he couldn't have been God! That doesn't make sense to us." Polycarp didn't just disagree with these people; he wrote books about what he believed. Polycarp held on to his belief and stood up for what was right. Eventually, Polycarp died for his faith in Jesus.

> SOME CHRISTIANS DIDN'T THINK THAT THE WRITINGS OF SAINT PAUL (JAN. 24) WERE WORTH READING, BUT SAINT POLYCARP SHOWED THAT SAINT PAUL'S LETTERS TAUGHT THE TRUTH.

Jesus, help me know and speak the truth—
the truth that You are God!

SAINT ETHELBERT

552–616 • ENGLAND

UNSEEN GOD

No one has ever seen God; if we love one another,
God lives in us, and his love is perfected in us.

1 JOHN 4:12

Ethelbert wasn't too sure about his new wife's faith. Ethelbert was used to the way his people worshipped, and he was unfamiliar with the way his wife would go into her room by herself to pray and worship her God. Why did she have a God whom she couldn't see? Ethelbert had always worshipped idols in the temples. One day another Christian named Augustine came to his court. Augustine answered Ethelbert's questions. Ethelbert decided to become a Christian too. He helped his country, England, convert to Christianity as a nation. Ethelbert got rid of all of the idols, and he turned the temples into churches.

> SAINT ETHELBERT WAS THE FIRST KING OF ENGLAND WHO WAS A CHRISTIAN.

Jesus, I want my faith to be an example to others.

FEBRUARY 25

SAINT NESTOR OF MAGYDOS

UNKNOWN–250 • PAMPHYLIA (MODERN-DAY TURKEY)

FEARLESS

There is no fear in love, but perfect love casts out
fear; for fear has to do with punishment, and whoever
fears has not reached perfection in love.

1 JOHN 4:18

Nestor served as a bishop. He lived a long time ago, about two hundred years after Jesus died. Nestor must have been an amazing leader to the other Christians. The Romans, who were trying to kill Christians during Nestor's lifetime, singled out Nestor. They knew that unless they killed Nestor, they would never be able to control the spread of Christianity. The Romans found Nestor and demanded that he sacrifice to their gods. Nestor knew that Jesus is the one true God, and he refused to sacrifice to the Romans' gods. Nestor was killed at their hands and became a martyr.

> THE ROMANS NOTED THAT SAINT NESTOR OF MAGYDOS WAS A MAN OF COURAGE AND AUTHORITY.

*Jesus, I want to love You fearlessly, just
as Saint Nestor of Magydos did.*

SAINT MARIA BERTILLA BOSCARDIN

1888–1922 • ITALY

UNWANTED

*We urge you, beloved, to . . . encourage the fainthearted,
help the weak, be patient with all of them.*

1 THESSALONIANS 5:14

Maria heard the cries of the children, echoing down from the hospital rooms where they slept. These were children whom no one else wanted. Maria rose from her bed to take care of them every night. When Maria was a child, she feared her own father and felt unwanted. Her father did not think that Maria was special and sent her to work at a young age instead of sending her to school. Maria later found out that she had important work to do—to care for children who were forgotten and rejected, just as she was. Maria spent her life tending to children whom other people saw as worthless.

SAINT MARIA BERTILLA BOSCARDIN WORKED AT THE HOSPITAL DURING WORLD WAR I. SHE OFTEN HEARD SIRENS THAT SIGNALED HER CITY WAS GOING TO BE BOMBED.

Jesus, You love everyone. Help me see and love people who feel unloved and unwanted.

SAINT GABRIEL OF OUR LADY OF SORROWS

1838–1862 • ITALY

FIFTEEN MINUTES

I will extol you, my God and King, and bless
your name forever and ever.

PSALM 145:1

Gabriel prayed in the chapel every single day. While other young men were out in the streets finding ways to make money and get into trouble, Gabriel decided to do something that wouldn't make him any money at all. He prayed! Gabriel's father may have been confused by his habit because Gabriel wrote to him, telling him how much he loved prayer. He said he didn't want to give up even fifteen minutes of prayer, not even in exchange for years of fun and money. Gabriel died when he was young; he was only twenty-four. But he had spent more time in prayer during his short life than some people spend in their whole lives.

SAINT GABRIEL OF OUR LADY OF SORROWS WAS BORN IN ASSISI, JUST LIKE SAINT CLARE (AUG. 11) AND SAINT FRANCIS (OCT. 3), JUST SEVEN HUNDRED YEARS LATER.

Jesus, help me love spending time talking to You.

BLESSED DANIEL BROTTIER

1876–1936 • FRANCE

A FUTURE FULL OF LIFE

Is it not to share your bread with the hungry, and bring the homeless poor into your house; when you see the naked, to cover them, and not to hide yourself from your own kin?

ISAIAH 58:7

Daniel's country, France, had been torn apart by a long and terrible war. Soldiers had left for battle and never returned. Many people in cities had died, and their children had become orphans. Daniel knew that if these orphaned children didn't experience love, they would grow up with anger and bitterness in their hearts. Daniel, who was a priest, worked hard to give these children food, clothing, education, and a safe place to sleep. Daniel helped give them a future full of life and love, even though their past had been so difficult.

BLESSED DANIEL BROTTIER WAS ALSO A MISSIONARY TO WEST AFRICA AND A CHAPLAIN IN THE WAR.

Jesus, I want to help create a better future by loving people today.

BLESSED DANIEL BROTTIER IS ON TRACK TO BECOME A SAINT.

SAINT DAVID OF WALES

UNKNOWN–589 • WALES

KINGDOM STRENGTH

Jesus answered, "My kingdom is not from this world. If my kingdom were from this world, my followers would be fighting to keep me from being handed over to the Jews. But as it is, my kingdom is not from here."

JOHN 18:36

David lived in Wales during the sixth century. It was a time of knights and castles, and as the story goes, David may have been the great-nephew of King Arthur. But David wasn't interested in conquests and castles. David wanted to bring the good news of Jesus to the people in Wales. He built churches and monasteries and taught about Jesus. Under David's guidance, the monks who lived and worked with him grew crops and kept bees so they could feed people who came by the monastery. Just like Jesus, David taught people that strength is more than might in battle. The Welsh people loved David and gave him the Welsh name "Dewi." All over Wales, people would gather to hear what Dewi taught.

SAINT DAVID OF WALES NEVER DRANK ANYTHING EXCEPT WATER.

Jesus, Your battle is more important than the battles of knights and kings. I want to fight for You.

SAINT AGNES OF BOHEMIA

1200–1281 • BOHEMIA (MODERN-DAY CZECHIA)

A PROMISE

More than that, I regard everything as loss because of
the surpassing value of knowing Christ Jesus my Lord. For
his sake I have suffered the loss of all things, and I regard
them as rubbish, in order that I may gain Christ.

PHILIPPIANS 3:8

Frederick II didn't often hear the word *no*. Frederick was the emperor of Germany, and he had armies at his command. He certainly didn't want to hear the word *no* from Agnes, who was supposed to become his wife. But Agnes refused. She didn't think marriage was bad, but she had already promised herself to Jesus. Frederick asked Agnes to marry him many times, but he couldn't undo her promise to Jesus. Frederick said that if she'd chosen another man over him, he would have fought the man with a sword. But he couldn't fight God in heaven. So instead of being an empress, Agnes became an abbess, someone who is devoted to a life of prayer and serving the poor.

> SAINT AGNES OF BOHEMIA ONCE PREDICTED THE OUTCOME OF A BATTLE. SHE KNEW HER BROTHER WOULD BE VICTORIOUS—AND SHE WAS RIGHT!

*Jesus, help me keep my promises to You and to all
people, just as Saint Agnes of Bohemia did.*

MARCH 3

SAINT KATHARINE DREXEL

1858–1955 • THE UNITED STATES

WHO WILL GO?

*I heard the voice of the Lord saying, "Whom shall I send, and
who will go for us?" And I said, "Here am I; send me!"*

ISAIAH 6:8

Katharine knew of a problem in her country, the United States. Katharine saw huge communities of poor people, many of whom were Black or Native American, who needed schools and hospitals. Katharine had money, but money could only do so much! Who was going to help these people? Katharine brought this issue all the way to the pope. She offered him her money. Maybe with these extra funds more priests could be sent to these communities. The pope told her that people needed more than her money and her influence—they needed her heart and her hands. He said Katharine should go to help them herself. So she did! She gave up her beautiful home and life of wealth to serve these communities.

> SAINT KATHARINE DREXEL LIVED TO BE NINETY-SIX YEARS OLD.

*Jesus, show me the needs in my community, and help
me volunteer to help as Saint Katharine Drexel did,
not to wait for someone else to take care of it.*

MARCH 4

SAINT CASIMIR

1458–1484 • POLAND

CHOOSE YOUR BATTLES WISELY

Not by might, nor by power, but by my spirit, says the LORD of hosts.

ZECHARIAH 4:6

Casimir and his father, the king of Poland, disagreed about power. His father said power was about winning battles; Casimir said power was about winning souls for Christ. His father relied on swords, and Casimir relied on prayer. At his father's request, Casimir led their army into battle, but after he returned, he promised to never join a war again. When his father insisted that Casimir go into another battle, Casimir said he would battle in prayer. His father couldn't change his mind. During his short life, Casimir rejected the comforts of his father's kingdom so he could focus on God's heavenly kingdom.

SAINT CASIMIR SLEPT ON THE GROUND, EVEN THOUGH HE COULD HAVE HAD A BEAUTIFUL AND COMFORTABLE BED.

Jesus, You are more powerful than any king or kingdom of this world. I want to know Your power, just as Saint Casimir did.

SAINT JOHN JOSEPH OF THE CROSS

1654–1739 • ITALY

IMPORTANT JOBS

"I was naked and you gave me clothing, I was sick and you took care of me, I was in prison and you visited me."

MATTHEW 25:36

John Joseph ran out to the man lying beside the gate and offered him a coat. The poor man was begging for money and clothes. Every day, people in need came to the church where John Joseph lived. John Joseph was in charge of the church and had many responsibilities. But he had made a rule, which he expected the people who worked for him to follow: whenever poor people sat at the gate of their church, someone needed to offer them food and clothes right away. No other job at the church was as important as this.

> WHEN SAINT JOHN JOSEPH OF THE CROSS TRAVELED, HE DIDN'T TELL PEOPLE WHO HE WAS, BECAUSE HE DIDN'T WANT TO RECEIVE ANY SPECIAL TREATMENT.

Jesus, Saint John Joseph of the Cross knew that being famous and having important jobs were less important than taking care of the poor. Help me know what's important too and to help those in need.

SAINT MARY ANN OF JESUS OF PAREDES

1618–1645 • ECUADOR

BREAD ALONE

*One does not live by bread alone, but by every word
that comes from the mouth of the LORD.*

DEUTERONOMY 8:3

People say breakfast is the most important meal of the day, but Jesus and His words are even more important than food—even breakfast! Mary Ann knew this well. She fasted regularly and ate only an ounce of bread every ten days! Her strict fasts helped her remember that the real bread that her soul needed was Jesus. By relying on Jesus for all of her needs, Mary Ann was able to meet the needs of others. She started a school in Ecuador for children who weren't welcomed into schools that already existed. She made certain that these children were given the knowledge they needed—that Jesus Christ is all we need.

> DURING A PLAGUE, SAINT MARY ANN OF JESUS OF PAREDES SET ASIDE CONCERNS FOR HER OWN SAFETY SO SHE COULD NURSE THE SICK BACK TO HEALTH.

*Jesus, You are the true Bread of Life.
Help me rely on You alone.*

MARCH 7

SAINTS PERPETUA AND FELICITY

UNKNOWN–203 • CARTHAGE (MODERN-DAY TUNISIA)

PRISONERS

*Remember those who are in prison, as though
you were in prison with them.*

HEBREWS 13:3

The name *Christian* was worth so much to Perpetua and Felicity that they died for it. They lived in Carthage, about two hundred years after Jesus had died, and the emperor had made Christianity illegal. Perpetua and Felicity were Christians but hadn't been baptized yet. Even though they were risking their lives, they chose to go through with their plans for baptism. Soldiers caught and arrested the two women, but that still didn't stop their plans. They were baptized in prison. They were soon sentenced to death and were thrown into an arena. The crowd cheered in excitement. Perpetua and Felicity themselves were joyful but for an entirely different reason. They knew that they were going to heaven.

> SAINT FELICITY SAID THAT SHE KNEW SHE COULD BRAVE HER DEATH BECAUSE JESUS WOULD HELP HER ENDURE THE SUFFERING.

*Jesus, I want to understand the worth of the name
Christian, just as Saints Perpetua and Felicity did.*

SAINT JOHN OF GOD

1495–1550 • SPAIN

FEED MY LAMBS

Jesus said to him, "Feed my lambs."

JOHN 21:15

John was a shepherd and a soldier, but he knew that there had to be more to life than raising flocks or fighting in battles. He wanted to work for a different kind of kingdom. One day, John heard a powerful new perspective from a respected teacher, and John had the answers he needed. Living in God's kingdom meant caring for the people who no one else wanted to care for. He gave up his life as a shepherd and a soldier to become a nurse. He tended a different kind of flock—the flock of God's children. And he fought a different kind of battle—the battle against sickness.

SAINT JOHN OF GOD RENTED A HOUSE IN SPAIN AND SPENT HIS TIME HOSTING AND CARING FOR SICK STRANGERS WHOM HE WOULD INVITE TO THE HOUSE.

Jesus, thank You for the teachers in my life who show me how to follow You. I want to take care of Your children, just as Saint John of God did.

SAINT FRANCES OF ROME

1384–1440 · ITALY

LET'S TRADE

He has filled the hungry with good things,
and sent the rich away empty.

LUKE 1:53

Frances walked out of her home, holding her plate of rich food. She walked out of the gate and approached a poor, hungry person on the street. The poor person had nothing for lunch but a dry crust of bread, and Frances knew it. She traded him her plate anyway. She took his dry crust of bread back into her home, thanked God for providing for her, and ate the crust. She knew that Jesus would provide everything she needed. After all, in God's kingdom, anything could happen. The hungry could be filled. A carpenter could be a King. Sins could be forgiven. Since she understood the way that God traded, Frances could give away what she had to others.

> SAINT FRANCES OF ROME WAS MARRIED FOR FORTY YEARS. DURING THAT TIME, SHE AND HER HUSBAND NEVER HAD AN ARGUMENT.

Jesus, I want to trade what You've given me to
those in need, just as Saint Frances of Rome did.
Remind me that You provide for our needs.

SAINT JOHN OGILVIE

1579–1615 · SCOTLAND

HOUSE DIVIDED

*Now I appeal to you, brothers and sisters, by the name
of our Lord Jesus Christ, that all of you be in agreement
and that there be no divisions among you.*

1 CORINTHIANS 1:10

John wanted the Church to be united. During John's life, the Church had split into many different groups, even though each group claimed to love Jesus! John knew that the division among these groups was not what Jesus would have wanted. So John went to Scotland, even though he disagreed with the king of Scotland about

BEFORE SAINT JOHN OGILVIE DIED, SOMEONE ASKED IF HE FEARED DEATH. HE SAID, "I FEAR DEATH AS MUCH AS YOU DO YOUR DINNER."

church. John knew his choice could cost him his life. After a few years of trying to do something about the divisions, John was locked in prison. He was tortured and executed because he would not name anyone else he knew who disagreed with the king. Even through pain and death, John didn't regret his mission to bring unity and understanding to the church groups.

Jesus, please make us united in our love for You.

MARCH 11

SAINT TERESA MARGARET OF THE SACRED HEART

1747–1770 • ITALY

GOD IS LOVE

Whoever does not love does not know God, for God is love.

1 JOHN 4:8

Teresa Margaret joined a convent, or a group of women dedicated to loving Jesus and serving others, when she was only eighteen. Saint Teresa of Ávila (Oct. 15) created this convent in the 1500s. Even though it was two hundred years later, Teresa Margaret believed that she felt a call

> SAINT TERESA MARGARET OF THE SACRED HEART WAS ALWAYS CHEERFUL, EVEN WHEN OTHERS MADE FUN OF HER.

from Saint Teresa of Ávila herself to join the convent. As a nun, Teresa Margaret took on difficult jobs. She worked as a nurse and often did the jobs that no one else wanted to do. Teresa Margaret used hand gestures to speak to the nuns who couldn't hear. She was calm and gentle with the nuns who couldn't speak and think quickly. By loving the women who weren't loved often enough, Teresa Margaret knew God.

Jesus, give me the desire to be with the people that no one else wants to be with.

BLESSED ANGELA SALAWA

1881–1922 • POLAND

THE CHOICE

He said to them all, "If any want to become my followers, let them
deny themselves and take up their cross daily and follow me."

LUKE 9:23

Angela loved Jesus. At least, she had loved Him once. When she was a child, her parents and many siblings often found Angela praying. But all of that changed after she grew up and moved away from her home and small town. She became a maid and worked in large and wealthy houses. She wanted less of Jesus and more of the wealth she saw all around. Jesus wanted Angela back, though, and He found a way to tell her. While Angela was dancing at a wedding, she believed she saw Jesus across the room. "Would you rather dance than follow Me?" He seemed to ask her. Angela stopped dancing and went to the nearest church, falling on her knees in prayer. Angela made her choice, and her choice was Jesus.

BLESSED ANGELA SALAWA HAD ELEVEN BROTHERS AND SISTERS.

*Jesus, I want to choose You, just as Blessed
Angela Salawa did. Help me listen to You.*

BLESSED ANGELA SALAWA IS ON TRACK TO BECOME A SAINT.

MARCH 13

SAINT LEANDER OF SEVILLE

534–600 · SPAIN

BROTHERLY LOVE

Therefore, my beloved, be steadfast, immovable,
always excelling in the work of the Lord, because you
know that in the Lord your labor is not in vain.

1 CORINTHIANS 15:58

Leander would not compromise what he knew about Jesus. He worked in the Church in Spain, and during his life, people were convinced of the false teaching that Jesus was not actually both God and man. It can be very difficult for people to believe that Jesus is who He says He is—that's still true now. But Leander was able to convince two powerful royal brothers, Hermenegild and Reccared, that his view of Jesus was the true one, and Christianity kept spreading throughout Europe.

> SAINT LEANDER OF SEVILLE AND SAINT ISIDORE OF SEVILLE (APR. 4) WERE BROTHERS, AND TWO OTHER SIBLINGS OF THEIRS ARE SAINTS TOO!

*Jesus, I want to share Your truth with the world
so that more people will know You.*

SAINT MATILDA

895–968 · GERMANY

QUEEN MOTHER

She opens her mouth with wisdom, and the teaching of kindness is on her tongue.

PROVERBS 31:26

Matilda was married to King Henry the Fowler and ruled as queen of Germany. Her five kids were princes and princesses, and she loved them dearly. She not only provided for their needs of food, clothing, and shelter, but she also provided for their spiritual needs and showed them how to be like Jesus. She set an example of being humble, moral, and generous. Matilda also showed her kids how important it is to care for the children in their country who didn't have money or parents. Even though Matilda was a queen, she gave away her wealth to children so they could have food, clothing, and shelter just as her own kids had.

SAINT MATILDA WAS RAISED BY HER GRANDMOTHER, WHO ENCOURAGED HER TO PRAY AND HELP OTHERS.

Jesus, thank You for my mother. Help me honor her in ways that honor You.

SAINT LOUISE DE MARILLAC

1591–1660 · FRANCE

FREE OF DOUBT

Ask in faith, never doubting, for the one who doubts is like a wave of the sea, driven and tossed by the wind.

JAMES 1:6

Louise often doubted herself, which means she wasn't sure she made the right choices. She spent time thinking about ways she could have done better, and she was afraid that she would not make the right choice in the future. Louise took all of her doubts to God in prayer, and God answered her! Louise struggled with doubt for a long time before His answer came. She wrote that one day, while she was praying in church, she suddenly felt free from her doubts. After that, Louise was free to do great work for God. She served the poor, built churches, and cared for people in prison.

SAINT LOUISE DE MARILLAC WAS GREAT FRIENDS WITH SAINT VINCENT DE PAUL (SEPT. 27), WHO TAUGHT HER HOW TO SERVE THE POOR.

Jesus, I want to believe You completely. Free me from doubt, just as you freed Saint Louise de Marillac.

SAINT CLEMENT MARY HOFBAUER

1751–1821 • MORAVIA (MODERN-DAY CZECHIA)

WAIT YOUR TURN

Those who wait for the LORD shall renew their strength,
they shall mount up with wings like eagles, they shall run
and not be weary, they shall walk and not faint.

ISAIAH 40:31

Clement wanted only one thing—to serve God as a priest. If he had been given the chance, he would have run to the school where priests were educated and willingly spent hours a day in study and in prayer. But often God doesn't give people exactly what they want when they want it. Sometimes Christians have to wait for God's perfect timing. As a young man, Clement needed to help his family. So Clement worked as a baker's assistant, even though he would have rather been studying. Later in his life, he became a priest, and he made up for lost time! Clement tackled his work as a priest with energy and excitement, grateful that he had the opportunity to do what he had always wanted to do.

> SAINT CLEMENT MARY HOFBAUER'S FRIEND ONCE SAID CLEMENT HAD SUPERHUMAN ENERGY.

Jesus, there are things that I want right now. Help me be patient and wait, just as Saint Clement Mary Hofbauer did.

MARCH 17

SAINT PATRICK

387–493 • IRELAND

THE BEST THING

We know that all things work together for good for those who love God, who are called according to his purpose.

ROMANS 8:28

Patrick's parents taught him to love Jesus and to pray often, and Patrick willingly learned. But when Patrick was sixteen, his life took a strange turn. Patrick was captured by thieves and sold as a slave. He was taken away from his parents and from his home. But the thieves couldn't take Patrick's God. For six whole years, Patrick worked as a slave, tending sheep for his owners in an unfamiliar place called Ireland. Patrick kept praying, and he even learned the language of the people who captured him. He eventually escaped slavery, but one day he did the unthinkable. He went back to spread Christianity to the Irish people who had captured him, and many became Christians!

AS THE STORY GOES, SAINT PATRICK USED A SHAMROCK, WHICH IS A THREE-LEAF CLOVER, TO EXPLAIN THE TRINITY TO THE IRISH.

Jesus, You used Saint Patrick's suffering to make him more like You and to prepare him for important work. Do the same for me!

MARCH 18

SAINT CYRIL OF JERUSALEM

315–386 • PALESTINE (MODERN-DAY ISRAEL)

SEE AND KNOW

The Word became flesh and lived among us, and we have seen his
glory, the glory as of a father's only son, full of grace and truth.

JOHN 1:14

What does the garden of Gethsemane look like? Where is the hill Jesus was crucified on? Christians often wonder about the places where Jesus lived and died, and when they see those places, they grow in their faith. Even today people from all over the world travel to Jerusalem, Israel, to see the places where Jesus and His disciples actually walked, talked, and changed lives. Cyril knew that seeing these places and praying there would be helpful for Christians, so he encouraged people, saying, "Go! See where Jesus lived, died, and rose again! Pray by the places where He lived so that you might know that He was fully God and fully man."

> SAINT CYRIL OF JERUSALEM WAS EXILED, OR SENT AWAY, BY THE PEOPLE OF HIS CHURCH SEVERAL TIMES BECAUSE OF DISAGREEMENTS.

*Jesus, I know that You are both God and man and
that You lived and walked on earth, just as I do.*

MARCH 19

SAINT JOSEPH

FIRST CENTURY • GALILEE (MODERN-DAY ISRAEL)

MEASURE UP

*An angel of the Lord appeared to him in a dream and said,
"Joseph, son of David, do not be afraid to take Mary as your
wife, for the child conceived in her is from the Holy Spirit."*

MATTHEW 1:20

Since he was a carpenter, Joseph knew the importance of a measurement. If he measured the wood incorrectly, he wouldn't be able to use it. So when he heard that Mary was pregnant, Joseph started measuring. Could his and Mary's relationship measure up? Or should he break off their engagement? Then an angel appeared to him and told him Mary would be the mother of the Savior of the world. He said Joseph should become Mary's husband and Jesus' earthly father, and Joseph agreed, even though it was going to be difficult. He knew that God would help him measure up to the job.

ANGELS VISITED SAINT JOSEPH AGAIN AFTER JESUS WAS BORN AND TOLD HIM TO FLEE TO EGYPT. JOSEPH LISTENED TO THE ANGELS AND HELPED KEEP HIS FAMILY SAFE.

*Jesus, I know You will prepare me for any job You
have for me. Help me obey when You call me.*

MARCH 20

SAINT MARTIN OF BRAGA

520–580 • HUNGARY AND PORTUGAL

UNAFRAID

When I am afraid, I put my trust in you.

PSALM 56:3

When Martin was a leader in the Church, other leaders worried about the people practicing other religions. *How dare they worship other gods and idols!* they thought. They clucked their tongues and shook their heads. The strange ceremonies of these non-Christians made many leaders afraid. But living in fear doesn't spread the love of God, and Martin knew this. He was not afraid of the people who didn't believe in Jesus. Martin spoke to them in ways they would understand, writing speeches that used words they would know. He spoke to them and asked them questions. Over time, many of these people became Christians. They were open to learning about Jesus because Martin was kind and didn't treat them like unwanted strangers.

> SAINT MARTIN OF BRAGA HAD TO FLEE FROM PERSECUTION IN ROME AND, BECAUSE OF THIS, WAS ABLE TO TEACH PEOPLE IN PORTUGAL ABOUT JESUS.

Jesus, help me become friends with people who are different from me. Help me share You with people who haven't heard about You yet.

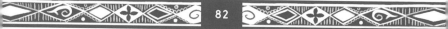

82

MARCH 21

SAINT NICHOLAS OF FLÜE

1417–1487 • SWITZERLAND

TIME ALONE WITH GOD

For dominion belongs to the LORD, and he rules over the nations.

PSALM 22:28

Nicholas had been alone for so long that he had almost forgotten what the voices of other people sounded like. Nicholas was a hermit, but at one time he had lived on his farm with ten children! Things had been noisy and busy. Now his ten children and wife ran the farm without him because God gave Nicholas a unique mission. God called Nicholas to live by himself so he could focus on praying. Both Nicholas and his wife were confused by the call, but they obeyed God. After six years of solitude, the leaders of his country, Switzerland, came to Nicholas with an important set of questions. The country was about to go to war with itself! With all the wisdom he had gained in the years by himself, Nicholas was able to help these leaders come to an agreement.

IN THE SPIRIT OF SAINT NICHOLAS OF FLÜE, SWITZERLAND OFTEN REFRAINS FROM TAKING SIDES IN GLOBAL CONFLICTS.

*Jesus, help me spend time alone with You
each day so that I can grow in wisdom.*

SAINT NICHOLAS OWEN

1562–1606 · ENGLAND

HIDING PLACE

For he will hide me in his shelter in the day of trouble.

PSALM 27:5

Nicholas peered into the dark, waiting and watching. In the distance he heard quiet footsteps, then the clatter of hooves. Nicholas whispered a prayer, asking God to speed the steps of the priests who were headed his way so he could hide them from the soldiers. The priests reached Nicholas just in time. He swept them into a hole he had dug right before the men on horses came rushing over their hiding place. At least for the moment, the priests were safe. The Church was divided during Nicholas's life, and many men who dedicated their lives to Jesus were being hunted and killed. To protect these men, Nicholas made places for them to hide from the servants of the king who wanted them killed. Because of Nicholas's special skill, many priests who would have been killed were spared.

SAINT NICHOLAS OWEN WAS A CARPENTER, A SKILL SET THAT PROBABLY HELPED HIM BUILD HIDING PLACES TO KEEP PRIESTS SAFE.

Jesus, when I'm afraid, I will hide under Your shelter.

SAINT TURIBIUS OF MOGROVEJO

1538–1606 • PERU

WORTH MORE THAN GOLD

*My brothers and sisters, do you with your acts of favoritism
really believe in our glorious Lord Jesus Christ?*

JAMES 2:1

In Peru, Turibius saw the native people living in poverty and the colonists from Spain being cruel to the natives. He knew only one thing could fix this—the love of Jesus Christ. Turibius taught the native people the gospel. He also reminded the people from Spain that Jesus wanted His followers to love God and people more than money. He improved life for both communities, building hospitals and schools that could be used by both the colonists from Spain and the native people of Peru. He reminded all of them that a single soul is worth more than silver and gold, no matter where a person is from.

> SAINT TURIBIUS OF MOGROVEJO THOUGHT DANGEROUS TRAVEL WAS WORTH THE RISK IF IT MEANT HE COULD TELL THE STORY OF JESUS TO JUST ONE PERSON WHO HAD NOT HEARD IT YET.

*Jesus, I can tell the world that I believe in
You by showing love to everyone.*

SAINT OSCAR ARNULFO ROMERO

1917–1980 • EL SALVADOR

CAUGHT IN THE MIDDLE

Those who oppress the poor insult their Maker, but
those who are kind to the needy honor him.

PROVERBS 14:31

Oscar was caught in the middle. His country, El Salvador, was torn apart by two different sides. Each side wanted Oscar to say they were right. But Oscar refused. He argued that the violence caused by each side created one loser, and that loser was the poor people in El Salvador. Neither side was happy that he stood up for the poor, and Oscar knew his life was in danger. He was right. Oscar was shot in the middle of a church service, and he is remembered as a martyr—a person who gave his life for his faith in Jesus.

> SAINT OSCAR ARNULFO ROMERO WAS NOMINATED FOR THE 1979 NOBEL PEACE PRIZE.

Jesus, help me be brave and stand up for people who don't have a voice, just as Saint Oscar Arnulfo Romero did.

SAINT LUCY FILIPPINI

1672–1732 • ITALY

TRAINED RIGHT

Train children in the right way, and when old, they will not stray.

PROVERBS 22:6

Lucy loved school. She lost her parents when she was young, and she took comfort in her daily trip to school. Lucy became a great teacher herself. She believed that all children, boys and girls, poor and rich, needed the comfort and hope that a good education provided. Even though some people didn't agree with her, Lucy knew that girls could be wonderful students and women could be wonderful teachers. The pope agreed with her. Lucy's schools were dedicated to training all students, especially young girls who didn't have money.

SAINT LUCY FILIPPINI FOUNDED MORE THAN FIFTY SCHOOLS.

Jesus, help me do my best in school and love and appreciate my teachers.

SAINT CATHERINE OF GENOA

1447–1510 • ITALY

LUKEWARM

"I know your works; you are neither cold nor hot.
I wish that you were either cold or hot."

REVELATION 3:15

Catherine felt lost. She had once loved Jesus with everything, but now life felt worthless. Catherine married a man who loved entertainment and wanted nothing to do with her faith in Jesus. Her husband's choice made her so sad that she became "lukewarm" in her faith. People who are lukewarm don't try to be close to God or ask for His help. They still believe in God but don't try to increase their faith. They are lost in the middle. Finally Catherine prayed, asking God for that same love for Jesus that she once had. God answered her. She felt God's light enter her heart. Catherine was given the same love for God that she had when she was young. One day, her husband would come back to faith in Christ too.

> SAINT CATHERINE OF GENOA SERVED THE POOR AND SICK PEOPLE AT THE HOSPITALS IN HER CITY.

*Jesus, I do not want to be lukewarm in my faith. Help me give
my whole heart to You, just as Saint Catherine of Genoa did.*

SERVANT OF GOD BLANDINA SEGALE

1850–1941 • ITALY AND THE UNITED STATES

OUT WEST

The LORD will fight for you.

EXODUS 14:14

"Stop!" Sister Blandina yelled, rushing into the crowd. The angry people pushed and shoved against each other. Some of them were even waving guns in the air. But Sister Blandina was not afraid. She knew that God would help her break up the fight. After Blandina encouraged the crowd to talk through their problems, everyone went home peacefully. These were the kinds of troubles Sister Blandina dealt with in the Wild West, where she moved at age twenty-two. She lived in the Colorado and New Mexico territories before they became states, helping people in need and showing people how to live in peace. She worked in hospitals, taught children, and even broke up gunfights. She helped the people in that part of the United States understand the love of Jesus.

> SERVANT OF GOD BLANDINA SEGALE'S LIFE WAS SO EXCITING THAT THERE ARE BOOKS, COMICS, AND TV SHOWS ABOUT HER! ONE OF THE SHOWS CALLED SISTER BLANDINA "THE FASTEST NUN IN THE WEST."

Jesus, You are with me, even in dangerous places. Show me how to share Your love and peace with others.

SERVANT OF GOD BLANDINA SEGALE IS ON TRACK TO BECOME A SAINT.

SAINT CATHERINE OF BOLOGNA

1413–1463 • ITALY

BEAUTIFUL WORDS

Open my eyes, so that I may behold wondrous things out of your law.

PSALM 119:18

Catherine wrote the holy words carefully. She knew that an excellent copy of the breviary, or book of prayers and psalms, would help other people pray the same way that she was able to. And she knew that getting the words right was important, but that it was also important to make the copy beautiful because it was more likely that people would want to read it if it were beautiful. Copies of prayer books and writing about living life for Jesus were not available everywhere when Catherine was alive, and she worked diligently to create more copies for others. While she copied the words of scriptures, she thanked God for His beautiful words.

PART OF SAINT CATHERINE OF BOLOGNA'S JOB IN HER CONVENT, THE PLACE SHE LIVED WITH OTHER WOMEN WHO DEDICATED THEIR LIFE AND WORK TO CHRIST, WAS TO TAKE CARE OF THE ANIMALS.

Jesus, Your Word is wonderful. Help me love Your Word just as Saint Catherine of Bologna did.

SAINT LUDOVICO OF CASORIA

1814–1885 · ITALY

TO LOVE EVERYONE

"The blind receive their sight, the lame walk, the lepers
are cleansed, the deaf hear, the dead are raised, and
the poor have good news brought to them."

MATTHEW 11:5

Ludovico knew that when Jesus said to love everyone, He meant *everyone*—even people others didn't think were important. *Everyone* meant children. *Everyone* meant people who had been slaves. *Everyone* included people who couldn't see or hear. Ludovico spent his whole life building organizations that were designed to help people who had no one else to help them, and he trained other people to help those in need too. These helpers were called the Gray Friars of Charity and the Franciscan Sisters of Saint Elizabeth, and they taught people to love Jesus.

WHEN HE WAS YOUNG, SAINT LUDOVICO OF CASORIA WORKED AS A CABINET MAKER.

*Jesus, train me to love everyone, just as You
trained Saint Ludovico of Casoria.*

SAINT JOSEPH OF ARIMATHEA

FIRST CENTURY · JUDEA (MODERN-DAY ISRAEL)

STONE TOMB

This man went to Pilate and asked for the body of Jesus.
Then he took it down, wrapped it in a linen cloth, and laid it
in a rock-hewn tomb where no one had ever been laid.

LUKE 23:52–53

Joseph held Jesus' body in his arms, feeling His weight. Even though he was a member of the council that accused Jesus and said He should die, Joseph didn't agree with those men. Joseph believed that Jesus is the Savior of the world. After Jesus had died, Joseph went quickly to the scene. He knew people would try to take Jesus' body and treat it poorly, but Joseph knew His body should be treated with respect. He gave Jesus a beautiful burial place on his property. And when he found out that Jesus didn't need the stone tomb any longer, he rejoiced!

WHEN JESUS WAS ALIVE, SAINT JOSEPH OF ARIMATHEA WAS AFRAID TO SAY THAT HE FOLLOWED HIM, BUT AFTER HE DIED, JOSEPH BOLDLY DECLARED THAT HE FOLLOWED JESUS.

*Jesus, I want to give You a place in my heart,
just as Saint Joseph of Arimathea did.*

SAINT STEPHEN OF MAR SABA

725–796 • PALESTINE (MODERN-DAY WEST BANK)

IN SILENCE

My people will abide in a peaceful habitation, in
secure dwellings, and in quiet resting places.

ISAIAH 32:18

Stephen loved silence. Without any noise to distract him, he could concentrate on listening to God. He loved silence so much that he spent time as a hermit, or a person who lives alone and spends time in prayer—sometimes in total silence. Imagine that! By spending time alone in the quiet, Stephen could hear God answer his questions, and he became wise. People would often go to his home and ask him for his advice. Stephen's advice was so good that he had to put a sign on his door asking people to only ask for his advice on Saturdays and Sundays!

SAINT PETER DAMIAN (FEB. 20) AND SAINT NICHOLAS OF FLÜE (MAR. 21) WERE HERMITS TOO. HERMITS OFTEN HELPED PEOPLE RESOLVE TROUBLING SITUATIONS IN THEIR LIVES.

*Jesus, I want to spend time alone with You in the
quiet, just as Saint Stephen of Mar Saba did.*

SAINT HUGH OF GRENOBLE

1053–1132 • FRANCE

RESTORED

For I will restore health to you, and your
wounds I will heal, says the LORD.

JEREMIAH 30:17

Hugh might have wanted to throw his hands up in the air and shout, "This is too big of a mess! It will never get done!" Instead, Hugh took the job the pope offered him. The pope put him in charge of the church in his city, Grenoble, France. For years, foolish church leaders had wasted time and money. They should have been working, studying the Bible, and serving the poor, but they hadn't done any of that. They kept money for themselves and hardly ever talked about Jesus. Those foolish leaders hadn't helped people love Jesus at all! The church in Grenoble was struggling, but Hugh helped restore the church's commitment to God. To help everyone remember Jesus, Hugh built two new buildings, used only for worship and prayer, not for wasting time.

> DURING A FAMINE, SAINT HUGH OF GRENOBLE SOLD ITEMS FROM HIS CHURCH. HE USED THE MONEY TO FEED PEOPLE WHO WERE STARVING. OTHER PEOPLE WITH VALUABLE ITEMS WERE INSPIRED TO DO THE SAME.

Jesus, sometimes life is messy. Help me set things right again.

SAINT FRANCIS OF PAOLA

1416–1507 • ITALY

HEALING HANDS

He sent them out to proclaim the kingdom of God and to heal.

LUKE 9:2

Francis clasped the sick man's hand and bowed his own head. He prayed that the sick man would know and love Jesus and that, if it were God's will, he would be healed. Francis prayed for the sick all over his country, Italy. Many times, God healed them! When people died, Francis was at their side, reminding them that they were going to be with God. Francis was known for praying for people across his country, so the sick king of France was confused when Francis refused to come to him. The king had said he'd pay anything! But Francis was not interested in the king's money. When Francis finally went to the king's bedside, he told the king to pray earnestly for his healing, trust God completely, and place himself in God's hands. The king eventually died, but Francis had helped him prepare to meet the heavenly King.

> SAINT FRANCIS OF PAOLA FOUNDED AN ORDER CALLED THE "MINIMS." THE MEN IN HIS ORDER PROMISED TO HAVE ONLY THE "MINIMUM."

Jesus, Your healing is worth more than money!

SAINT BENEDICT THE AFRICAN

1526–1589 • AFRICA AND SICILY

SERVANT LEADER

"So the last will be first, and the first will be last."

MATTHEW 20:16

Benedict didn't need to be in charge. Benedict didn't even *want* to be in charge! But the people who lived with him recognized that Benedict was such a good leader, he should probably be in charge anyway. Benedict's parents had been slaves, and he was a slave, too, when he was a child, but he was freed when he turned eighteen. Then he spent many years as a hermit, living alone in silence and prayer. A few other hermits lived in the same area as Benedict. They recognized Benedict's gentleness and asked him for leadership. Benedict eventually said yes after they asked many times. Benedict was the servant of those he led, and he often asked them for help and forgiveness.

> SAINT BENEDICT THE AFRICAN NEVER USED THE WORD *MINE*. HE REPLACED IT WITH *OURS* INSTEAD!

Jesus, help me love and serve the people around me, just as Saint Benedict the African did.

SAINT ISIDORE OF SEVILLE

560–636 • SPAIN

DEFEND THE TRUTH

"The Father and I are one."

JOHN 10:30

Isidore studied hard. He could speak and write in Greek, Hebrew, and Latin. Since he knew these languages, he could read and study about Jesus. Isidore learned the truth about Jesus and often defended it.

During his life, some teachers didn't believe Jesus was and is really God. They acted like Jesus was a lesser god or just a prophet. Isidore called out those teachers and told them the truth. Jesus wasn't a lesser god or a prophet. He is *truly* God. Jesus and His Father are one! Isidore helped the Church remember this truth. His life teaches an important lesson: to defend the truth, a person must know the truth.

> SAINT ISIDORE OF SEVILLE WROTE A HUGE BOOK FOR A FRIEND WHO ASKED HIM TO WRITE DOWN EVERYTHING THAT THEIR SOCIETY KNEW. THE BOOK, *ETYMOLOGIAE,* WAS SO LONG THAT HIS FRIEND SPLIT IT INTO TWENTY BOOKS.

Jesus, You and Your Father are one. Help me know this truth, defend it, and live by it.

APRIL 5

SAINT VINCENT FERRER

1350–1419 · SPAIN AND FRANCE

CONFLICT

Those conflicts and disputes among you, where do they come from?
Do they not come from your cravings that are at war within you?

JAMES 4:1

Vincent felt caught in the middle. Two men, Martin and Benedict, claimed to be the pope, or the person in charge of the Catholic Church. Only one person could be pope, and each man said, "It must be me!" Their disagreement caused division in the Catholic Church and in the world. Families argued, churches divided, and armies even went to war! Vincent knew that the Catholic Church was meant to have peace. Jesus hated to see fighting in church. So Vincent begged Benedict to back down. But Benedict didn't listen to Vincent right away. Vincent spent many years praying for an end to the conflict, and two years before he died, the Church declared that Martin would be the pope. The division was over.

> ONE DAY, AFTER SAINT VINCENT FERRER PREACHED TO THEM, A CROWD OF OVER FIVE THOUSAND PEOPLE BELIEVED THAT JESUS IS THE SAVIOR OF THE WORLD.

Jesus, help me put an end to arguments and love peace, just as Saint Vincent Ferrer did.

APRIL 6*

SAINT CRESCENTIA HÖSS

1682–1744 · GERMANY

FEW ARE CHOSEN

"For many are called, but few are chosen."

MATTHEW 22:14

A good church is a big church, right? Crescentia didn't believe that for a minute. She knew that God could gather large numbers of people together, but she also knew that He didn't need big numbers to make big changes. Crescentia was a Sister, which means she lived in a community of women who dedicated their lives to Jesus. Often, groups of Sisters lived in a building called a convent. Together, they devoted their lives to service to others and to prayer. Crescentia was also very wise. She helped decide which women were going to become Sisters. Many women asked to become Sisters, but only a few were chosen, especially when Crescentia was making the decision. The other Sisters wondered why Crescentia didn't just ask them all to join. More Sisters meant a bigger group, and bigger was better! Crescentia knew this was wrong. It was better to have a few Sisters who really loved Jesus than a large crowd not fully devoted to Him.

SAINT CRESCENTIA HÖSS RECOMMENDED THAT ALL OF THE SISTERS IN HER CARE READ THE GOSPELS.

Jesus, help me see that bigger isn't always better. I want to care more about what You care about—having a heart devoted to You.

SAINT JOHN BAPTIST DE LA SALLE

1651–1719 · FRANCE

HEAR THE CRY

*If you close your ear to the cry of the poor,
you will cry out and not be heard.*

PROVERBS 21:13

John wanted every child to learn to read and write, even if a child's family could not pay for school. John found ways to educate the students whom no one else paid attention to. Even though John was passionate about helping students, other teachers didn't like John's ideas. Teaching poor students meant sacrificing money—money that could be earned by focusing on richer families. John didn't want that money, though. He preferred teaching every child he could over having a comfortable life. He even sold his possessions and gave the money to the poor. Later he created a group of teachers who dedicated themselves to poor students. This group was called the Christian Brothers, but while John was alive, the group was very small. After he died, it grew and grew! The Christian Brothers spread around the world, answering the cries of the poor.

EVEN TODAY, THERE ARE 560 SCHOOLS RUN BY THE CHRISTIAN BROTHERS ALL OVER THE WORLD!

*Jesus, help me hear the poor and help them,
just as Saint John Baptist de la Salle did.*

APRIL 8*

SAINT CASILDA

950–1050 · SPAIN

MADE WELL

He said to her, "Daughter, your faith has made you well; go in peace."

LUKE 8:48

Casilda's father was an important ruler in Spain, so Casilda had servants and power. She could have done anything she wanted with her time, but she chose to spend her time visiting people in prison. Casilda heard about Jesus from the Christian prisoners in her father's dungeons. These Christians, Casilda learned, had a hope that she didn't have! She had been suffering from a terrible sickness. The Christians told her about a spring where they had heard many had been healed. Casilda set out in faith, taking a journey to the same spring. Her sickness was healed, but more importantly, her heart was made well too! She finally had peace, and she professed faith in Jesus, just like those Christian prisoners she had visited.

BEFORE SHE BECAME A CHRISTIAN, SAINT CASILDA WAS A MUSLIM.

Jesus, You gave peace to Saint Casilda's heart. Make my heart well by giving me Your peace too.

SAINT JULIE BILLIART

1751–1816 • FRANCE

WALK AGAIN

*The lame shall leap like a deer, and the tongue
of the speechless sing for joy.*

ISAIAH 35:6

Julie wanted to be a teacher. Even as a young girl, she would clamber up on haystacks and teach the people working in the fields! The priests and teachers in Julie's town just knew she was going to be an incredible teacher. One day Julie suffered a terrible shock—someone tried to kill her father! Julie was so scared that her legs stopped working. She was paralyzed. How could Julie become a great teacher? Well, Julie kept teaching and praying from her bedside. Twenty-two years later, Julie walked again! Even before God gave her the ability to walk again, Julie started new schools. She kept starting schools, teaching, and praying for the rest of her life.

DURING SAINT JULIE BILLIART'S LIFE, MANY BATTLES WERE FOUGHT IN FRANCE. SAINT JULIE BILLIART'S SCHOOLS WERE OFTEN NEARBY THESE BATTLES. YET NONE OF THE WOMEN IN HER CHARGE WAS HURT.

*Jesus, You did the impossible in Saint Julie Billiart's
life—she walked again! Help me put my hope in You.*

SAINT MAGDALENA OF CANOSSA

1774–1835 • ITALY

GOD'S PLAN

The human mind plans the way, but the LORD directs the steps.

PROVERBS 16:9

Magdalena hoped so badly that her plan would work that she tried it twice! But God told her to try something else. Magdalena had tried to join a religious group called the Carmelites. Being a Carmelite Sister was all that Magdalena had ever wanted! But God knew that becoming a Carmelite wasn't the right path for Magdalena. God was preparing her for something special, a plan that would be even better than her plan. After a few more years, God led Magdalena to create a different group, a group of men and women who would serve the poorest of the poor. What could Magdalena give to these people in desperate need? She would share the love of Christ with them. The people who joined Magdalena's mission would help the poor all around the world.

> SAINT MAGDALENA OF CANOSSA FOUNDED THE CANOSSIAN SISTERS, THE SAME GROUP THAT SAINT JOSEPHINE BAKHITA (FEB. 8) JOINED.

Jesus, Your plan is the best plan. Direct my steps, just like You directed Saint Magdalena of Canossa.

SAINT STANISLAUS

1030–1079 • POLAND

SPEAK UP

They did not listen or incline their ear; they stiffened their
necks and would not hear or receive instruction.

JEREMIAH 17:23

Stanislaus wanted his country, Poland, to be at peace. When Stanislaus became the bishop of his city, he could see problems everywhere. Some people wanted a new king. Others declared that a new king would mean war. And people across the city were starving. Something had to be done. Stanislaus believed that their king, Boleslaw, was leading his people away from Jesus. Stanislaus spoke out against King Boleslaw and was executed. After his death, the people of Poland were amazed by his courage. They were inspired to speak up against the things they knew were wrong, just as Stanislaus had. Many people remembered Stanislaus and his dedication to the Church and were inspired to love Jesus more.

SAINT STANISLAUS WAS THE FIRST PERSON FROM POLAND TO BE NAMED A SAINT.

Jesus, help me speak up about what's right just as Saint Stanislaus did, even when it's unlikely that people will listen.

SAINT TERESA OF LOS ANDES

1900–1920 • CHILE

CHANGE OF HEART

A new heart I will give you, and a new spirit I will put within you.

EZEKIEL 36:26

Teresa rested on her bed peacefully, even though she knew that she would die soon. She remembered the unrest she had felt when she was a child, often throwing temper tantrums when she didn't get what she had wanted. Many times during Teresa's childhood, she felt so angry that she couldn't control her actions. Later, that all changed. Teresa read the story of the great Saint Thérèse of Lisieux (Oct. 1). Teresa learned that even the incredible Saint

> SAINT TERESA OF LOS ANDES LIKED TO SING, DANCE, SWIM, AND PLAY THE PIANO.

Thérèse had struggled with overwhelming feelings when she was a child. But Jesus had changed the Saint's heart, and He could change Teresa's heart too! Teresa decided to give her life over to God. Teresa no longer felt so angry—she felt God's peace. Teresa died when she was only twenty years old, but she died with a totally changed heart.

Jesus, change my heart! Make me more like You.

APRIL 13

SAINT MARTIN I

598–655 • ITALY

STICK BY THE TRUTH

*If anyone proclaims to you a gospel contrary to
what you received, let that one be accursed!*

GALATIANS 1:9

Martin pushed the letter back across his desk, still blank in the spot that wanted his signature. Martin knew that his enemies would use this refusal against him, but he didn't budge. The Church needed to know the truth about Jesus, and if Martin signed these letters, countless people would be confused and led away from the truth. Another powerful Church leader had written many lies about Jesus in this letter; he said Jesus couldn't be both God and man and expected the other leaders to agree with him. Martin, and many others, refused. Martin, who served as pope, knew that Jesus and God are one. Martin, who was supposed to be in charge of the Church, was tortured for his refusal, but he stuck by the truth.

SAINT MARTIN I DIDN'T WANT ANY OF THE EMPEROR'S SOLDIERS TO LOSE THEIR LIVES TRYING TO CAPTURE HIM, SO HE WENT WITH THEM WITHOUT A FIGHT.

*Jesus, You gave Saint Martin I the courage to
stick by the truth. Give me that courage too.*

SAINT DAMIEN OF MOLOKAI

**1840–1889 • BELGIUM AND HAWAII
(MODERN-DAY UNITED STATES)**

GOD'S MERCY

*As he entered a village, ten lepers approached him. Keeping their
distance, they called out, saying, "Jesus, Master, have mercy on us!"*

LUKE 17:12–13

Everywhere Damien looked, he saw suffering. He had come to the Hawaiian Islands to be a missionary. Hawaiian people who had Hansen's disease, or leprosy, were being isolated. They were left totally alone with no help because no one else wanted to get the disease. But Damien knew that Jesus went where no one else was willing to go, and Damien wanted to be like Jesus. So Damien moved to Hawaii and showed these people God's mercy. He became friends with them—so much so that he didn't want to leave, even when another missionary volunteered to take his place. Damien eventually did contract the disease. Even so, Damien loved where Jesus had placed him because it gave him an opportunity to serve.

SAINT DAMIEN OF MOLOKAI'S DAY OF DEATH, APRIL 15, IS CELEBRATED AS A MINOR HOLIDAY IN HAWAII.

*Jesus, help me show Your mercy to everyone I
meet, just as Saint Damien of Molokai did.*

BLESSED LUIS MAGAÑA SERVÍN

1902–1928 • MEXICO

GREAT LOVE

We know love by this, that he laid down his life for us—
and we ought to lay down our lives for one another.

1 JOHN 3:16

Luis walked toward the soldiers, intending to surrender. While Luis had been away from his house, soldiers had arrived to arrest him. Since Luis wasn't home, they arrested his brother instead. Why? The government thought that Luis was joining a revolt against the government, like some Christians were doing. Luis was a Christian, but he wasn't trying to fight against the government. Luis loved being at church, and he often prayed with the people who worked with him. He wasn't joining a rebellion. But he would show the government something that they had never seen before—an act of great love. Luis went to the jail where his brother was held and turned himself in, even though he wasn't guilty. He courageously took his brother's place so his brother could live. Before he was killed, Luis told the soldiers that he forgave them.

> BLESSED LUIS MAGAÑA SERVÍN LOVED BASEBALL.

*Jesus, help me love my brothers and
sisters with Your great love.*

BLESSED LUIS MAGAÑA SERVÍN IS ON TRACK TO BECOME A SAINT.

APRIL 16

SAINT BERNADETTE SOUBIROUS

1844–1879 • FRANCE

SPRINGS OF LIFE

"As the scripture has said, 'Out of the believer's heart shall flow rivers of living water.'"

JOHN 7:38

Bernadette faced many struggles. Her whole family lived in one room that was cold and damp. They were so poor that Bernadette couldn't even go to school when she was young. Throughout these trials, Bernadette remained humble and at peace. One day Bernadette believed that she saw Mary, the mother of God. Many people in Bernadette's city of Lourdes did not believe her story. Some of them even said that Bernadette was insane and needed to be kept away from everyone else! One time Bernadette believed Mary told her to drink from a spring, but she didn't see a spring. So Bernadette started digging in the ground. People watching must have thought Bernadette was insane! But only days later, a spring bubbled up from the exact spot where Bernadette dug.

PEOPLE STILL TRAVEL TO THE SPRING THAT SAINT BERNADETTE SOUBIROUS FOUND IN LOURDES TO PRAY AND ASK JESUS FOR HEALING.

Jesus, You show up in all kinds of unexpected places. Thank You for Your surprises.

APRIL 17*

SAINT BENEDICT JOSEPH LABRE

1748–1783 • FRANCE AND ITALY

JESUS IS EVERYTHING

The LORD will keep your going out and your coming
in from this time on and forevermore.

PSALM 121:8

Benedict longed to tell the world that Jesus is everything. He thought about becoming a priest or a monk. He thought about living in several different churches. But none of his plans worked! God was calling him to a completely different way of life. He wasn't supposed to stay in one church or even one city—Benedict would travel the world, and he would point everyone he came across to Jesus. He kept almost nothing with him. In fact, he had only one coat! He even slept on the ground outside. He visited different beautiful and holy places, praying all the way, witnessing to all he met. "Why don't you need beautiful things or warm clothes? You don't even have a house!" people would say to him. "Well," Benedict would reply, smiling, "I don't need those things. Jesus is everything." He stayed on the move for thirteen years.

> SAINT BENEDICT JOSEPH LABRE OWNED ALMOST NOTHING, BUT HE DID CARRY A FEW BOOKS WITH HIM—INCLUDING A COPY OF THE NEW TESTAMENT.

Jesus, You are everything! Help me believe this and share it with others, just as Saint Benedict Joseph Labre did.

SAINT APOLLONIUS

UNKNOWN–185 • ROMAN EMPIRE (MODERN-DAY ITALY)

GREATEST WISDOM

Happy are those who find wisdom, and
those who get understanding.

PROVERBS 3:13

Other Romans called Apollonius wise because he was known for studying books and reasoning the best possible solutions to problems. Apollonius was even wiser than most Romans knew because he had learned about Jesus and decided to follow Him. Unfortunately, Christianity was illegal in the Roman Empire, so Apollonius only told others about Jesus in secret. A man Apollonius knew told his secret to other powerful men. Apollonius was then given a choice—he could deny Jesus before the senate (the governing council of the empire) and live, or he could say that he was a Christian and be condemned to death. He chose to tell the truth. Apollonius made a beautiful speech to the senate about Jesus. However, the senate did not believe his wise words about Jesus, and Apollonius died for his faith.

> SAINT APOLLONIUS SAID IN HIS SPEECH THAT CHRISTIANITY GAVE HIM HOPE TO LIVE A GOOD LIFE, EVEN WHEN HE ENDURED SUFFERING.

Jesus, knowing You is the greatest wisdom.

VENERABLE FULTON J. SHEEN

1895–1979 · THE UNITED STATES

ROCK AND REDEEMER

Let the words of my mouth and the meditation of my heart
be acceptable to you, O LORD, my rock and my redeemer.

PSALM 19:14

Whether he was bent over his desk answering a letter or on his knees in prayer in the chapel, Fulton understood that words had great power. He chose his words carefully because with every word, he wanted to glorify God. Fulton was a priest, and even as a young priest, he was considered a wonderful preacher. In addition to being a priest, he was a professor, a speaker, an author, and the host of a television program. He spoke to crowded lecture halls and wrote personal answers to letters, sometimes as many as one hundred a day! He also wrote sixty-six books. The many words he spoke and wrote were all for his Rock and Redeemer—the Lord whom he trusted with his life and his words.

> VENERABLE FULTON J. SHEEN'S TELEVISION SHOW, *LIFE IS WORTH LIVING,* ATTRACTED OVER 30 MILLION VIEWERS EACH WEEK DURING THE HEIGHT OF ITS POPULARITY.

*Lord, You are my Rock and Redeemer. I
want all my words to honor You.*

VENERABLE FULTON J. SHEEN IS ON TRACK TO BECOME A SAINT.

SAINT CONRAD OF PARZHAM

1818–1894 · GERMANY

EVERYWHERE

The eyes of the LORD are in every place, keeping
watch on the evil and the good.

PROVERBS 15:3

Conrad worked through the field, the sun beating down on his bare head. "What is he doing?" the other workers wondered aloud. "Why isn't he wearing a hat to protect himself from the sun?" When Conrad heard their questions, he only smiled. He took his hat off everywhere he went to remind himself that God is everywhere. Men took off their hats in church as a way to say, "God is here!" Conrad never wore his hat so that he would always be aware of God's presence and constantly be in prayer. His prayers kept his heart focused on Jesus. Whenever groups of people saw Conrad coming, they knew they had to stop gossiping. Conrad didn't tolerate it when people spoke poorly of others because he was always thinking of Jesus and what He says to do.

> SAINT CONRAD OF PARZHAM WORKED AS A DOORKEEPER AT A CHURCH FOR FORTY-ONE YEARS, WELCOMING PEOPLE INTO THE CHURCH.

*Jesus, help me remember that You are everywhere,
just as Saint Conrad of Parzham did.*

SAINT ANSELM

1033–1109 · ENGLAND

DEBT PAID

The free gift is not like the trespass. For if the many died through the one man's trespass, much more surely have the grace of God and the free gift in the grace of the one man, Jesus Christ, abounded for the many.

ROMANS 5:15

Why did God become man?" Anselm wrote the question out and considered the different ways that he could answer it. Anselm was both a scholar and a monk. He lived and studied for the Church, so he was in a good position to provide great answers to difficult questions.

Many Christians couldn't answer that question well, so Anselm set to work to answer it. Here's what he found: Humans sinned. They did the opposite of what God told them to do. This sin was a crime against God, so humans owed a debt to God. But humans couldn't pay God—only God could pay Himself back. So God had to become a man, and He did this in Jesus. Jesus died on the cross for our sins. His death was the payment for our debt!

> SAINT ANSELM'S FATHER WANTED HIM TO BE A POLITICIAN, BUT HE KNEW FROM AN EARLY AGE THAT GOD CALLED HIM TO WORK FOR THE CHURCH.

Jesus, thank You for paying back my whole debt!

APRIL 22*

SAINT ADALBERT OF PRAGUE

956–997 • BOHEMIA (MODERN-DAY CZECHIA)

STAND UP

So then, brothers and sisters, stand firm and hold
fast to the traditions that you were taught by us,
either by word of mouth or by our letter.

2 THESSALONIANS 2:15

Adalbert stood up for what he believed. He served the Church as a priest in many different European countries. He moved around so much because so many people disagreed with him. Adalbert was often faced by a group of angry people, and many times, these people were priests too! Once, Adalbert declared that the priests needed to start living according to God's will. Adalbert also said that priests needed to dedicate their whole lives to the Church, and they couldn't take the money given to the Church to buy themselves lavish gifts. Just for saying that, he was told to leave the country! Even though he had to stand up against people in his own church, Adalbert did what was right.

SAINT ADALBERT OF PRAGUE BECAME A MARTYR ON A MISSIONARY TRIP TO THE REGION NEAR THE BALTIC SEA. HE AND THE OTHER MISSIONARIES STOOD UP FOR THEIR FAITH, EVEN WHEN FACING DEATH.

*Jesus, give me the courage to stand up for what is right,
even when those around me want to do what is wrong.*

APRIL 23

SAINT GEORGE

280–303 • ROMAN EMPIRE (MODERN-DAY TURKEY)

GOD'S ARMY

Put on the whole armor of God, so that you may be able to stand against the wiles of the devil.

EPHESIANS 6:11

George fought in the ranks of the Roman soldiers, and he became a tribune, which meant that the other soldiers recognized his bravery. But George's most important identity wasn't that of a soldier, tribune, or Roman—it was being a Christian. George lived about 250 years after Jesus lived, and a cruel emperor named Diocletian ruled over Rome. Diocletian hated Christians and often condemned them to terrible deaths. Once, when George's army started making sacrifices to Roman gods before battle, the other soldiers noticed that George wasn't worshipping. When they asked him why, George told them about Jesus. Because of his testimony, George was tortured and killed. George wasn't just brave as a soldier; he was brave enough to choose his faith in Jesus over his own life.

> A FUN LEGEND TELLS OF SAINT GEORGE KILLING A DRAGON WITH A LANCE, SO PICTURES OF SAINT GEORGE OFTEN SHOW HIM FIGHTING A DRAGON.

Jesus, Saint George stood against temptation because he had on the armor of God. Help me be brave in my battles too.

APRIL 24

SAINT FIDELIS OF SIGMARINGEN

1577–1622 • GERMANY

CHEERFUL GIVER

Each of you must give as you have made up your mind, not
reluctantly or under compulsion, for God loves a cheerful giver.

2 CORINTHIANS 9:7

Fidelis was a friar, which means he lived and preached in a church and served the poor. He lived during a time of division among countries and churches. Amid the confusion, people who loved Jesus were often killed. But Fidelis preached about Jesus without fear, and he made many enemies for doing so. Fidelis accepted that his faith in Jesus would likely result in his death. The fact that some people wanted him to die didn't make him sad—it made him cheerful! He considered it an honor to give his life *and* death to Jesus. Eventually, Fidelis was killed by a group of soldiers. As he was dying, Fidelis asked God to forgive the people who were killing him.

> BEFORE SAINT FIDELIS OF SIGMARINGEN BECAME A FRIAR, HE WORKED AS A LAWYER, DEFENDING CLIENTS WHO COULD NOT PAY WELL.

*Jesus, I want to be like Saint Fidelis of Sigmaringen,
who gave You his life cheerfully.*

APRIL 25

SAINT MARK

FIRST CENTURY • JUDEA (MODERN-DAY ISRAEL)

GOOD NEWS EVERYWHERE

*They went out and proclaimed the good news everywhere,
while the Lord worked with them and confirmed the
message by the signs that accompanied it.*

MARK 16:20

After Jesus' death and resurrection, Mark helped the apostles in their mission to proclaim the good news everywhere. When the apostle James was killed and the apostle Peter had been captured by the authorities and sent to prison, Mark's mother opened their home to other believers, who gathered there to pray. "May the will of God be done," they prayed over and over again. The next morning Peter knocked at their door! The believers were overjoyed that God had freed Peter from prison. Mark would go on to do missionary work and write amazing testimonies to tell the world about what Jesus could do.

SAINT MARK AND SAINT BARNABAS (JUNE 11) WERE COUSINS.

*Jesus, I want to share the good news
everywhere I go, just as Saint Mark did.*

SAINT PEDRO DE SAN JOSÉ BETANCUR

1626–1667 • GUATEMALA

FAITHFUL SHEPHERD

He said to him, "Lord, you know everything; you know
that I love you." Jesus said to him, "Feed my sheep."

JOHN 21:17

Pedro loved the people of Guatemala. He loved the rich, and he loved the poor. He spent the first part of his adulthood as a shepherd, but he left the countryside to look for a job in the city. He found that there was certainly enough work to go around! He became a kind of shepherd to the people in the city, guiding them and helping them. The poor had undeniable needs; they needed hospitals and schools. But the rich had needs too—spiritual needs! They needed to know the love of Jesus, to admit the wrongs they had done, and to offer up some of their wealth to support the poor. Pedro's faithful shepherding of the Guatemalan people showed that Jesus can meet anyone's needs.

> SAINT PEDRO DE SAN JOSÉ BETANCUR IS THE FIRST SAINT OF GUATEMALA.

*Jesus, I am one of Your sheep. You can give me anything
I need. Help me see and fill the needs of others.*

SAINT LOUIS-MARIE GRIGNION DE MONTFORT

1673–1716 • FRANCE

PRAISE GOD!

The LORD gave, and the LORD has taken away;
blessed be the name of the LORD.

JOB 1:21

When crowds listened to Louis preach, they didn't yawn or rub their eyes, even when he talked for a long time. They stood with rapt attention, their eyes fixed on him. Louis brought the news of Jesus to people with great passion. His passion inspired others to take action for God. In fact, he inspired a group of people to build a large wall, decorated with gigantic bronze crosses, that would encourage the whole city. Anyone walking by it would remember Jesus and His sacrifice and would pray. Everyone worked on the project enthusiastically. Unfortunately, the king ordered for the entire wall, called a calvary, which took hundreds of people an entire year to build, to be torn down. How did Louis respond? He said simply, "Praise God! God's still in control of everything."

> SAINT LOUIS-MARIE GRIGNION DE MONTFORT OFTEN TRADED CLOTHES WITH THE POOR PEOPLE HE MET ON HIS TRAVELS.

Jesus, help me accept the good and the bad with the same grace that Saint Louis-Marie Grignion de Montfort accepted them.

SAINT PETER CHANEL

1803–1841 • FRANCE AND OCEANIA

HOLD ON TO BELIEF

If I take the wings of the morning and settle at the
farthest limits of the sea, even there your hand shall
lead me, and your right hand shall hold me fast.

PSALM 139:9–10

Peter waited when God asked him to wait, and he worked cheerfully when God gave tasks that seemed impossible. No matter what, Peter held on to the belief that God loved him and that He was in control. Peter always wanted to be a missionary, but first he was called to spend time serving God in his country of France. When Peter was a young priest, he was sent to a church that had fallen on difficult times. He helped the church grow and become more faithful to God by simply showing them how to serve the sick. Eventually,

EVEN THOUGH SAINT PETER CHANEL'S MISSION DIDN'T LOOK SUCCESSFUL, FUTUNA ISLAND HAS MANY CHRISTIANS LIVING ON IT TODAY.

Peter was sent on a mission to a faraway island in the middle of the ocean: a place called Futuna. For most of the time Peter spent on Futuna, no one was interested in his message about Jesus. Finally, the chief's son asked to be baptized, and the chief, in a fit of rage, killed Peter.

*Jesus, thank You for Saint Peter Chanel's courage. Help
me hold on to my belief that You are in control.*

APRIL 29

SAINT CATHERINE OF SIENA

1347–1380 • ITALY

SMALL START

"For truly I tell you, if you have faith the size of a mustard seed, you will say to this mountain, 'Move from here to there,' and it will move."

MATTHEW 17:20

Catherine would eventually do big things. She would help people who were sick and poor. She would help whole cities resolve conflicts. She would even enter a worldwide dispute about who should be the pope. But when Catherine was young, she started small—at least, it looked small. Catherine spent three whole years in prayer in a small room attached to her father's house. She wasn't trapped—she was free in Jesus. She talked to Jesus, sang to Him, and learned from Him. When she left her small room three years later, she was ready to do big things.

SAINT CATHERINE OF SIENA WROTE THOUSANDS OF LETTERS DURING HER LIFE—TO HER FAMILY, TO HER FRIENDS, AND EVEN TO THE POPE.

Jesus, I want to start changing the world by letting You change my heart.

SAINT PIUS V

1504–1572 • ITALY

ON THE SAME PAGE

I revere your commandments, which I love,
and I will meditate on your statutes.

PSALM 119:48

When he became pope, Pius already knew that some things needed to change. People were abandoning the Catholic Church left and right. Priests were abusing their powers, demanding that members of their families be given powerful roles in city and church leadership. Priests also took large amounts of money from people who were poor. Ultimately, Pius decided all the priests needed to be on the same page. Maybe, if everyone read the same scriptures every day, the Church would grow in its faithfulness to God. Pius published

SAINT PIUS V ORDERED THAT THE WATERWAYS BE FIXED IN HIS CITY, DRAINING THE DIRTY WATER OUT OF THE CITY. THIS HELPED REDUCE THE AMOUNT OF ILLNESS THE POOR PEOPLE WERE EXPERIENCING.

and promoted a missal, which is a book that detailed which prayers and songs should be used at each church service. The missal said that every priest would use the same readings from the Bible at their services.

Jesus, Saint Pius V loved Your Word.
Help me love Your Word too.

SAINT JEREMIAH THE PROPHET

**SEVENTH AND SIXTH CENTURIES BC · KINGDOM
OF JUDAH (MODERN-DAY ISRAEL)**

WORD OF THE LORD

Now the word of the LORD came to me.

JEREMIAH 1:4

Jeremiah was a prophet, or a person who delivered messages from God. He lived hundreds of years before Jesus was born. Jeremiah spent hours in prayer, talking to God, and God gave Jeremiah many messages to deliver. Jeremiah knew that his people, the Jews, wouldn't like hearing what God had told him. Some of Jeremiah's messages said that the Jews were disobeying God. They had forgotten Him and decided to worship other gods. Some of the messages said that if the Jews kept disobeying God, they would lose their homes and be forced to live somewhere else. Many of the messages said that God loved the Jews, and He wanted them to ask for forgiveness and put their trust in Him again. Jeremiah was right—the Jews didn't want to hear these messages from God. According to tradition, Jeremiah was stoned to death.

> SAINT JEREMIAH THE PROPHET LIVED DURING THE REIGN OF THE RIGHTEOUS KING JOSIAH, THE "BOY KING" WHO RULED WHEN HE WAS ONLY A CHILD.

*Jesus, help me listen to Your words and obey
them, even when they aren't easy to hear.*

SAINT ATHANASIUS

296–373 • EGYPT

ONE GOD

"For just as the Father has life in himself, so he has granted the Son also to have life in himself."

JOHN 5:26

Athanasius lived during a time when the Church was facing many changes. One of the biggest changes was that the emperor of Rome had declared that belief in Jesus was no longer illegal. For two hundred years, Christians had sometimes been dying at the hands of the government for their beliefs. Now that Christianity was legal, Christians could join together to worship without any secrets or hiding. But since the Church had been in hiding so long, they didn't have a system of beliefs. Athanasius fought against the false belief that Jesus was not God, just a creation of God. Athanasius knew there is one God in three Persons—God the Father, God the Son, and God the Holy Spirit. He and many other Church leaders helped produce a creed, or statement, that Christians could memorize, helping them remember who Jesus is—the Son of God.

> SAINT ATHANASIUS STUCK TO HIS BELIEFS. DIFFERENT EMPERORS KEPT EXILING HIM TO TRY TO GET HIM TO CHANGE HIS MIND, BUT IT DIDN'T WORK. HE WAS EXILED FIVE TIMES!

Jesus, I believe that You are God's Son.

MAY 3

SAINT PHILIP

**FIRST CENTURY · GAZA DESERT AND
GALILEE (MODERN-DAY ISRAEL)**

GOOD NEWS

The Spirit said to Philip, "Go over to this chariot
and join it." So Philip ran up to it.

ACTS 8:29–30

Right before He returned to heaven, Jesus told His followers to go and tell the whole world about Him. His followers didn't have radios or televisions or other ways to tell people in different countries about Jesus. But Jesus made a way for them. The Holy Spirit guided His followers to different parts of the world so they could spread the good news about Jesus. One of Jesus' followers, Philip, listened carefully when the Holy Spirit told him what to do. Once, when Philip was walking through the desert, he came upon a man sitting in a chariot, reading some of the scriptures. The man asked Philip about the scripture he was reading, and the Holy Spirit told Philip to respond. Philip told the man what the scriptures meant. He shared the good news and explained who Jesus is. The man became a Christian!

> THE MAN WHOM SAINT PHILIP LED TO CHRIST WAS FROM ETHIOPIA, A COUNTRY IN AFRICA.

*Jesus, I want to share the good news with
others. Help me listen to the Holy Spirit.*

VENERABLE MOTHER MARIA KAUPAS

1880–1940 · LITHUANIA AND THE UNITED STATES

DONE IN LOVE

Let all that you do be done in love.

1 CORINTHIANS 16:14

When she was seventeen, Maria traveled across the ocean to visit her brother, who was working in a town in Pennsylvania as a priest. Maria, who was born in Lithuania, relished the adventure. Maria also noticed that many people from her country lived as immigrants in the United States. Maria saw that the lives of immigrants were hard—the jobs they were offered, like work in the mines, had incredibly long hours and dangerous risks. Because of their circumstances, it was difficult for the Lithuanian immigrants to be true to the traditions and the faith of their home country. Maria knew she had to do something about this. Inspired by the great love God gave her for her countrymen, she dedicated her life to teaching the children and adults about their faith and helping them hold on to their traditions.

> VENERABLE MOTHER MARIA KAUPAS'S PERSONAL MOTTO WAS "ALWAYS MORE, ALWAYS BETTER, ALWAYS WITH LOVE."

*Jesus, help me do things for others in great love,
like Venerable Mother Maria Kaupas did.*

VENERABLE MOTHER MARIA KAUPAS IS ON TRACK TO BECOME A SAINT.

MAY 5

SAINT NUNZIO SULPRIZIO

1817–1836 · ITALY

FOR CHRIST

He has graciously granted you the privilege not only of
believing in Christ, but of suffering for him as well.

PHILIPPIANS 1:29

Many Saints built schools and hospitals and cathedrals; they spoke to thousands about the love of Jesus and gave their possessions to the poor. But not every Saint had these opportunities. As a young boy, Nunzio loved learning about the Saints. He hoped to be a priest or a missionary one day, just like his heroes.

But Nunzio had to work in his family's black-smith shop instead of continuing school. And because he was often sick, he couldn't work quickly. Nunzio died of a leg injury he received in the shop. As he lay in the hospital, Nunzio remembered that Jesus suffered too. He used

> THE WORDS OF SAINT PHILIP NERI (MAY 26) ABOUT THE STRENGTH OF BEING CHEERFUL ENCOURAGED SAINT NUNZIO SULPRIZIO WHILE HE WAS IN THE HOSPITAL.

his time in the hospital to pray. The constant prayer and the cheerful attitude that Nunzio had in the hospital were his great works for Christ.

*Jesus, I want to commit everything
to You, even the hard times.*

MAY 6

SAINT DOMINIC SAVIO

1842–1857 · ITALY

TURN TOWARD THE GOOD

*Who shall stand in his holy place? Those who have clean
hands and pure hearts, who do not lift up their souls
to what is false, and do not swear deceitfully.*

PSALM 24:3–4

Dominic studied hard in obedience to both God and his beloved teacher, Saint John Bosco (Jan. 31). Like his great teacher, Dominic spent a lot of time around unruly boys. But Dominic had a gift for turning unkind conversation and activity toward what's good. When other boys would start to gossip, Dominic offered something else to talk about. When other boys made bad choices, Dominic spoke up and found something better for everyone to do. Dominic wanted to be friends with Jesus, and he wanted to show others how to be friends with Jesus, too, and turn toward what's right.

> EVEN THOUGH SAINT DOMINIC SAVIO WAS SERIOUS ABOUT HIS RELIGIOUS STUDIES, HE LOVED TO PLAY GAMES AND MAKE JOKES TOO.

*Jesus, help me use my words for good. I want to turn
away from evil things toward what is good and right.*

SAINT ROSE VENERINI

1656–1728 • ITALY

GOOD TEACHER

I will instruct you and teach you the way you should go.

PSALM 32: 8

Rose knelt in the front room of her house, repeating the prayers she had known since she was a child. She was surrounded by other women and girls from the neighborhood; she had known many of them since she was young. A few months before, Rose had been surrounded in a convent, or a house where women devoted their lives to Jesus together, saying these same prayers. But God had different plans for Rose. Though she had wanted to stay in the convent, Rose left to help take care of her mother. As Rose looked around the room, she noticed that

> SAINT ROSE VENERINI WAS ONCE VISITED BY THE POPE, WHO THANKED HER FOR THE WORK SHE WAS DOING, SAYING, "YOU ARE DOING THAT WHICH WE CANNOT DO."

many of the girls didn't know the prayers at all! She had to do something! She started a preschool in her town, and her amazing teaching skills made the school a success. Her reputation as a good teacher spread, and church leaders asked her to help organize more schools. Rose realized this had been God's plan for her life all along.

Jesus, help me listen to good teachers
like Saint Rose Venerini.

MAY 8

SAINT PETER OF TARENTAISE

1102–1175 • FRANCE AND SWITZERLAND

HOUSEHOLD FAITH

As for me and my household, we will serve the LORD.

JOSHUA 24:15

Some Saints became priests and nuns because their parents encouraged them to. But in Peter's family, the encouragement went in the other direction! Peter loved God and wanted to dedicate his whole life to Him by serving as a monk. He was so confident of his choice that he convinced his whole household— his father, his two brothers, and his sister—to dedicate their lives to God too. During his ministry, Peter worked with the sick and with people who were traveling, and he also worked on behalf of the poor. After he became a bishop, he started a tradition called "May bread"—he gathered food from different churches and donated the food to the poor. The "May bread" tradition lasted for six hundred years.

EVEN THOUGH HE WAS BORN IN FRANCE, SAINT PETER OF TARENTAISE DID MOST OF HIS MINISTRY IN SWITZERLAND.

Jesus, I want to share my love for You with my family, just as Saint Peter of Tarentaise did.

SAINT PACHOMIUS

292–348 • EGYPT

RULES OF LIFE

Do not turn aside from any of the words that I am
commanding you today, either to the right or to the left.

DEUTERONOMY 28:14

Pachomius fought in the Egyptian army. While he was a soldier, he met some Christians. These Christians were willing to give up anything for their God. Pachomius never forgot those Christians. After his time in the army was over, Pachomius decided he was going to follow Jesus. Being a soldier had taught Pachomius many things—one of these things was the importance of having rules for everyone to follow. Rules helped everyone work together as a team. So when Pachomius and another Christian decided to live as monks, they gave themselves a set of rules to live by, guided by what they knew about Jesus' life and the teachings of His followers. By the time Pachomius died, more than seven thousand monks lived in houses that he had founded, living by the rules he had written.

> SAINT BASIL (JAN. 2) AND SAINT BENEDICT (JULY 11) ALSO WROTE SETS OF RULES FOR CHRISTIANS TO LIVE BY, CALLED "RULES OF LIFE." THEY WERE INSPIRED BY SAINT PACHOMIUS.

*Jesus, help me follow Your commands. I know
Your rules help make my life better.*

SAINT JOHN OF ÁVILA

1500–1569 • SPAIN

RICH INHERITANCE

By his great mercy he has given us a new birth into a living hope through the resurrection of Jesus Christ from the dead, and into an inheritance that is imperishable, undefiled, and unfading.

1 PETER 1:3–4

When John's parents died, they left him a large amount of money as an inheritance. John didn't have any siblings, so if he had wanted to spend it all on himself, he could have. He could have lived comfortably in a large house with many servants. But John knew something about money—any money he was given was just a gift to be given back to God. John gave the money that his parents left him back to God by giving it away to the poor. He dedicated himself to God and to educating young people. He talked about Jesus in ways that were beautiful, in ways that people could understand. John's thoughts were a rich inheritance for the people who heard him.

SAINT JOHN OF ÁVILA ATTENDED A UNIVERSITY AS A STUDENT WHEN HE WAS ONLY FOURTEEN YEARS OLD.

Jesus, I want to understand the value of Your love.

SAINT IGNATIUS OF LACONI

1701–1781 • ITALY

LISTENING WITH KINDNESS

Lead a life worthy of the calling to which you have been called, with all humility and gentleness, with patience, bearing with one another in love.

EPHESIANS 4:1–2

Ignatius took slow and steady steps toward the next house. On his back he carried a large sack of donations he'd received. At the end of the day, he would take them to the place he lived with the other friars.

Ignatius was not their leader or even an inspiring teacher. He spent his time making materials for the community and walking from house to house in the surrounding countryside, asking for donations that would help the friars continue their life of prayer. Sometimes the townspeople would ask Ignatius to come into their houses. Ignatius always listened to them with kindness and patience. He would cheer up anyone in the house who was sick or lonely. When he left, he looked ahead with kindness to the next house.

WHEN HE WAS ABOUT TWENTY YEARS OLD, SAINT IGNATIUS OF LACONI ALMOST LOST HIS LIFE WHEN HIS HORSE GOT SPOOKED. MIRACULOUSLY, THE HORSE CALMED, AND SAINT IGNATIUS THEN COMMITTED HIS LIFE TO SERVING GOD SINCE HE BELIEVED THAT GOD HAD SAVED HIM.

Jesus, sometimes You ask me to do something as simple as listen to others. Help me listen well.

MAY 12

SAINTS NEREUS AND ACHILLEUS

FIRST CENTURY • ROMAN EMPIRE (MODERN-DAY LOCATION UNKNOWN)

BEAUTIFUL SACRIFICE

Therefore be imitators of God, as beloved children,
and live in love, as Christ loved us and gave himself up
for us, a fragrant offering and sacrifice to God.

EPHESIANS 5:1–2

Nereus and Achilleus fought for the empire of Rome, but they wanted to fight for something more. They lived during the days of the early Church. Most leaders hated the Christians. These Christians were calling Jesus their king, and there couldn't be two kings! But Nereus and Achilleus loved Jesus more than they loved the emperor and even more than they loved their own lives. Giving up their jobs as soldiers to become Christians would be very dangerous, but Nereus and Achilleus knew that it was worth it. They were killed for their faith in Jesus. An artist made a sculpture of the moment when Achilleus gave up his life for Jesus. The sculpture is the earliest known artwork depicting martyrdom. But Nereus and Achilleus's love for Jesus was even more beautiful than any sculpture.

> SAINTS NEREUS AND ACHILLEUS MAY HAVE BEEN SERVANTS OF THE EMPEROR'S NIECE.

*Jesus, I want to know the beauty of Your sacrifice
and praise You as the one true King.*

SAINT LEOPOLD MANDIC

1866–1942 • CROATIA AND ITALY

ONE BY ONE

"Just so, I tell you, there will be more joy in heaven
over one sinner who repents than over ninety-nine
righteous persons who need no repentance."

LUKE 15:7

Leopold was a priest, but unlike other priests, he did not often preach to large crowds. His voice wasn't loud enough, and he couldn't stand up for long periods of time because of his poor health.

But God knows how to use everyone. Even though Leopold couldn't preach, he could still work as a priest and love people. Leopold spent hour after hour listening to people talk about their sins and struggles. People came to Leopold one by one. He heard people's confessions. Privately, people told Leopold about the ways they had sinned. He heard them say that they felt like they weren't good enough for God. Leopold listened with kindness and encouraged them, telling them over and over that God loved them and forgave them. Leopold spoke to thousands of hearts—he just did it one by one.

> SAINT LEOPOLD MANDIC ALWAYS WANTED TO BE A MISSIONARY, BUT HE WAS NOT ABLE TO TRAVEL BECAUSE OF HIS HEALTH.

*Jesus, help me share Your love with the world. I'll
start by sharing it with one person today.*

MAY 14

SAINT MATTHIAS

FIRST CENTURY • GALILEE (MODERN-DAY ISRAEL)

CHOSEN

They cast lots for them, and the lot fell on Matthias;
and he was added to the eleven apostles.

ACTS 1:26

Matthias followed Jesus before His death and resurrection. He saw Jesus heal people and perform miracles. Matthias, along with the other disciples, abandoned Jesus when He was arrested. Matthias wept when Jesus was killed and rejoiced when he saw Jesus again after He rose from the grave. Matthias was chosen to replace Judas, the disciple who betrayed Jesus. After the disciples received the Holy Spirit, Matthias traveled away from Jerusalem to follow Jesus' command to take the good news everywhere and to everyone. Matthias eventually came to the place that is now called Turkey. Matthias, like the other disciples, was killed for refusing to give up his faith in Jesus.

> SAINT MATTHIAS WAS CHOSEN BY THE OTHER APOSTLES TO REPLACE JUDAS ISCARIOT. THEY CHOSE HIM BY CASTING LOTS—LIKE FLIPPING A COIN AND EXPECTING GOD TO CONTROL IT.

Jesus, thank You for choosing me to be one of Your disciples. Show me how to share Your love with the world.

SAINT ISIDORE THE FARMER

1070–1130 · SPAIN

WALK HUMBLY

What does the LORD require of you but to do justice, and
to love kindness, and to walk humbly with your God?

MICAH 6:8

Isidore wasn't an incredible scholar or priest who preached to thousands of people. He was a farmer who worked on another man's land. Isidore lived a very simple life. He didn't travel much. He spent time praying and worshipping God in the church that was near his home, and he loved and cared for the poor people who were living close by. Sometimes, Isidore would even have to rush to get to work after attending church or serving others. He would even wake up earlier than he needed to so he could go to church before work. Isidore loved being with God in prayer. He loved God exactly where he was, and he walked humbly with his God.

> SAINT ISIDORE THE FARMER LOVED ANIMALS AND INSISTED THAT PEOPLE TREAT ANIMALS WITH CARE.

Jesus, help me love You exactly where I am.

MAY 16*

BLESSED MICHAEL MCGIVNEY

1852–1890 • THE UNITED STATES

LIKE A CHILD

"Truly I tell you, unless you change and become like children, you will never enter the kingdom of heaven."

MATTHEW 18:3

Michael pursued the life of a priest from the time he was a young man. After his ordination, Michael stayed true to himself and his mission. He was kind, animated, and enthusiastic. He was even called "childlike" by some. That's not to say he was childish—he trusted God, believing himself to be one of God's beloved children. Michael noticed that many young men didn't have the same trust. They suffered from not only a lack of faith but a lack of good things to do. Michael started a group called the Knights of Columbus, which helped men grow in their faith and organize works of service for them to do for their communities.

> WHEN HE WAS THIRTEEN, BLESSED MICHAEL MCGIVNEY WORKED IN A FACTORY THAT MADE SPOONS. THE MONEY HE MADE HELPED SUPPORT HIS LARGE FAMILY—HE WAS THE OLDEST CHILD.

Jesus, help me be like a child—that is, totally trusting in You.

BLESSED MICHAEL MCGIVNEY IS ON TRACK TO BECOME A SAINT.

SAINT PASCHAL BAYLON

1540–1592 • SPAIN

DEFEND THE TRUTH

Do your best to present yourself to God as one
approved by him, a worker who has no need to be
ashamed, rightly explaining the word of truth.

2 TIMOTHY 2:15

What is the best way to defend the truth about Jesus? It's not always about reading a ton of books and having the best answers in arguments. Knowledge is good, but knowledge alone skips a very important step. To defend the truth about Jesus, a person has to love Jesus. Paschal loved Jesus. He was a friar, and he loved spending time with Jesus in prayer. He spent his life loving the poor and talking to people who had no one else to talk to. And when the time came, Paschal defended the truth about Jesus to people who disagreed with him and tried to hurt him.

SAINT PASCHAL BAYLON WAS KNOWN FOR TREATING PEOPLE WITH COURTESY, NO MATTER HOW RICH OR POOR THEY WERE.

*Jesus, help me explain the truths about You with
kindness, just as Saint Paschal Baylon did.*

144

SAINT JOHN I

470–526 • ITALY

UNITY

Put things in order, listen to my appeal, agree with one another,
live in peace; and the God of love and peace will be with you.

2 CORINTHIANS 13:11

John wanted to end a worldwide conflict, even though he knew he would probably have to sacrifice his life to do it. During his life, the Church was split in two. This would be a problem that happened again and again throughout history, but as the pope, John knew he needed to do his part to keep the Church unified. John unified the Church with Emperor Justin I of the Byzantine Empire, which ended hundreds of years of conflict. Unfortunately, the ruler in Rome, Theodoric the Great, didn't approve. Theodoric captured Pope John and starved him to death in prison. But John was willing to make this sacrifice for the sake of unity in the Church.

THE DATE OF EASTER CHANGES EVERY YEAR. THIS IS BECAUSE EASTER IS ALWAYS CELEBRATED ON A SUNDAY. SAINT JOHN I HELPED THE CHURCH CHOOSE A SYSTEM FOR PICKING THE DATE OF EASTER EACH YEAR, A SYSTEM CALLED THE ALEXANDRIAN COMPUTATION.

Jesus, I want to ask You for help when I'm in the middle
of a disagreement. Help me unite those who disagree.

SAINT YVES

1253–1303 • FRANCE

JUSTICE

When justice is done, it is a joy to the
righteous, but dismay to evildoers.

PROVERBS 21:15

Yves wanted justice for everyone. *Justice* is what happens when wrongs
are put right. Say a girl tears a page of her brother's favorite book.
Should she lie about it? That's not justice. Should her brother become
angry and say mean things to her? That's not justice. Justice looks like
the girl telling her brother exactly what happened. And justice looks like
her brother forgiving her and telling her how she can make things right
again, maybe by paying for some tape so they can tape the page back
together. Yves knew that it was difficult to put wrongs
right again—especially without someone to help people
find solutions. So Yves became that helper by becoming a lawyer. As a lawyer, he helped sort out the many
different wrongs that can happen between people.
Yves even helped people who couldn't pay him for his
help. To Yves, money wasn't as important as justice.

SAINT YVES
WAS ABLE TO
HELP PEOPLE
FOR FREE
BECAUSE HE
KEPT HIS OWN
COSTS OF
LIVING LOW.

Jesus, You love justice. Help me love justice too.

SAINT BERNARDINE OF SIENA

1380–1444 • ITALY

PRAISEWORTHY

Finally, beloved, whatever is true, whatever is honorable,
whatever is just, whatever is pure, whatever is pleasing,
whatever is commendable, if there is any excellence and if
there is anything worthy of praise, think about these things.

PHILIPPIANS 4:8

Bernardine didn't want to think about anything that didn't glorify God. He asked Jesus for a pure heart and Jesus answered him. Because his heart was pure, Bernardine was able to serve people who had nothing, who often lived in terrible conditions. He hated hearing anyone say anything rude or crude. Bernardine loved the example of Jesus' mother, Mary, and wanted to imitate her purity of heart. He wanted a heart that was so pure that it was able to say yes to God, just like Mary had. Bernardine spoke across Italy about truth and excellence. A biography was written about Bernardine's life after he died. His biographer called him a light in the darkness because he chose to do what is pure and just in a world full of dark deeds.

JUST LIKE SAINT DOMINIC SAVIO (MAY 6), SAINT BERNARDINE OF SIENA DIDN'T PARTICIPATE IN RUDE CONVERSATION OR GOSSIP. PEOPLE WOULD STOP BACKBITING IMMEDIATELY WHEN THEY SAW BERNARDINE COMING!

Jesus, I only want to speak about things that glorify You.

MAY 21

SAINT CRISTÓBAL MAGALLANES JARA

1869–1927 • MEXICO

KINDNESS TO ALL

"Bless those who curse you, pray for those who abuse you."

LUKE 6:28

Cristóbal was born in Mexico. During his life, bitter divisions existed among the people living in Mexico. There were frequent wars and hostility among the different groups. Cristóbal wanted the wars to end. He helped the people who attended his church build up their city by improving schools, creating carpentry jobs, and even taking part in planning new water systems for the town. He dedicated his life to serving people who spoke a different language and had unfamiliar customs. His kindness was misinterpreted terribly, and he was accused of starting a rebellion.

ONE OF SAINT CRISTÓBAL MAGALLANES JARA'S FIRST JOBS WAS HERDING SHEEP.

Cristóbal just wanted the fighting to end, and he willingly gave up his life for it. On his way to prison, where he knew he would wait to die, he gave his last pieces of clothing to the people who escorted him to prison. He spoke to them kindly and reminded them of God's forgiveness.

Jesus, help me show kindness to all people,
even those who don't deserve it.

MAY 22

SAINT RITA OF CASCIA

1381–1457 • ITALY

FORGIVING FAMILY

"Will not God grant justice to his chosen ones who cry to him day and night? Will he delay long in helping them?"

LUKE 18:7

When Rita was still young, her husband was killed. Other people thought that Rita and her children should hate the men who killed her husband. That was how everyone else felt, even the other people in Rita's own family! But Rita openly forgave the men who killed her husband, and she told her own sons to never kill those men in return. Even after her sons died, Rita kept loving Jesus. She asked to serve at a church nearby. She wanted to be a Sister, one of the women who dedicated their lives to serving Jesus and the Church. Rita asked again and again, only to be refused. The Sisters said that first Rita's whole family had to show forgiveness to the men who killed her husband. So Rita begged her family day and night, she prayed for them, and she constantly reminded them that Jesus forgave the people who killed Him. Her family finally agreed to forgive.

SAINT RITA OF CASCIA'S GIVEN NAME, MARGHERITA, MEANS "PEARL."

Jesus, help me forgive like You forgave and just as Saint Rita of Cascia forgave—with my whole heart.

SAINT JOHN BAPTIST DE ROSSI

1698–1764 • ITALY

PERFECT IN WEAKNESS

He said to me, "My grace is sufficient for you, for power is made perfect in weakness." So, I will boast all the more gladly of my weaknesses, so that the power of Christ may dwell in me.

2 CORINTHIANS 12:9

Even though he suffered from epilepsy, or frequent seizures, John was a priest on the move. He also knew that the sick and dying in the hospital didn't just need doctors; they needed company. He knew that the prisoners in the jails didn't just need their freedom; they needed to be free in Christ. Everywhere he went, John saw opportunities to help others. With his small salary, John kept enough savings to buy a house for women and girls who had no home and no way of providing themselves with one. Even though John suffered from an illness, Jesus used John's weakness to give him compassion for other people. John trusted in Jesus, knowing that He could use anyone to do His work.

> SAINT JOHN BAPTIST DE ROSSI WOULD PREACH UP TO SIX TIMES A DAY!

Jesus, my weaknesses are made perfect in Your love!

SAINT MARY MAGDALENE DE PAZZI

1566–1607 • ITALY

TAUGHT TO PRAY

He was praying in a certain place, and after he had finished, one of his disciples said to him, "Lord, teach us to pray, as John taught his disciples."

LUKE 11:1

Mary spent her life in conversations with Jesus. She loved God and prayer. When she was only nine years old, she asked to be taught more about how to pray. Many people prayed with "rote" prayers, or prayers written by someone else and then memorized. The words of these prayers were beautiful, and Mary wanted more. She was taught to make "mental prayers"—that is, to sit in the quiet and speak to God with her own thoughts. She would think about Jesus and picture His cross, growing closer to Him as she better understood His suffering. Later, she would become a Sister, a woman who lived in a convent with other women, who dedicated her life to service and prayer.

> SAINT MARY MAGDALENE DE PAZZI BELIEVED THAT GOD ASKED HER TO GO BAREFOOT. TO KEEP HER SACRIFICE HIDDEN, SHE REMOVED THE BOTTOMS OF HER SHOES. EVEN THOUGH SHE WAS BAREFOOT, IT STILL LOOKED LIKE SHE WAS WEARING SHOES.

Jesus, teach me to pray!

SAINTS MARIAN AND JAMES

UNKNOWN–259 • NORTH AFRICA

LAST NIGHT

Your sons and your daughters shall prophesy, your old men shall dream dreams, and your young men shall see visions.

JOEL 2:28

What does a person think about the night before they know they will die? Marian and James lived during the persecutions of the early Church. Many Roman emperors killed those who were loyal to Christ above all else, and Marian and James were two of these persecuted Christians. They were imprisoned and spent a cold night in a cell, awaiting their deaths. Like many other Christians, Marian and James prayed and prayed during that final night, asking God for courage and, most of all, to feel His presence. Because of these prayers, many Christians went to their deaths praising God. This was the case for Marian and James, who, as the story goes, were each granted a vision from God as a way to encourage them right before they died.

> BEFORE THEIR DEATHS, BOTH SAINT MARIAN AND SAINT JAMES SPENT THEIR TIME SERVING THE CHURCH.

Jesus, You give courage to anyone who asks for it. Give me courage too.

MAY 26

SAINT PHILIP NERI

1515–1595 • ITALY

SINGING TO THE LORD

O come, let us sing to the LORD; let us make a
joyful noise to the rock of our salvation!

PSALM 95:1

The large audience bustled around the front of the church, searching for more seats. Everyone had gathered at the church to hear from Philip, a passionate priest and teacher.

Philip noted the lack of seats and started planning—if big crowds wanted to come and learn about Jesus, the church would just have to get larger! Philip organized the construction of a large room over the front of his church so that every person who came to hear his teachings could have a place. The room could be used for

> "ORATORIOS," NAMED AFTER THE ROOM THAT SAINT PHILIP NERI HAD BUILT OVER THE CHURCH, ARE PIECES OF MUSIC THAT USE THE WORDS FROM SCRIPTURE.

all kinds of worship—including singing beautiful music. So Philip organized music for people to enjoy and learn from too. People gathered in the "oratory," the large room Philip built above the front of the church, to learn more about Jesus and to hear songs that brought them closer to God.

Jesus, I want to sing songs about You and Your Word.

MAY 27

SAINT AUGUSTINE OF CANTERBURY

UNKNOWN–605 • ENGLAND

SECOND CHANCE

The word of the LORD came to Jonah a second time, saying, "Get up, go to Nineveh, that great city, and proclaim to it the message that I tell you."

JONAH 3:1-2

Augustine needed a second chance. The pope sent Augustine and forty other monks to tell the good news about Jesus to the people living in England. The first time, Augustine and the other monks gave up when they heard how fierce the English people were. "Even the water around England is fierce and violent," Augustine was told. Augustine thought to himself, *Maybe it's not worth trying! Even if we don't die on the way, we'll be killed by the people.* But after they returned to Rome, the pope told them to try again. Augustine didn't give up the second time. He crossed the choppy waters between France and England, and within a year of his arrival, the king of England became a Christian.

THE KING OF ENGLAND WHOM SAINT AUGUSTINE OF CANTERBURY LED TO FAITH IN CHRIST WAS SAINT ETHELBERT (FEB. 24).

Jesus, You give me new chances every day. I don't want to give up on obeying You.

VENERABLE PIERRE TOUSSAINT

1766–1853 • HAITI AND THE UNITED STATES

RICH IN GOOD WORKS

They are to do good, to be rich in good works, generous, and ready to share, thus storing up for themselves the treasure of a good foundation for the future, so that they may take hold of the life that really is life.

1 TIMOTHY 6:18–19

Pierre grew up in slavery in Haiti. After moving to New York, Pierre learned to cut and style hair. He was freed when his owners died, and he continued to work as a hairdresser, giving much of the money he earned to poor people. Pierre married Juliette, a woman who shared his faith in God and his love for the poor. Many people enjoyed Pierre and Juliette's hospitality, including priests, orphans, and travelers. Pierre and Juliette helped many people without jobs find work, and they gave money to help rebuild a beautiful cathedral. Together, Pierre and Juliette helped the poor, loved their neighbors, and lived lives of faith.

> WHEN VENERABLE PIERRE TOUSSAINT DIED, NEW YORK CITY PAPERS PUBLISHED ARTICLES ABOUT HOW MUCH HE LOVED GOD AND HOW KIND HE WAS TO THE POOR.

Jesus, help me to be rich in good works just as Venerable Pierre Toussaint was.

VENERABLE PIERRE TOUSSAINT IS ON TRACK TO BECOME A SAINT.

SAINT MADELEINE-SOPHIE BARAT

1779–1865 • FRANCE

REORDERED

All things should be done decently and in order.

1 CORINTHIANS 14:40

Madeleine-Sophie was a child during the French Revolution. In France, many terrible things had been said about people who loved Jesus and lived for Him. It was dangerous for Christians in France, just as it had been dangerous for Christians in Rome more than fifteen hundred years before Madeleine's life. After things settled down in France, just like the years after the persecution of those earliest Christians, the ideas about the best ways to live a Christian life had become somewhat scattered and confused. When should Christians pray, and how often? What was a Christian supposed to do for the poor? Madeleine-Sophie became a nun and dedicated her life to revealing Jesus' heart to people all over the world— she told them how much He loved them. She was so successful that she was sent on missionary trips around the world to help reestablish order.

SAINT MADELEINE-SOPHIE BARAT CREATED THE SOCIETY OF THE SACRED HEART, A GROUP TO HELP EDUCATE YOUNG GIRLS. OVER THE YEARS, THE GROUP GREW AND SPREAD ALL THE WAY TO SOUTH AMERICA.

Jesus, You put everything right again. Help me trust You.

SAINT JOAN OF ARC

1412–1431 • FRANCE

THE COURAGE TO LISTEN

*You come to me with sword and spear and javelin; but
I come to you in the name of the LORD of hosts.*

1 SAMUEL 17:45

Many people tried to tell Joan that she was too young. She was only thirteen. But Joan had all she needed to be a mighty warrior. She believed that she had heard from God and from the Saints, all of whom gave her orders that would help her save her homeland, France. And she had the courage to listen. She shared the orders with the French forces, and because they listened, they won battles that they otherwise would have lost. Joan had commanded the king of England to leave France with all his soldiers, and when he didn't listen, she led the French forces into battle against him. But there were many who didn't think Joan had actually heard from God— they doubted her visions. The powerful French men who couldn't fight their own battles didn't interfere when she was imprisoned by the English and executed. Even in the face of powerful people who didn't believe her, Joan kept believing that she had heard from God.

SAINT JOAN OF ARC'S STANDARD, OR FLAG, THAT SHE CARRIED INTO BATTLE HAD LILIES ON IT.

*Jesus, You gave Saint Joan of Arc the courage to
listen for Your voice. Give me that courage too.*

SAINT FELIX OF NICOSIA

1715–1787 • SICILY

TREASURED POSSESSION

"Now therefore, if you obey my voice and keep my covenant,
you shall be my treasured possession out of all the peoples."

EXODUS 19:5

Felix wasn't a king or a pope. He never traveled the world, and he never became a scholar. He didn't lead anyone into battle. He never spoke in front of huge crowds or advised powerful kings. He lived his whole life in the same town. He helped his group of religious brothers—men who lived, worshipped, and served together—keep and dispense their money, but he never took any of it for himself. Felix taught the young people in his town, spoke often and lovingly about Jesus, and instructed all he met to obey God. He was obedient to God, even though it seemed like God never asked Felix to do great things. Even so, Felix was God's treasured possession. Felix's very great work for God was his obedience.

> SAINT FELIX OF NICOSIA'S LAST WORDS WERE "MAY I DIE NOW?" HIS SUPERIORS THEN GAVE HIM PERMISSION. HE WAS OBEDIENT UNTIL THE VERY END.

Jesus, I want to obey You.

SAINT JUSTIN MARTYR

100–165 • JUDEA (MODERN-DAY ISRAEL) AND ITALY

DISCOVERING THE TRUTH

I pray that the God of our Lord Jesus Christ, the Father of glory, may
give you a spirit of wisdom and revelation as you come to know him.

EPHESIANS 1:17

To find out more about God, Justin learned diligently. He learned what the Romans and the Greeks said about God. He learned what the Jews said about God. And he learned what the religion of these new Christians said about God. Justin found Christianity to be true and became a Christian himself. And because he understood and studied other religions respectfully, Justin could explain the Christian beliefs in ways that could be understood by people of other religions. But not everyone agreed with Justin, and some saw him as a threat. They told Justin to renounce, or give up, the truths he had discovered, but he refused. He was then killed for his faith in Jesus.

SAINT JUSTIN MARTYR WAS THE FIRST KNOWN WRITER TO QUOTE FROM THE BOOK OF ACTS.

*Jesus, help me learn more about You and share what
I learn with others, just as Saint Justin Martyr did.*

JUNE 2

SAINT MARCELLINUS

UNKNOWN–304 • ROMAN EMPIRE (MODERN-DAY ITALY)

REPAY WITH KINDNESS

Do not repay evil for evil or abuse for abuse; but, on
the contrary, repay with a blessing. It is for this that you
were called—that you might inherit a blessing.

1 PETER 3:9

The Christians who lived a few hundred years after Jesus told a wonderful story about Marcellinus. Marcellinus was a priest. He served other Christians, even though Christianity was illegal and the cruel Roman emperor named Diocletian tried to kill every Christian he could find. Marcellinus served anyway. After he was caught and imprisoned for the crime of being a Christian, he kept on serving. He was so kind to the jailer that the jailer listened to Marcellinus's stories about Jesus. Even though Marcellinus was killed, the jailer and his family came to believe in Jesus. Marcellinus paid back kindness, even when he was treated with cruelty.

> OTHER CHRISTIANS LOVED AND RESPECTED SAINT MARCELLINUS, SO THEY CAREFULLY SEARCHED FOR HIS BODY SO THEY COULD HONOR HIM BY BURYING HIM PROPERLY.

*Jesus, I want to always repay good for
evil, just as Saint Marcellinus did.*

JUNE 3

UGANDAN MARTYRS

UNKNOWN–1886 • UGANDA

BRAVE BELIEVERS

I hereby command you: Be strong and courageous;
do not be frightened or dismayed, for the LORD
your God is with you wherever you go.

JOSHUA 1:9

During the 1800s, many missionaries came to the country of Uganda in Africa to spread the good news about Jesus. These missionaries were from many different Christian traditions, like Anglicanism and Catholicism. In response to the brave witness of the missionaries, many of the Ugandans showed incredible bravery too—the bravery of believing in Jesus. Their new Christian beliefs clashed with Ugandan religious practices. So the Ugandan king tried to stop the spread of Christianity in his kingdom by using fear and cruelty. Over the course of several years, almost fifty Ugandan Christians were killed for their faith. But the killings had the opposite effect that the king wanted. Even more Ugandans became Christians!

UGANDANS NOW CELEBRATE JUNE 3, THE DAY THAT MOST OF THE UGANDAN MARTYRS WERE KILLED, AS A NATIONAL HOLIDAY.

*Jesus, make me brave, just like You made
the Ugandan martyrs brave.*

SERVANT OF GOD JULIA GREELEY

1833–1918 • THE UNITED STATES

THE HEART TO SERVE

The LORD is near to the brokenhearted,
and saves the crushed in spirit.

PSALM 34:18

Julia rolled her wagon through the dark streets, the light for her steps coming only from streetlamps. Inside the wagon were parcels of food and clothing. She rolled the wagon up to a door and knocked gently. Julia often handed out packages to the poor and needy people in her city of Denver. If she delivered these goods at night, the people who received her gifts wouldn't have to be embarrassed by begging for help. Julia understood, better than most, what it was like to be downtrodden. She grew up in slavery, so she understood the hearts of the poor. And she knew that Jesus understood the poor too. It was Jesus who had given her the heart to serve.

SERVANT OF GOD JULIA GREELEY IS REMEMBERED AS DENVER'S "ANGEL OF CHARITY."

Jesus, Servant of God Julia Greeley loved the poor like You love them. Help me find ways to serve others as she did.

SERVANT OF GOD JULIA GREELEY IS ON TRACK TO BECOME A SAINT.

SAINT BONIFACE

672–754 • GERMANY

ONE TRUE GOD

We know that the Son of God has come and has given us understanding so that we may know him who is true; and we are in him who is true, in his Son Jesus Christ. He is the true God and eternal life.

1 JOHN 5:20

When he was a young man, Boniface dedicated his life to Jesus, even though his parents disapproved. He would make a point of doing what God wanted him to do, even when other people didn't agree with him. Boniface left his home country of England to spread the good news of Jesus across Europe. In Germany, he encountered a group of people who were worshipping Thor, their god of thunder, by a large oak tree. These German people believed that nothing could destroy this tree, which represented the mighty power of their god. Boniface disagreed. In the middle of their worship, Boniface took an axe to the large tree and chopped it down. Staring at their fallen god in disbelief, the people heard Boniface's account of the one true God. They became Christians.

SAINT BONIFACE OFFERED THE GERMANS A NEW PRACTICE: TO PUT LITTLE FIR TREES IN THEIR OWN HOMES AS A REMINDER OF THE ONE TRUE GOD. THESE WERE THE FIRST CHRISTMAS TREES!

Jesus, You are the one true God.

BLESSED FRANZ JÄGERSTÄTTER

1907–1943 • AUSTRIA

THE RIGHT WAY

For the word of the LORD is upright, and all
his work is done in faithfulness.

PSALM 33:4

When he said no, Franz defied a powerful army. The Nazi leaders insisted that the men of Franz's country, Austria, join their army. Most men joined, but not Franz. Franz believed that the Nazi leaders were evil. How did Franz know? Franz studied the Bible every evening. He read it with his family, a wife and three daughters whom he loved very much. Even though he would be killed for his choice and his faith, Franz stayed true to what he had learned in the Bible. Franz went the right way, even when it was difficult, because he knew the right way, God's Word, by heart.

OVER 99 PERCENT OF AUSTRIANS WHO COULD VOTE AGREED WITH THE NAZIS. BLESSED FRANZ JÄGERSTÄTTER WAS ONE OF A SMALL NUMBER OF AUSTRIANS WHO DISAGREED.

*Jesus, give me the wisdom to go the right way,
just as Blessed Franz Jägerstätter did.*

BLESSED FRANZ JÄGERSTÄTTER IS ON TRACK TO BECOME A SAINT.

SAINT NORBERT

1080–1134 · GERMANY

COMMITTED TO CHANGE

*Repent therefore, and turn to God so that
your sins may be wiped out.*

ACTS 3:19

Norbert's story starts with his disobedience. Even though Norbert had told Jesus, his church, and his city that he would live a life of sacrifice and obedience, he didn't keep his promise. He ate rich food, even though he had promised to help the poor find food to eat. He went to wild parties, even though he had promised to spend his time serving at the church. He didn't pray, and he didn't want to listen to God. So God got Norbert's attention. While Norbert was traveling, a bolt of lightning struck near the path where he was riding. His horse bucked him off and ran away. Norbert lay on the ground, stunned. Miraculously, he lived. Norbert repented. He told God that he was sorry for his selfishness and lies, and he committed to change. Norbert became a holy priest and servant of the Church.

> LATER, WHEN A CHURCH WOULD BE BUILT IN HIS HONOR, SAINT NORBERT CHOSE A VALLEY THAT WAS SHAPED LIKE A CROSS.

*Jesus, thank You that when I do wrong, I can repent
and commit to change. You are so gracious.*

JUNE 8

SAINT WILLIAM OF YORK

1090–1154 · ENGLAND

GOOD SENSE

Whoever belittles another lacks sense, but
an intelligent person remains silent.

PROVERBS 11:12

William was a faithful young man living in England. His family was wealthy and provided an excellent education for him. He decided to become a priest. He was a good priest, and he was offered the very important job of archbishop. Unfortunately, other powerful families disliked William's family, and even though William would have been the right person for the role, they told him that he couldn't have it. He must have felt very disappointed since he had worked and studied hard

SAINT WILLIAM OF YORK'S FAMILY WAS VERY POWERFUL. HIS UNCLE WAS IN LINE TO BE KING OF ENGLAND.

for this job. But William was unlike the people who disliked him so much. He showed good sense. Instead of saying terrible things about them in return, William quietly went about his work as a priest. Fourteen years later, William was finally given the job of archbishop.

*Jesus, help me know when to keep quiet
and focus on serving You.*

JUNE 9

SAINT EPHREM

306–373 • ROMAN EMPIRE (MODERN-DAY TURKEY)

SHARING THE TRUTH

If you confess with your lips that Jesus is Lord and believe in your heart that God raised him from the dead, you will be saved.

ROMANS 10:9

Ephrem knew what it felt like to be in the middle. Even when he was young, Ephrem chose to live differently from his parents. His father was a priest for a false god, but Ephrem decided to become a Christian. His decision must have confused his parents. After Ephrem became a Christian, he traveled around the world and served many different churches. On his travels he met many people who claimed to be Christians but did not believe that Jesus is really God. Since Ephrem had changed his own childhood beliefs, he was able to point out the lies and false beliefs that were misleading other people, then share the truth.

SAINT EPHREM WAS AN INCREDIBLE POET. HIS POEMS WERE READ HUNDREDS OF YEARS AFTER HE DIED, AND OTHER GREAT POETS, LIKE DANTE, WERE INSPIRED BY HIM.

Jesus, help me share the truth about You to others.

SAINT JOACHIMA DE VEDRUNA

1783–1854 · SPAIN

LIFELONG SERVANT

*Whatever your task, put yourselves into it, as done
for the Lord and not for your masters.*

COLOSSIANS 3:23

Joachima loved Jesus and wanted to serve Him. When she was a young wife, she served Jesus by loving her husband, Theodore. When she and Theodore were blessed with children, Joachima served Jesus by caring for her children. After Theodore died and her children were grown, Joachima wondered how Jesus would call her to serve Him next. As she was riding her horse through her town one day, her horse stopped in front of a church and refused to move. Joachima got off her horse and went into the church. There, a wise priest gave her some directions. Joachima would serve Jesus by leading a group of women. These women would serve Jesus by teaching children and nursing the sick.

SAINT JOACHIMA DE VEDRUNA WAS ONE OF EIGHT CHILDREN, AND SHE HAD EIGHT CHILDREN HERSELF!

*Jesus, show me how to serve You so that I can be a
lifelong servant just as Saint Joachima de Vedruna was.*

SAINT BARNABAS

UNKNOWN–61 • CYPRUS AND JUDEA (MODERN-DAY ISRAEL)

ENCOURAGER

There was a Levite, a native of Cyprus, Joseph, to whom the apostles
gave the name Barnabas (which means "son of encouragement").

ACTS 4:36

Barnabas believed that Paul could change. And though few people
would encourage Paul in his new faith, Barnabas was there by Paul's
side. A few years before, Paul had tried to kill anyone who said they believed in Jesus. But after his
conversion, Paul was on a mission for Jesus with
Barnabas. They brought donations from the city
of Antioch to the city of Jerusalem, which was
experiencing a terrible famine. Together, Paul and
Barnabas brought food to the people who needed it
the most—people whom Paul would have once considered enemies. But
the love of Jesus had changed Paul, just like it had changed Barnabas.
Barnabas knew that the love of Jesus made any change possible.

SAINT BARNABAS WAS ONE OF THE FIRST FOLLOWERS OF JESUS TO ACCEPT SAINT PAUL (JAN. 24) AFTER HIS CONVERSION.

Jesus, help me encourage everyone,
just as Saint Barnabas did.

JUNE 12

SAINT ONUPHRIUS

FOURTH CENTURY · EGYPT

WISDOM IN THE DESERT

I will make a way in the wilderness and rivers in the desert.

ISAIAH 43:19

Paphnutius wandered through the desert, wondering why God had sent him there. This part of Egypt felt like a sandy waste. He spotted a cave and decided to take shelter in it. Inside the cave, Paphnutius had the surprise of his life—a great hairy being sat in the middle of the cave! The being wasn't surprised by Paphnutius, though. It—he—was a hermit named Onuphrius. He was very old, and he hadn't cut his hair since entering the cave, so his beard was huge. Onuphrius had been sitting in the desert listening to God for most of his life, and he had much wisdom to share with Paphnutius. After Onuphrius died, Paphnutius buried him and returned to the monastery to tell everyone else about the wonderful things he had learned from Onuphrius.

AS THE LEGEND GOES, SAINT ONUPHRIUS ATE ALMOST NOTHING EXCEPT DATES FROM A TREE THAT GREW NEAR HIS CAVE.

Jesus, help me listen to wisdom, even when I'm not expecting it!

JUNE 13

SAINT ANTHONY OF PADUA

1195–1231 • ITALY

SAVE THE LOST

"For the Son of Man came to seek out and to save the lost."

LUKE 19:10

Anthony's life changed when five other lives were lost. He was inspired to become a Franciscan priest after he saw the bodies of Berard and his companions (Jan. 16) in a procession through the Portuguese city where he was studying. Berard and his friends had gone on a dangerous mission to spread the good news about Jesus, and they were killed for their faith. Anthony heard their story and decided he wanted to go on the same dangerous mission! But God had a different mission for Anthony. After Anthony's bad health prevented him from staying on the mission, Anthony was assigned to preach and teach in Italy. Even though he was young, he became a passionate preacher. Gigantic crowds of more than thirty thousand would gather at a time to hear Anthony's incredible teachings. Many who heard the gospel for the first time were saved, and believers who already knew the gospel deepened their faith.

> SAINT ANTHONY OF PADUA IS THE PATRON OF LOST OBJECTS. HE ONCE PRAYED TO RECEIVE HIS LOST BOOK OF PSALMS, WHICH HAD BEEN STOLEN. THE BOOK WAS RETURNED.

Jesus, You can save anyone who is lost.
Thank You for saving me.

JUNE 14

SAINT ELISHA

NINTH CENTURY BC · ANCIENT ISRAEL (MODERN-DAY ISRAEL)

FOLLOWING GOD

Then he set out and followed Elijah, and became his servant.

1 KINGS 19:21

Elisha needed to make a choice. He could stay with his family business of farming, or he could follow the prophet Elijah. One choice meant sticking with what he knew, and the other meant a life of complete unknowns. The prophet had many enemies, and following him could lead to Elisha's death. But following the prophet would also be following God. Elisha decided he was done farming. He left the next day and traveled with Elijah until the day when Elijah was taken up to heaven in a chariot. Elisha kept doing miracles and telling people about the power of God, just like Elijah had. Wherever Elisha went, people were amazed and said to themselves that the God of Elisha must be the real God!

SAINT ELISHA'S NAME MEANS "GOD IS SALVATION."

God, Saint Elisha followed You even when it meant giving up everything. Help me do the same.

JUNE 15*

SAINT MARGUERITE D'YOUVILLE

1701–1771 • CANADA

WHEN THINGS GO WRONG

I consider that the sufferings of this present time are not worth comparing with the glory about to be revealed to us.

ROMANS 8:18

Marguerite understood how fast things could go wrong. She was married, but her husband didn't keep his promises to her. She had children, but many of her children died when they were only babies. But Marguerite knew that God's love was stronger than everything that could go wrong. She felt His love so deeply that she was able to deal with her difficult family life. Even though so much had gone wrong, Marguerite believed that God loved her and her family. And that was enough. After her husband died, Marguerite founded a group of women whose mission was to love people with terribly difficult lives. She spent the rest of her life loving people when things went wrong.

> ONCE, AFTER A FIRE HAD DESTROYED SAINT MARGUERITE D'YOUVILLE'S HOUSE FOR THE POOR, SHE KNELT IN THE ASHES AND THANKED GOD. GOD GAVE HER OTHER HOUSES TO USE FOR HER MISSION.

Jesus, Saint Marguerite d'Youville held on to Your promises during hard times. Help me do the same.

JUNE 16

SAINT JOHN FRANCIS REGIS

1597–1640 · FRANCE

STRONG SPIRIT

For God did not give us a spirit of cowardice, but rather
a spirit of power and of love and of self-discipline.

2 TIMOTHY 1:7

When John was young, he felt absolutely crushed when anyone said anything critical about his schoolwork. The teacher only had to say that John's answers could have been a little better written, and John dissolved into tears. Later, after he became a priest, he was able to endure shouts and threats from people who disagreed with him. People even threatened to kill him, and John was calm and collected. What had changed? John had grown in his faith in Jesus, and his spirit had been strengthened by Him. As John grew older and learned more about Jesus, he prayed and asked for courage, and it was given to him.

> SAINT JOHN FRANCIS REGIS NEVER SLEPT IN A BED. HE USED A SPOT ON THE FLOOR INSTEAD!

Jesus, give me a spirit of power and love and self-discipline, just as You gave to Saint John Francis Regis.

SAINT JOSEPH CAFASSO

1811–1860 • ITALY

NEAR TO GOD

Draw near to God, and he will draw near to you.

JAMES 4:8

J oseph kept hearing the same words from the other priests. They sighed and said, "I'm just not good enough for God, and I never will be." Joseph couldn't stand this. Teachers, many of them priests too, kept telling people that they should keep themselves at a distance from God because they would never be good enough for Him. "No!" Joseph told the other priests. "Run *to* God, not away from Him!

> SAINT JOSEPH CAFASSO LOVED PRISONERS, AND HE SAT WITH MANY OF THEM AS THEY DIED, HELPING THEM ASK JESUS FOR FORGIVENESS.

No matter what you've done, God wants to be with you. He loves you more than you can imagine." Joseph pointed to the words of Saint Francis de Sales (Jan. 25) to prove his point. He pointed many priests toward the unending love of God, including Saint John Bosco (Jan. 31)!

*Jesus, Saint Joseph Cafasso knew that You
are near. Help me know that too.*

VENERABLE MATT TALBOT

1856–1925 · IRELAND

TRUE THIRST

"Those who drink of the water that I will
give them will never be thirsty."

JOHN 4:14

M att never did anything halfway. He worked a difficult job on the docks, unloading cargo from ships.
After his workday was done, he took the money he had
earned and spent it on alcohol. He did this for years.
One day his heart was changed. Matt had no money,
so he stood outside the pub where he usually drank.
None of his friends offered to buy him a drink this
time. Embarrassed and ashamed, he returned to his mother's house.
He promised he would never drink again. Matt spent every spare hour
in prayer, even the break time on the docks. Instead of going straight
to the pub after work, he went straight to the chapel to pray. For the
rest of his life, he only thirsted for time with God.

VENERABLE
MATT TALBOT
TAUGHT
HIMSELF TO
READ. HE
SAID THAT HE
ASKED THE
HOLY SPIRIT
FOR HELP.

*Jesus, help me thirst only for You, just
as Venerable Matt Talbot did.*

VENERABLE MATT TALBOT IS ON TRACK TO BECOME A SAINT.

SAINT ROMUALD

950–1027 • ITALY

OF THE WORLD

"If you belonged to the world, the world would love you as its own. Because you do not belong to the world, but I have chosen you out of the world—therefore the world hates you."

JOHN 15:19

Romuald wanted to love Jesus with everything, but some temptations always drew him back. He didn't believe he could give up the pleasures of the world to live for Jesus. But the events of one day changed Romuald's heart. Romuald's father insisted that Romuald attend his duel. Romuald's father disagreed deeply with one of his enemies, and to solve the problem, they agreed to fight. Whoever lived was the winner. Romuald's father won the duel, but Romuald was so dismayed by watching the other man die that he prayed for forty days in a monastery. He was so full of sorrow that it seemed like Romuald himself had killed the man! The days of prayer changed Romuald's heart. He committed his life to Jesus and to prayer.

SAINT ROMUALD WENT ON TO ESTABLISH MANY MORE MONASTERIES.

Jesus, help me give up whatever You ask me to.

SAINT PAULINUS OF NOLA

353–431 • GAUL (MODERN-DAY FRANCE) AND ITALY

FINDING COMFORT

"Blessed are those who mourn, for they will be comforted."

MATTHEW 5:4

Paulinus and his wife wept. They had lost their only child. Paulinus had lived a life of success. He was a successful soldier and politician. He had wealth and a beautiful home. But none of his accomplishments could compare to the love that he had felt for his small child, and now that child was gone. What were he and his wife going to do? Instead of falling into despair and bitterness, Paulinus and his wife decided to give everything to God. They left their life of power and wealth and dedicated the rest of their days to serving the poor. Their old friends couldn't believe it, but Paulinus wrote them beautiful letters and poetry describing the incredible love of God. Paulinus told them about the gift of giving up everything.

SAINT PAULINUS OF NOLA ALSO WROTE LETTERS TO SAINT AUGUSTINE (AUG. 28) AND SAINT JEROME (SEPT. 30).

Jesus, comfort me when I'm sad, just as You comforted Saint Paulinus of Nola. Show me how to find comfort in serving You.

JUNE 21

SAINT ALOYSIUS GONZAGA

1568–1591 · ITALY

BEGINNING TO END

You hem me in, behind and before, and lay your hand upon me.

PSALM 139:5

From the beginning to the end of Aloysius's life, God had a plan for him. The first words Aloysius spoke were the names of Jesus and His mother, Mary, so it should not have been a surprise to his parents when Aloysius wanted to be a priest, even from a young age. But his father was determined that Aloysius would be a soldier, and from the time Aloysius was five years old, his father sent him to be trained and educated for a high-ranking position in the army. Even after that training, Aloysius followed God's call to be a priest anyway. His father eventually gave up his plans for his son, and Aloysius threw himself into the service of the poor. He died while caring for sick people during a terrible plague.

SAINT ALOYSIUS GONZAGA WAS FROM A WEALTHY FAMILY, BUT HE GAVE UP ALL THE RIGHTS TO HIS INHERITANCE SO HE COULD FOCUS ON SERVING GOD.

Jesus, You know everything from beginning to end. Guide me so that I can serve You for my whole life, just as Saint Aloysius Gonzaga did.

SAINT THOMAS MORE

1478–1535 • ENGLAND

CHANGING TIMES

Jesus Christ is the same yesterday
and today and forever.

HEBREWS 13:8

Thomas refused to change, even when the times changed. For most of Thomas's life, the king of England held him in high esteem and favor. Thomas's education was thorough—he learned Latin, logic, and history. Thomas became a lawyer and an author, and he wrote about complicated problems with clarity and conviction. He loved the poor and helped them often. Thomas even gave good counsel to the king. Then the king made a decision that Thomas disagreed with on moral grounds. The king divorced his wife, Catherine, and married another woman, Anne Boleyn. Thomas refused to attend the crowning ceremony of the king's new wife. Because of this, the king, who had once praised Thomas, ordered his execution. Thomas never wavered or backed down, and he was executed for refusing to change.

FOR THE TITLE OF ONE OF HIS BOOKS, SAINT THOMAS MORE CREATED THE WORD *UTOPIA,* WHICH MEANS "NO PLACE."

*Jesus, help me stay committed to You and to what
You say is right—today, tomorrow, and forever.*

SAINT JOHN FISHER

1469–1535 · ENGLAND

THE RIGHT THING

Anyone, then, who knows the right thing to
do and fails to do it, commits sin.

JAMES 4:17

Like Saint Thomas More (June 22), John stood firm when it would have been easy to give up. Saint Thomas More was a lawyer and John was a priest, but they were involved in the same conflict. The king of England had divorced his wife, Queen Catherine, and married another woman, Anne Boleyn. John stood by the queen even when powerful people, like the king, were against her. John knew he would probably die for his refusal to agree with the king. But John told his accusers that he was prepared to defend the king's marriage, even if the king wouldn't. John pointed to the example of Jesus' cousin, Saint John the Baptist (Aug. 29), who had been willing to tell King Herod that his actions regarding marriage were wrong too (Mark 6:14–29).

> SAINT JOHN FISHER WAS CALM AND DIGNIFIED EVEN UP TO THE MOMENT OF HIS EXECUTION.

*Jesus, give me the courage to stand up for
what is right, no matter the cost.*

SAINT ZECHARIAH

FIRST CENTURY • JUDEA (MODERN-DAY ISRAEL)

ANYTHING IS POSSIBLE

You, child, will be called the prophet of the Most High;
for you will go before the Lord to prepare his ways.

LUKE 1:76

Zechariah stared at his impossible baby. His wife, Elizabeth, gave birth to a beautiful baby boy, even though she was too old to have children. They thought that they would never be given children, but here he was! Zechariah had waited for decades for a gift from God like this, and he had even given up. But God had given the gift anyway. Feeling God's blessing in this moment, Zechariah, filled with the Holy Spirit, sang over his family: "Blessed be the Lord God of Israel, for he has looked favorably on his people and redeemed them" (Luke 1:68). Zechariah sang and sang, filled with hope. If God could give him a son, God could do anything. God could deliver Israel again!

> SAINT ZECHARIAH'S WHOLE TOWN OF JUDEA WAS SO AMAZED BY SAINT JOHN THE BAPTIST'S BIRTH THAT THEY COULDN'T STOP TALKING ABOUT IT!

Jesus, You can do the impossible!

JUNE 25*

SAINT FIACRE

600–670 • IRELAND AND FRANCE

GARDEN OF PRAYER

*Let us not grow weary in doing what is right, for we
will reap at harvest time, if we do not give up.*

GALATIANS 6:9

Fiacre believed in the importance of peace and quiet for prayer. He was willing to make big sacrifices for God—he left his native land of Ireland for France. There, he made himself a cell in the middle of the forest to be reserved for his own use for prayer and solitude. The ground around his hermitage was very beautiful, which is why he is the patron of gardening and gardeners. Saint Fiacre did not allow any women in his presence so that he wouldn't become interested in getting married. Fiacre made a promise to Jesus to commit his life to service instead of marriage. Fiacre used the land in his hermitage to grow vegetables and herbs, and he used the space in the buildings to host travelers and offer quiet spaces for prayer.

WHEN QUEEN ANNE OF FRANCE VISITED SAINT FIACRE'S HERMITAGE A THOUSAND YEARS LATER, SHE STAYED OUTSIDE OF IT TO RESPECT SAINT FIACRE'S PROMISE TO JESUS.

*Jesus, help me make time to pray and
to keep my promises to You.*

JUNE 26

SAINT JOSEMARÍA ESCRIVÁ

1902–1975 • SPAIN

SACRIFICES

Do not neglect to do good and to share what you
have, for such sacrifices are pleasing to God.

HEBREWS 13:16

Josemaría lived through the struggles of ordinary life. His father suffered bad business deals and job losses. His family had to survive on a much lower salary. Josemaría even suffered with his family through the deaths of several of his siblings. While Josemaría was studying to be a priest, his father died, and he was asked to help take care of his family. Josemaría knew that ordinary life was full of opportunities for holiness. Holiness wasn't just for priests; holiness was for everyone! Josemaría eventually became a priest, but he knew that there were other ways of living that were just as important. He traveled the world, encouraging people who had ordinary jobs and ordinary lives, telling them, "You don't have to be a hermit or a martyr to make incredible sacrifices for God."

> SAINT JOSEMARÍA ESCRIVÁ WAS INSPIRED TO BECOME A PRIEST WHEN HE SAW THE BARE FOOTPRINTS OF ANOTHER PRIEST IN THE SNOW.

*Jesus, I want to worship You with my life. Show
me what sacrifices I can make for You.*

JUNE 27

SAINT CYRIL OF ALEXANDRIA

375–444 • EGYPT

KIND AND FORGIVING

Return to the LORD, your God, for he is gracious and merciful, slow to anger, and abounding in steadfast love, and relents from punishing.

JOEL 2:13

Cyril brought the truth into the complicated situations he faced in churches. Even Christians could be misled by bad ideas and false teachings. Cyril passionately set things right again.

During Cyril's life, Christians were being persecuted. Many Christians chose to die rather than to worship false gods. But other Christians weren't as strong, and they worshipped the false gods. Later, when they tried to repent, a few churches said these weaker Christians couldn't be forgiven. Cyril knew that they were wrong, and he declared that

> SAINT CYRIL OF ALEXANDRIA CONFRONTED AN EMPEROR WHO HAD BEEN BROUGHT UP AS A CHRISTIAN BUT REVERTED TO PAGANISM.

those churches were teaching lies. "Jesus is forgiving," Cyril said, "and Jesus gives second chances." After all, Saint Peter himself had denied Jesus, and Jesus forgave him!

> *Jesus, You are kind and forgiving. Help me*
> *repent when I realize I've done wrong.*

189

SAINT IRENAEUS

UNKNOWN–202 • SMYRNA (MODERN-DAY TURKEY) AND FRANCE

FAITH IN ACTION

What good is it, my brothers and sisters, if you say you
have faith but do not have works? Can faith save you?

JAMES 2:14

Irenaeus believed that knowledge wasn't enough—real faith meant action! In the first days of the Church, many Christians were influenced by a terrible teaching called Gnosticism. The teachings of Gnosticism seemed to completely ignore the stories about and the writings of the first apostles. The false teachers said that God created the world by accident and just knowing *about* God was the only way to be saved. For the Gnostics, knowledge was seen as the way to escape the evils of the world. Irenaeus knew that their wrongheaded "knowledge" wouldn't save anyone. Jesus alone offered salvation. Irenaeus read what Saint Polycarp (Feb. 23) and the apostles had to say, and Irenaeus wrote five lengthy books that explained how Gnosticism was wrong. Jesus served others and offered His own life as a sacrifice. And when we have faith in Him, we don't just have knowledge of God—we live out our faith by serving Him!

SAINT IRENAEUS TAUGHT AND PREACHED ABOUT THE IMPORTANCE OF THE FOUR GOSPELS, THE BOOKS WRITTEN BY SAINT MATTHEW, SAINT MARK, SAINT LUKE, AND SAINT JOHN.

*Jesus, help me put my faith in action. I
want to know You and serve You.*

JUNE 29

SAINTS PETER AND PAUL

FIRST CENTURY • GALILEE (MODERN-DAY ISRAEL)

RECONCILED

All this is from God, who reconciled us to himself through
Christ, and has given us the ministry of reconciliation.

2 CORINTHIANS 5:18

Peter and Paul couldn't have been more different. One was raised to be a fisherman, the other to be a religious leader. One spent his childhood in a tiny town near a lake, the other in a bustling city. One pursued a simple life; the other pursued the demanding studies of the Pharisees. Peter was the fisherman, and Paul was the Pharisee. At one point, Paul wanted Peter dead! But Christ can reconcile anyone—that is, Christ can bring anyone together. Paul became a follower of Jesus, and Peter welcomed him into the mission. Through Christ, both of these men became united in one mission—to spread the good news of Jesus everywhere.

THE CALENDAR OF SAINTS CELEBRATES THESE TWO MEN ON THE SAME DAY BECAUSE TRADITION SAYS THAT BOTH OF THEM WERE KILLED FOR THEIR FAITH IN JESUS BY THE SAME CRUEL EMPEROR, EMPEROR NERO, ON THE SAME DAY.

Jesus, help me reconcile with others who aren't like me.

THE FIRST MARTYRS OF THE CHURCH OF ROME

FIRST CENTURY • ROMAN EMPIRE

RIGHTEOUS REWARD

"Blessed are those who are persecuted for righteousness'
sake, for theirs is the kingdom of heaven."

MATTHEW 5:10

Following Jesus was unpopular right after He died. In many places, being a Christian was considered a crime! The consequences could be severe—His followers were often killed when they were caught. But about twenty years after Jesus died, the persecution started growing worse—much worse. Persecution is cruelty that is experienced by people who believe certain things. And these first Christians, who believed Jesus is the Son of God, were persecuted by being ridiculed, tortured, and killed. An emperor named Nero hated followers of Jesus and killed many of them. There were so many of them that we don't have a record of all these martyrs' names. They died with the hope that people all over the world and throughout history would love Jesus.

EVEN THOUGH CHRISTIANS WERE KILLED, PEOPLE KEPT JOINING THE CHURCH. THEY'VE NEVER STOPPED!

Jesus, You give the kingdom of heaven to the Christians who give their lives for You.

SAINT JUNÍPERO SERRA

1713–1784 • SPAIN AND MEXICO

ON THE PATH

You must follow exactly the path that the
LORD your God has commanded you.

DEUTERONOMY 5:33

Junípero walked a long path to spread the good news of Jesus. He grew up in Spain and chose to become a priest at just fifteen years old. Junípero longed to take the news of Jesus to people who had never heard it before, and he'd go a long way to do it. He boarded a boat in Spain and landed in Mexico. Then he and another priest walked 250 miles to the university in Mexico City, walking the path that God had set for them. Along the way, Junípero suffered a leg injury, but it didn't stop him. Junípero kept walking. Even though the injury would hurt him for the rest of his life, he didn't let long distances or injuries stop him from completing his mission.

SAINT JUNÍPERO SERRA DEFENDED THE NATIVES IN MEXICO WHEN SPANISH SOLDIERS TREATED THEM POORLY.

Jesus, Saint Junípero Serra walked the path You told him to walk. Help me do the same.

JULY 2*

SAINT OLIVER PLUNKETT

1625–1681 · IRELAND

DIVIDED HOUSE

He knew what they were thinking and said to them,
"Every kingdom divided against itself is laid waste, and
no city or house divided against itself will stand."

MATTHEW 12:25

Oliver stood firm in the middle of a storm of disagreements. The priests in Ireland were told by the leaders from England that they could not worship the way they wanted to worship. This wasn't their biggest problem, though. Even worse, the priests in Ireland couldn't agree with each other! They were a divided house. Leaders in England were causing them trouble, but there was real trouble in their own hearts too. They argued about which priest should get to live and teach at which church in Ireland. Oliver knew that these priests couldn't stand against the English persecution if they were always angry with the priest who lived in the next town. Oliver helped the priests in Ireland find ways to agree.

SAINT OLIVER PLUNKETT LOVED ROME AND ENCOURAGED OTHER PRIESTS TO STUDY THERE.

Jesus, help me point back to You when people disagree.

JULY 3

SAINT THOMAS THE APOSTLE

FIRST CENTURY · GALILEE (MODERN-DAY ISRAEL)

NO DOUBT

Thomas answered him, "My Lord and my God!"

JOHN 20:28

Jesus was alive again? Thomas knew that was impossible. Jesus, his leader and his teacher, was dead. He had been sealed in a tomb. And now the other disciples were believing something false. They kept telling Thomas that they had seen Jesus again. But it couldn't be true. Thomas told them as much, saying, "Unless I see the mark of the nails in his hands, and put my finger in the mark of the nails and my hand in his side, I will not believe" (John 20:25). The next week, Jesus appeared to Thomas and the other disciples in the house where they were meeting, even though none of the doors had been opened! Jesus gave an answer to Thomas's doubts. He looked directly at Thomas and told him to touch Him so he could believe! Then Thomas believed and said to Jesus, "My Lord and my God!" (v. 28).

AS THE STORY GOES, SAINT THOMAS THE APOSTLE DIED FOR HIS FAITH IN INDIA. THOMAS WAS WOUNDED BY A SPEAR IN HIS SIDE, JUST LIKE JESUS HAD BEEN.

Jesus, help me believe in You and not doubt, just as You helped Saint Thomas the Apostle.

JULY 4

SAINT ELIZABETH OF PORTUGAL

1271–1336 • PORTUGAL

GOOD CONDUCT

Keep your conscience clear, so that, when you are maligned, those who abuse you for your good conduct in Christ may be put to shame.

1 PETER 3:16

Elizabeth married the king of Portugal when she was young—*very* young. She was only twelve years old! She did her best to be a good queen, praying for her people and giving money and time to help the poor. At first her husband, the king, was kind to her. But his kindness faded away. He turned cold toward her and looked down on her dedication to her faith. Even though her husband changed, Elizabeth didn't! She kept praying for him, and she never wavered in her good conduct. After many difficult years, her husband finally realized that he had been treating her poorly. He asked for her forgiveness, and Elizabeth forgave him.

SAINT ELIZABETH OF PORTUGAL WENT TO CHURCH EVERY SINGLE DAY.

Jesus, Saint Elizabeth of Portugal forgave freely. Help me do the same.

JULY 5

SAINT ANTHONY MARY ZACCARIA

1502–1539 • ITALY

HEALING

Jesus answered, "Those who are well have no need of
a physician, but those who are sick; I have come to call
not the righteous but sinners to repentance."

LUKE 5:31–32

Anthony arrived at the university ready to study hard, and he worked tirelessly over the next few years to become an excellent doctor. But as he traveled around the countryside, he discovered that people were suffering from more than their physical ailments—their spirits needed help too. Maybe he could help them heal their bodies, but Anthony knew they needed a different healer. They needed Jesus. So Anthony heard God's call in his life. He was going to point people to the Doctor of their souls! He became a priest at age twenty-six and lived for only ten more years, but he brought spiritual healing to people all over Italy.

A BEAUTIFUL STORY IS TOLD ABOUT SAINT ANTHONY MARY ZACCARIA. SOME PEOPLE BELIEVED THEY SAW ANGELS AROUND THE ALTAR DURING THE MIDDLE OF THE FIRST SERVICE HE CELEBRATED AS A PRIEST.

*Jesus, You are the good Doctor. You
can heal our bodies and souls!*

JULY 6

SAINT ROMULUS OF FIESOLE

FIRST CENTURY • ROMAN EMPIRE (MODERN-DAY ITALY)

FAITH AND HOPE SET ON GOD

Through him you have come to trust in God, who raised him from the dead and gave him glory, so that your faith and hope are set on God.

1 PETER 1:21

Romulus heard the news about Jesus from one of His followers: Peter. Peter was a disciple of Jesus. He had followed Jesus and learned from Him while He walked on earth. Peter had showed enough faith to walk on water with Jesus and declare that He is the Christ, but he had also abandoned Jesus when He was arrested. Jesus loved Peter through everything, and after Jesus resurrected, Peter told many people about Him, including Romulus. Peter's faith and hope were set on God, and Romulus wanted that for his life too.

A LEGEND ABOUT SAINT ROMULUS OF FIESOLE TELLS THAT HE WAS RAISED BY WOLVES AND CAPTURED BY SAINT PETER.

Romulus became a brave and bold Christian. He didn't just hear Peter's message; he lived it! He told people all around Italy about Jesus.

Jesus, my faith and my hope are set on You.

BLESSED EMMANUEL RUIZ

1804–1860 • SYRIA

A BRAVE SACRIFICE

"I am the resurrection and the life. Those who
believe in me, even though they die, will live."

JOHN 11:25

Fighting broke out in the streets of Damascus, and Emmanuel Ruiz knew that he and the other priests would likely not survive the fighting. Many people in the city didn't love Jesus, and the priests would be targeted for their faith. The priests prayed together, then Emmanuel went into the church to guard it from the attackers as best as he could. The crowd of attackers came in, demanding that these priests say they never believed in Jesus. The priests refused and died shortly afterward, but the story of their brave sacrifice spread throughout the Church.

THE PRIESTS LIVING WITH BLESSED EMMANUEL RUIZ WERE STUDYING ARABIC SO THEY COULD TALK TO THE PEOPLE OF DAMASCUS IN THEIR OWN LANGUAGE.

*Jesus, Blessed Emmanuel Ruiz and his companions
trusted You completely. Help me trust You more.*

BLESSED EMMANUEL RUIZ IS ON TRACK TO BECOME A SAINT.

SAINT GREGORY GRASSI

1823–1900 · ITALY AND CHINA

HE LIVES IN ME

*It is no longer I who live, but it is Christ who lives in me.
And the life I now live in the flesh I live by faith in the
Son of God, who loved me and gave himself for me.*

GALATIANS 2:20

Gregory was a priest who lived with and served people in China. His ministry had wonderful results. Many people listened to the good news and believed in Jesus. But then the Chinese government noticed all of the conversions to Christianity, and considering this belief in Jesus dangerous, the powerful government decided to get rid of as many Christians as they could. Gregory was one of forty thousand Christians, most of them Chinese people, who were killed during the Boxer Rebellion, which was an uprising against the government. Gregory was able to give up his life because he'd already given it up—he'd given it to Jesus.

THE SACRIFICES OF SAINT GREGORY GRASSI AND THE OTHER CHINESE CHRISTIANS WERE REWARDED. FORTY THOUSAND DIED, BUT FEWER THAN THIRTY YEARS LATER, MORE THAN THREE HUNDRED THOUSAND CHRISTIANS LIVED IN CHINA.

*Jesus, Your love makes anything possible. Help
me see things the way You see them.*

JULY 9

SAINT AUGUSTINE ZHAO RONG

UNKNOWN–1815 • CHINA

THE WORD OF GOD IS NOT CHAINED

That is my gospel, for which I suffer hardship, even to the point of being chained like a criminal. But the word of God is not chained.

2 TIMOTHY 2:8–9

Zhao guarded the door of the prison and heard the words of the Chinese Christians inside. They had all been condemned to die for their belief in Jesus. *They should be terrified and sad*, thought Zhao, *but they are overjoyed!* He watched them die the next day, but he remembered their joy. Even though believing in Jesus and the gospel often led to death in China, Zhao couldn't stop thinking about the joy of the Christians. He converted to Christianity himself, and he even became a priest! Later when Christians were being persecuted again, Zhao was put in chains inside the kind of prison he used to guard. He would die for his faith, just like those Christians he once helped imprison. But now, Zhao was free in Christ.

> SAINT AUGUSTINE ZHAO RONG DIED WITH 120 OTHER CHRISTIANS, ALL OF WHOM REFUSED TO DENY CHRIST.

Jesus, You are not chained! Help me be free in You, like Saint Augustine Zhao Rong.

SAINT VERONICA GIULIANI

1660–1727 • ITALY

WRITE IT DOWN

Then the LORD answered me and said: Write the vision;
make it plain on tablets, so that a runner may read it.

HABAKKUK 2:2

Veronica walked into the small room where she slept after her long days of work. She wanted to go to her bed and sleep, but she still had important work to do—she believed Jesus wanted her to keep a detailed diary. Jesus has work for everyone to do, and Veronica's work was to write truths and words of wisdom, some of which were hard for her to understand at first. Veronica wrote and kept writing. Even when she felt terribly discouraged, Veronica kept writing! She wrote the diary for Jesus, but her words have encouraged Christians around the world.

SAINT VERONICA GIULIANI'S DIARY WAS MORE THAN TWENTY THOUSAND PAGES LONG!

*Jesus, help me do the work You have set
out for me, even when it is hard!*

SAINT BENEDICT

480–543 • WESTERN ROMAN EMPIRE (MODERN-DAY ITALY)

KEEPING COMMANDMENTS

"If you love me, you will keep my commandments."

JOHN 14:15

Benedict went to Rome hoping to learn truth. He was ready to study hard and to seek God at school. But before he even opened his books, he realized that his classmates were not truth seekers. They were pleasure seekers only! They spent their money and time gambling and doing whatever they wanted, even if it was wrong. When it came time for their exams, they just spat out eloquent lies! Their speeches were more about sounding good than about doing good. Benedict thought to himself, *If I stay here, I'll become just like them!* Benedict wanted no part of

> SAINT BENEDICT KNEW HIS RULES WOULD BE TOO STRICT FOR SOME PEOPLE. ONCE, A GROUP OF MONKS TRIED TO POISON HIS DRINK BECAUSE THE RULES WERE TOO MUCH FOR THEM, BUT HIS CUP SHATTERED BEFORE HE TOOK A DRINK.

their sinful lives. He wanted to keep God's commandments, not break them. He ran away from Rome, out into the mountains. There, he developed strict rules of life for other Christians, who, like him, wanted to live in a way that honored God.

Jesus, help me obey and love You.

JULY 12

SAINTS JOHN JONES AND JOHN WALL

1530–1598 (JONES), 1620–1679 (WALL) · ENGLAND

FIRM IN FAITH

Keep alert, stand firm in your faith, be courageous, be strong.

1 CORINTHIANS 16:13

Neither John Jones nor John Wall felt surprised when he wound up in prison. Both of them worked as priests, and both of them continued to serve the English people, even when practicing Catholicism became illegal. And both of them had the same first name. What made them different was the time they lived in—John Jones lived about a hundred years before John Wall. Many of the problems in England were still present a century later. But the death of John Jones didn't discourage John Wall. Because of John Jones's commitment to Christ, John Wall knew that he was part of a lineage of courage. Both of them were firm in their faith.

> BOTH SAINT JOHN JONES AND SAINT JOHN WALL WERE FRANCISCAN PRIESTS. THEY WERE PART OF THE ORDER STARTED BY SAINT FRANCIS OF ASSISI (OCT. 3) HUNDREDS OF YEARS BEFORE.

Jesus, help me remember the people who have believed in You, and help me have courage!

JULY 13

SAINT HENRY

973–1024 • GERMANY

KING OF KINGS

By justice a king gives stability to the land.

PROVERBS 29:4

Many earthly kings refuse to love God. Maybe they see their wealth and think they're so rich and powerful that they don't need help from the greatest King of all. But Henry was not one of those foolish kings. Even though King Henry had power and wealth, he devoted his life to the service of God. Henry was truly humble. He knew that even though he was a king, he was also a man in need of God. He knew that God loved the poor, and he used his power to help them, not to oppress them. Henry pledged to use his many resources and his great influence to make God known, not to make himself known. Even though King Henry had no children of his own, he left a rich legacy of love for Jesus and for His Church.

SAINT HENRY HELPED BUILD CHURCHES IN GERMANY.

*Jesus, You are the King of Kings. I want to use
all I have to make You known to the world.*

SAINT KATERI TEKAKWITHA

1656–1680 • MOHAWK TRIBE (MODERN-DAY UNITED STATES AND CANADA)

EXCLUDED

"Blessed are you when people hate you, and when they exclude you, revile you, and defame you on account of the Son of Man."

LUKE 6:22

Kateri would one day be remembered as the first Native American to become a Saint, but as a child, Kateri knew no other Christians besides her mother. Kateri grew up in the Mohawk tribe, and when she was only a little girl, Kateri's whole family died of smallpox. One day, a group of missionaries came to her tribe, and Kateri believed the gospel they shared. When the tribe realized that Kateri believed what these missionaries did, they became angry with her and treated her terribly. She fled north to the place the missionaries were living. Even though her tribe excluded her, Kateri never gave up praying for them.

> SAINT KATERI TEKAKWITHA IS ALSO CALLED THE "LILY OF THE MOHAWKS" BECAUSE SHE NEVER STOPPED PRAYING FOR HER TRIBE.

Jesus, Saint Kateri Tekakwitha prayed for people who hated her because of her love for You. Help me pray for the people who hate You and Your Church.

JULY 15

SAINT BONAVENTURE

1221–1274 · ITALY AND FRANCE

OVERSEER

Keep watch over yourselves and over all the flock, of which the
Holy Spirit has made you overseers, to shepherd the church
of God that he obtained with the blood of his own Son.

ACTS 20:28

Bonaventure gave the Church an important gift—he set the record straight about Saint Francis of Assisi (Oct. 3). Bonaventure joined the order that Saint Francis started. Saint Francis had inspired many men and women to dedicate their lives to Christ and live extraordinary lives of prayer. The works and words of Saint Francis were so popular that many legends—

SAINT BONAVENTURE LIVED AND WROTE DURING THE SAME TIME AS SAINT THOMAS AQUINAS (JAN. 28).

that is, stories that weren't exactly true—were told about him, even before he died! Because he was an important example for everyone in the Church, people needed to know what was true about his life and what wasn't. Bonaventure oversaw the collection and writing of the life of Saint Francis so people would know the truth about the life of the great Saint.

*Jesus, help me discover truth that builds up other
Christians, just as Saint Bonaventure did.*

VENERABLE AUGUSTUS TOLTON

1854–1897 • THE UNITED STATES

ALL PEOPLE

I looked, and there was a great multitude that no one could count,
from every nation, from all tribes and peoples and languages.

REVELATION 7:9

Augustus was born into slavery in Missouri, but his family escaped after the Civil War and found a home in Illinois. He and his family were Catholic, so they joined the Catholic church near their new home. Augustus knew that the church was a refuge for all people, but when he looked around at the other people in his church, he didn't see many others who looked like him. When Augustus grew up, he wanted to study to become a priest, but none of the seminaries in the United States would accept a Black student. Augustus was encouraged by priests from his town to study theology anyway. Augustus was ordained a priest in Rome. He returned to the United States to serve the churches in Illinois.

VENERABLE AUGUSTUS TOLTON PLAYED THE ACCORDION AND HAD A BEAUTIFUL VOICE.

*Jesus, thank You for the life and witness
of Venerable Augustus Tolton.*

VENERABLE AUGUSTUS TOLTON IS ON TRACK TO BECOME A SAINT.

JULY 17*

SAINT FRANCIS SOLANO

1549–1610 • SPAIN AND SOUTH AMERICA

NOT DISMAYED

It is the LORD who goes before you. He will be with you; he will
not fail you or forsake you. Do not fear or be dismayed.

DEUTERONOMY 31:8

Francis heard the crashing waves against the ship and felt the deck rock violently beneath him. The captain yelled at him again to get in the lifeboat with the crew. They would have to leave behind the rest of the people, a group of slaves from Africa. Francis looked around at the faces of the men in the cargo hold. Francis yelled back to the captain that the crew would have to go without him. For the whole voyage, Francis had been telling the people in the cargo hold about Jesus and His great love for them. Francis wouldn't leave them now, even as the ship sank and the storm raged. Francis would not give in to fear or despair. When others would have been dismayed, Francis held firm to his belief in God's love. Three days later, Saint Francis Solano and the survivors of the shipwreck were rescued.

IN A SMALL TOWN IN SPAIN, A BULL ESCAPED HIS PEN AND ATTACKED THE TOWNSPEOPLE. AS THE STORY GOES, SAINT FRANCIS SOLANO CONFRONTED THE BULL, WHO BECAME CALM AND LICKED HIS HAND. THE BULL ALLOWED FRANCIS TO TAKE HIM BACK TO HIS PEN.

*Jesus, You go before me, and You will be with me.
You help me do what's right, no matter the cost.*

SAINT CAMILLUS OF LELLIS

1550–1614 • ITALY

ARE ANY AMONG YOU SICK?

Are any among you sick? They should call for the
elders of the church and have them pray over them,
anointing them with oil in the name of the Lord.

JAMES 5:14

Before he followed Christ, Camillus followed his own whims. But then everything changed. Camillus started to understand the love of Christ, and he stopped wasting the time God had given him. Camillus committed to serve Christ by caring for the sick. He even created an order—a group of people living in community, focusing together on specific ways to live, serve, and pray. Camillus's order specialized in taking care of sick people. They were called the Ministers of the Sick, and they took excellent care of any patient, even those declared to be incurable. Even if a patient would die soon, Camillus and the other ministers of the sick treated that patient carefully and with dignity.

SAINT CAMILLUS OF LELLIS'S MINISTERS OF THE SICK WORE A RED CROSS ON THEIR ROBES.

*Jesus, help me care for and pray for the sick,
just as Saint Camillus of Lellis did.*

SAINT MARY MACKILLOP

1842–1909 • AUSTRALIA

BORN TO TEACH

*Show yourself in all respects a model of good
works, and in your teaching show integrity.*

TITUS 2:7

Mary's parents had moved to Australia before she was born. When
she was old enough, she moved to her aunt and uncle's home to help
educate their children. Mary started including some
of the poor children in her cousin's lessons. More
and more children gathered to learn from Mary, and
the town priest supported Mary's growing mission.
Together, the priest and Mary created a group of
women committed to service, prayer, and teaching
called an "order." For the rest of her life, Mary taught
children and helped grow her order. Mary and the other Sisters even
helped women who had just been released from prison find jobs and
places to live.

SAINT MARY MACKILLOP WAS THE FIRST PERSON FROM AUSTRALIA TO BE CALLED A SAINT.

*Jesus, Saint Mary MacKillop taught people from all walks
of life. Help me be a good student and a good teacher.*

SAINT APOLLINARIS

**UNKNOWN–79 • ANTIOCH (MODERN-DAY TURKEY)
AND ROMAN EMPIRE (MODERN-DAY ITALY)**

NOT WEARY

Brothers and sisters, do not be weary in doing what is right.

2 THESSALONIANS 3:13

As the story goes, Apollinaris simply wouldn't give up. Despite everything, he never got tired of trying to complete his mission. On his first missionary trip to Ravenna, Apollinaris told many people about Jesus. They believed him, and they abandoned their temples and false gods. Then the authorities in Ravenna beat Apollinaris and threw him out of the city. Apollinaris got up and walked right back. He was thrown out again, so he started preaching in the area around the city. When the authorities found out, they put him on a ship and sent him to Greece. Apollinaris tried to tell that country the good news too, but they sent him back to Ravenna! He walked back into the city that had thrown him out three times. Then he was killed for his faith in Jesus.

ACCORDING TO TRADITION, SAINT PETER THE APOSTLE (JUNE 29) SENT SAINT APOLLINARIS TO RAVENNA.

*Jesus, help me keep trying, even when
the right thing to do is difficult.*

SAINT MARY MAGDALENE

FIRST CENTURY • GALILEE (MODERN-DAY ISRAEL)

I HAVE SEEN THE LORD

Mary Magdalene went and announced to the
disciples, "I have seen the Lord."

JOHN 20:18

Mary Magdalene saw Jesus' miracles and heard His amazing parables, and He had healed her. When she saw Jesus betrayed by the people who had followed Him and when she saw Him die on a cross at the hands of soldiers, she was devastated. Early in the morning a few days after He died, she went to His tomb. But the stone was rolled away! *Who could have taken His body?* she wondered. *Who would have disrespected Him like this?* She told some of the disciples, and they came to see the empty tomb. After they left, Mary

IN THE GOSPEL WRITTEN BY SAINT LUKE (OCT. 18), SAINT MARY MAGDALENE IS MENTIONED BY NAME AS ONE OF THE MANY WOMEN WHO TRAVELED WITH JESUS.

Magdalene cried by herself. When she heard a voice, she assumed the gardener was speaking to her. But when she heard Him say her name, she knew. "Teacher!" she cried out. Jesus was back! She saw Him with her own eyes!

*Jesus, You are my teacher, just like You
were Saint Mary Magdalene's.*

SAINT LAWRENCE OF BRINDISI

1559–1619 • ITALY

BOY TEACHER

After three days they found him in the temple, sitting among the teachers, listening to them and asking them questions. And all who heard him were amazed at his understanding and his answers.

LUKE 2:46–47

When Jesus was only twelve, He amazed the teachers in the temple with His understanding of God. Churches in Italy remember and celebrate this story from Jesus' life by allowing young boys to preach in public at Christmas. Lawrence's Italian city celebrated this custom, and many boys could be seen during the Christmas season, preaching and teaching by the churches. Lawrence decided to join in when he was only six—and as it turned out, he was good at preaching. For Lawrence, this was only the beginning! He would become a priest and keep preaching for the rest of his life. He would offer his wisdom to leaders around the world.

AS THE STORY GOES, SAINT LAWRENCE OF BRINDISI SHED TEARS ON ALTAR LINENS THAT WERE LATER USED TO HEAL SICK PEOPLE.

Jesus, You gave Saint Lawrence of Brindisi wisdom when he was a young boy. Give me wisdom too.

JULY 23

SAINT BRIDGET OF SWEDEN

1303–1373 · SWEDEN

GENEROUS

Those who are generous are blessed, for they
share their bread with the poor.

PROVERBS 22:9

Bridget and her husband, Ulf, were Swedish nobles who loved Jesus and dedicated their lives to Him. Together, they raised eight children—four sons and four daughters. They taught their own children about the love of Jesus, and they used their wealth to serve the others around them. Bridget showed compassion to the women in her city who had children but didn't have husbands. These women needed extra support, which Bridget generously gave. Both Bridget and her husband traveled on a pilgrimage to see the places where Jesus had lived to learn more about Him and bring their knowledge back to Sweden. Her husband died on the journey home, but even after his death, Bridget continued serving Jesus by founding a religious order, now called the Brigittines, and building a monastery.

> SAINT BRIDGET IS THE PATRON SAINT OF SWEDEN.

*Jesus, help me give generously from the gifts that
You have given to me, just as Saint Bridget did.*

JULY 24

SAINT CHARBEL MAKHLOUF

1828–1898 • LEBANON

AT ALL TIMES

Pray in the Spirit at all times in every prayer and supplication. To that end keep alert and always persevere in supplication for all the saints.

EPHESIANS 6:18

Charbel's mother wanted him to get married, and his uncle thought that he should keep working in his shop. But Charbel made a decision that he knew neither of them would like—he wanted to become a monk. Even though Charbel helped his mother around the house and worked hard for his uncle, he also spent time contemplating God and sitting with Him in prayer. Charbel knew that he wanted to serve the world by prayer. He wanted to pray at all times. Charbel decided that the best way to follow God's direction was to leave his family quietly and walk all the way to the monastery. He would become both a priest and a monk. Charbel spent his life devoted to prayer and service to the Church.

ONE OF SAINT CHARBEL MAKHLOUF'S CHORES AS A YOUNG BOY WAS TO MILK HIS FAMILY'S COW.

Jesus, Saint Charbel Makhlouf spoke to You in the middle of his ordinary tasks. Help me do the same.

JULY 25

SAINT JAMES THE APOSTLE

UNKNOWN–44 • GALILEE (MODERN-DAY ISRAEL)

SON OF THUNDER

So he appointed the twelve: . . . James son of Zebedee
and John the brother of James (to whom he gave the
name Boanerges, that is, Sons of Thunder).

MARK 3:16–17

James's nickname was "Son of Thunder," and that may have been because of his hot temper that went in all directions, just like the rumbles of thunder in a thunderstorm. James once threatened a town near Jerusalem after they refused to accept Jesus, but Jesus immediately corrected James. Jesus can calm any storm—even the angry storms raging inside of people. After Jesus' death and resurrection, James replaced his anger with bold passion. King Herod didn't like what James had to say about Jesus' kingdom, and James was the first apostle to die for his faith.

SAINT JAMES THE APOSTLE IS BELIEVED BY MANY TO BE BURIED IN A CATHEDRAL IN SPAIN. PEOPLE FROM ALL OVER THE WORLD COME TO WALK A LONG PATH TO THE CATHEDRAL AND PRAY. IT'S CALLED THE WAY OF SAINT JAMES, OR EL CAMINO DE SANTIAGO.

Jesus, help me be passionate about the right things.

SAINTS JOACHIM AND ANNE

FIRST CENTURY · GALILEE (MODERN-DAY ISRAEL)

FOR THIS CHILD

For this child I prayed; and the LORD has granted me the petition that I made to him. Therefore I have lent him to the LORD; as long as he lives, he is given to the LORD.

1 SAMUEL 1:27–28

Joachim and Anne were married, but they had no children. Even though they had prayed and prayed, God had not given them a child to call their own. The couple isn't mentioned in the Bible, but as the story goes, an angel came to each of them, promising them that they would be given a child, even though it seemed completely impossible. After all, they had reached an old age, too old to have babies. But God can do anything. Anne eventually gave birth to a baby girl, and they named her Mary. One day Mary would have a baby too—an angel told her to name her baby Jesus.

> LIKE HANNAH, THE MOTHER OF SAMUEL, SAINT ANNE PROMISED THAT SHE WOULD GIVE ANY CHILD SHE WAS GIVEN INTO GOD'S SERVICE.

Jesus, children are a gift from You!

SAINT SIMEON STYLITES THE ELDER

388–459 • SYRIA

WITHDRAW AND PRAY

He would withdraw to deserted places and pray.

LUKE 5:16

Simeon wanted to hear from God. He practiced strict fasts, or periods of time when he went without food, to focus on praying. He knew that he needed time alone to hear from God, so he spent great amounts of time by himself. When he felt too crowded, he'd retreat farther away from people, but people often sought him out to ask questions since he was a wise man. Finally, after being bothered one too many times, Simeon made a platform on top of a pillar and sat on it. At first, his pillar was only nine feet high. Then he extended it to fifty feet high! Simeon spent the rest of his days sitting there and surrendering himself to the Lord in prayer. He sat on the pillar for thirty-six years!

> PEOPLE STILL WANTED TO TALK TO SAINT SIMEON STYLITES THE ELDER, EVEN WHEN HE WAS ON THE TOP OF HIS PILLAR. SO THEY PUT A LADDER AGAINST THE PILLAR AND CLIMBED UP!

Jesus, I want time alone with You. Help me find that time.

BLESSED STANLEY ROTHER

1935–1981 • THE UNITED STATES AND GUATEMALA

STRENGTH OF MY HEART

My flesh and my heart may fail, but God is the
strength of my heart and my portion forever.

PSALM 73:26

Stanley grew up serving his family and his church. He completed chores around his family's farm, and he assisted the priests at his church as an altar server. He wondered if God's plan for him was to join the priesthood, and after high school he went to seminary. Stanley was ordained and served as a priest for five years in Oklahoma. Then God called Stanley all the way to Guatemala. While he served the Guatemalan people, a terrible war broke out, and Stanley briefly left to go back to Oklahoma. But he knew that God's mission was more important than his own safety. Stanley returned to Guatemala, and soon he was killed for his faith in Jesus.

> BLESSED STANLEY ROTHER WAS THE FIRST PRIEST BORN IN THE UNITED STATES TO BE DECLARED A MARTYR.

Jesus, Blessed Stanley Rother gave You everything! Help me follow his example.

BLESSED STANLEY ROTHER IS ON TRACK TO BECOME A SAINT.

JULY 29

SAINT MARTHA

FIRST CENTURY • JUDEA (MODERN-DAY ISRAEL)

BELIEVING EVEN THEN

*Accordingly, though Jesus loved Martha and her sister
and Lazarus, after having heard that Lazarus was ill, he
stayed two days longer in the place where he was.*

JOHN 11:5–6

Martha believed that Jesus could do anything. So when her brother Lazarus got sick, she got the message to Jesus as fast as she could. If anyone could save Lazarus, it was Jesus. But Lazarus got sicker and sicker, and still, Jesus never came. Martha almost couldn't believe it when Lazarus died. This wasn't how it was supposed to end! When Jesus finally arrived, Martha couldn't help but tell Him, "Lord, if you had been here, my brother would not have died" (John 11:21). But she didn't stop there! Before Jesus raised Lazarus from the dead, Martha told Him that she believed He was the Son of God. Even then, in the middle of the tragedy, Martha believed in Him.

WHEN SAINT MARTHA WAS COOKING FOR JESUS AND HER SISTER WAS LISTENING TO HIM TALK, JESUS TOLD MARTHA THAT HER SISTER WAS DOING THE MORE IMPORTANT THING.

*Jesus, help me believe in You when it feels
like everything is going wrong.*

JULY 30*

BLESSED SOLANUS CASEY

1870–1957 • THE UNITED STATES

OPEN DOOR

"Ask, and it will be given you; search, and you will find;
knock, and the door will be opened for you."

MATTHEW 7:7

Solanus Casey stood by the door, opening it for anyone who wanted to enter. Solanus wasn't just opening doors to churches; he helped people open doors in their hearts to God. Solanus prayed, he heard confessions, and he sat with people who were sick and in pain. His kind eyes and his quiet voice inspired thousands of people to turn to God for help. Solanus's advice was often brief and showed how much wisdom and trust he placed in God. "Thank God ahead of time!" he would tell people. And to anyone mourning an unanswered prayer, he would gently say, "God answers every prayer. He does it in His way, though."

NO MATTER WHERE BLESSED SOLANUS CASEY SERVED, PEOPLE WOULD LINE UP FOR BLOCKS JUST FOR A CHANCE TO SPEAK WITH HIM.

Jesus, I want to open my whole heart to You. Help me see that You answer every prayer in Your own way.

BLESSED SOLANUS CASEY IS ON TRACK TO BECOME A SAINT.

JULY 31

SAINT IGNATIUS OF LOYOLA

1491–1556 • SPAIN

INTENTIONAL PRAYER

Indeed, the word of God is living and active. . . . It is able
to judge the thoughts and intentions of the heart.

HEBREWS 4:12

Ignatius knew that God wants people to hear His words and do them, and He wants to speak directly to people's hearts. Ignatius was a priest who understood the importance of knowing that God was speaking to him. But Ignatius also knew that hearing from God could be difficult. So Ignatius developed a system of exercises—or ways of thinking and praying—that people could complete to help them hear God. For example, Ignatius encouraged people to consider their daily actions before they fell into bed and went to sleep. What went well that day? Where could they see God? Ignatius was teaching people to be intentional in reading Scripture, in prayer, and in their actions. Ignatius helped people hear God and see His work in their lives.

BEFORE HE BECAME A PRIEST, SAINT IGNATIUS OF LOYOLA WAS A SOLDIER. HE WAS WOUNDED BY A CANNONBALL IN BATTLE!

Jesus, I want to hear You.

AUGUST 1

SAINT ALPHONSUS LIGUORI

1696–1787 · ITALY

LEAVE IT BEHIND

"Everyone who has left houses or brothers or sisters or
father or mother or children or fields, for my name's sake,
will receive a hundredfold, and will inherit eternal life."

MATTHEW 19:29

When he was only nineteen, Alphonsus was already defending people in court as a lawyer. He had completed law school, receiving his doctorate when he was only sixteen. He was way ahead and highly praised, but he decided to step off the path of fame and success and leave it behind. Alphonsus believed he had a vision while he visited a hospital. Alphonsus heard God calling him to a different way of life, so he gave up his early successes for a difficult life of prayer and service.

LATER IN HIS LIFE, SAINT ALPHONSUS LIGUORI SUFFERED FROM RHEUMATISM, WHICH IS A CONDITION THAT CAUSES PAIN IN MUSCLES OR JOINTS. HIS BACK WAS BENT SO FAR FORWARD THAT HE HAD TO DRINK OUT OF TUBES.

*Jesus, help me choose Your way over the ways of
the world, just as Saint Alphonsus Liguori did.*

AUGUST 2

SAINT EUSEBIUS OF VERCELLI

283–371 • ROMAN EMPIRE (MODERN-DAY ITALY)

TRUTH OF GOD

*In the beginning was the Word, and the Word
was with God, and the Word was God.*

JOHN 1:1

A few hundred years after Jesus' death, misunderstandings about Him were everywhere. People believed that Jesus was not really who He said He was. They thought Jesus couldn't be both God *and* man, but they were wrong. Jesus *is* both God and man. He said so Himself, and Eusebius knew it. When Eusebius's friend Athanasius (May 2) was told that he couldn't come to the meetings of Church leaders because he believed the truth about Jesus, Eusebius refused to attend the same councils himself. Later, Athanasius and Eusebius gathered faithful people together to help declare that Jesus is God. Even when so many people were against him, Eusebius bravely spoke the truth.

SAINT EUSEBIUS OF VERCELLI DEFENDED THE IDEA THAT THE HOLY SPIRIT IS GOD TOO.

*Jesus, help me know and defend the truth about
You, just as Saint Eusebius of Vercelli did.*

SAINT PETER JULIAN EYMARD

1811–1868 · FRANCE

AN HOUR WITH GOD

Then he came to the disciples and found them sleeping; and he said to Peter, "So, could you not stay awake with me one hour?"

MATTHEW 26:40

During Peter's life, more than a thousand years after Jesus' death, Christians were still suffering under false teachings and lies. The false teachers of Peter's day started with something true: all people are sinners in need of grace. But then they took it too far. They said that people were so bad that God wanted nothing to do with them, that God couldn't even look at them because they were so awful. Peter knew this was wrong. So after he became a priest, he decided to do something about it. Peter told people the opposite. He said to come into the church and just sit with God. He told churches to invite people to pray for an hour or more. Many churches started hosting these times of prayer for forty-hour stretches, with at least forty people in the church coming to be with God for an hour!

AT FIRST, SAINT PETER JULIAN EYMARD'S FATHER DID NOT WANT HIM TO BECOME A PRIEST. HE EVENTUALLY ACCEPTED IT.

Jesus, You want me to be with You, and I want to spend time with You too!

SAINT JOHN VIANNEY

1786–1859 • FRANCE

TROUBLED HEARTS

"Peace I leave with you; my peace I give to you. I do not
give to you as the world gives. Do not let your hearts
be troubled, and do not let them be afraid."

JOHN 14:27

John grew up in France during the French Revolution, a time when Christians were punished for practicing their religion. By the time the whole thing was over, French communities of Christians were disorganized. John became a priest in the middle of that big mess. How was he going to help put these communities back together again? He'd speak to hearts, one by one. He invited people to repent in the confessional. John spent over ten hours in the confessional every day, inviting people back into relationship with God. He saw about twenty thousand people every year for several years. When their troubled hearts were healed by God's forgiveness, the Christians were able to put their communities back together again.

SAINT JOHN VIANNEY WAS DRAFTED INTO NAPOLEON'S ARMY.

Jesus, help me when my heart is troubled.
I want to find my peace in You.

SERVANT OF GOD THEA BOWMAN

1937–1990 • THE UNITED STATES

BRINGING PEOPLE TOGETHER

All of you, have unity of spirit,
sympathy, love for one another, a
tender heart, and a humble mind.

1 PETER 3:8

Thea Bowman grew up in the southern United States and was a young woman in the 1960s, a time of racial tensions. She grew up going to church with her parents, and she wanted to dedicate her life to God as a Sister, or a woman who lived in a community of service and prayer. Most Sisters in Thea's part of the world were White, and she was Black. But Thea knew that she was called to give as much as she got and to teach as much as she learned. Thea spent her life singing joyfully to God and inviting others to sing with her. She was a highly praised teacher and writer. During the last few years of her life, she spoke to large audiences, who were amazed at her faith and dedication to bringing communities together.

> SERVANT OF GOD THEA BOWMAN'S FIRST NAME REFERS TO GOD.

Jesus, You bring people together. Help me do the same.

SERVANT OF GOD THEA BOWMAN IS ON TRACK TO BECOME A SAINT.

SAINTS PETER, JAMES, AND JOHN

FIRST CENTURY • GALILEE (MODERN-DAY ISRAEL)

THE TRANSFIGURATION

We ourselves heard this voice come from heaven,
while we were with him on the holy mountain.

2 PETER 1:18

Peter, James, and John followed Jesus back down the mountain. They were still trying to understand what they'd just seen. The day before, Jesus took the three of them up on a mountain to pray with Him. The three disciples almost fell asleep, but then they saw a light. As Jesus prayed, He was surrounded by brilliant light, and the light seemed to be coming from Him. Then two more men appeared. It was Moses and Elijah! The disciples watched as the two men talked with Jesus. *Could this really be?* the disciples wondered. As the

> SAINT PETER WROTE ABOUT JESUS' TRANSFIGURATION IN ONE OF HIS LETTERS, AND SAINT JOHN WROTE ABOUT IT IN HIS GOSPEL.

men left, Peter tried to make sense of what he had seen. Then a voice came from heaven, declaring, "This is my Son, my Chosen; listen to him!" (Luke 9:35). As they walked down the mountain, Jesus said not to tell anyone what they'd seen until He rose from the grave.

Jesus, You are who You say You are. Help me
share this good news with the world.

SAINT CAJETAN

1480–1547 • ITALY

TRULY A DISCIPLE

Jesus said to the Jews who had believed in him, "If you continue in my word, you are truly my disciples."

JOHN 8:31

Cajetan felt inspired by the stories of the first apostles, who lived and walked with Jesus. He knew that many priests in his country were teaching and doing things that didn't honor and serve God, and they certainly weren't living like the first apostles.

So Cajetan changed his own way of life and inspired others to do the same. He founded a group of priests who looked to the first apostles as their example for living faithfully as a true disciple of Christ. They focused on being pure and obedient, and they refused to store up wealth. In fact, Cajetan and the other priests wouldn't even beg for money when they were in need; they simply waited for God to provide for them.

SAINT CAJETAN WORE A SHIRT MADE OF HAIR EVERY DAY, AND HE SPENT HIS NIGHTS AND MORNINGS IN PRAYER, TAKING A BRIEF BREAK FOR SLEEP ON A STRAW BED.

Jesus, help me inspire good changes in the people around me, just as Saint Cajetan did.

AUGUST 8

SAINT DOMINIC

1170–1221 • SPAIN

IN NEED

Since there will never cease to be some in need on the
earth, I therefore command you, "Open your hand
to the poor and needy neighbor in your land."

DEUTERONOMY 15:11

Dominic took the money for his last shirt, adding it to the pile of coins that he would use to buy bread for the poor. Dominic was a student, but his next few weeks of study were going to be challenging—he'd sold his books, too, in order to help pay for the food that people desperately needed. A terrible famine left families and children hungry all across his country of Spain, so Dominic sold what he had to help them. His professors were confused. Why would their star student do this? Dominic insisted he wouldn't study from something that could be used to buy someone else food. Later in his life, Dominic would even try to sell himself into slavery in order to help people in need.

> SAINT DOMINIC
> WAS GIVEN
> THE NICKNAME
> "DOG OF
> THE LORD."

*Jesus, help me have open hands willing to help
people in need, just as Saint Dominic did.*

AUGUST 9

SAINT EDITH STEIN

1891–1942 • GERMANY

BECOMING A CHILD OF GOD

To all who received him, who believed in his name,
he gave power to become children of God.

JOHN 1:12

As a child, Edith practiced her Jewish faith with her large German family, but by the time she was a teenager, she declared that she was an atheist, which means she didn't believe in God at all. Edith studied hard and became a distinguished student. Once, on a school break, while she was reading a book that Saint Teresa of Ávila (Oct. 15) wrote, Edith became convinced that God is real after all. She believed that Jesus is God's Son, and she became a child of God. The next decades of Edith's life were dedicated to translating the works of Thomas Aquinas (Jan. 28) into German. She became a nun and lived in a religious community. Years later she was killed with many other people in a Nazi concentration camp because she refused to give up her faith in Jesus.

> SAINT EDITH STEIN IS ALSO KNOWN AS SAINT TERESA BENEDICTA OF THE CROSS.

Jesus, those who put their faith in You are Your children.
Help me keep believing in You even when it's difficult.

SAINT LAWRENCE

225–258 • ROMAN EMPIRE (MODERN-DAY ITALY)

BRAVE SOULS

"Do not fear those who kill the body but cannot kill the soul."

MATTHEW 10:28

Lawrence served the Church as a deacon in the days of the Roman emperors who proudly hunted Christians. Lawrence and six other deacons were challenged by the cruel emperor Valerian to give up their faith in Jesus. If the deacons didn't deny Him, they would be killed. Lawrence and the other deacons stayed true to their faith even as they faced death, knowing their souls belonged to God. The bravery of these martyrs inspired many people to believe in Jesus. Even some of the senators, who encouraged the emperor to kill Christians, had a change of heart. They thought, *If these deacons would rather die than give up believing in Jesus, then maybe Jesus is worth believing in.*

SAINT LAWRENCE GAVE MANY TREASURES OF THE CHURCH AWAY TO THE POOR BEFORE HE WAS MARTYRED.

Jesus, I can be brave because You are with me.

SAINT CLARE OF ASSISI

1194–1253 • ITALY

MORE PRECIOUS THAN GOLD

Jesus said to him, "If you wish to be perfect, go, sell your possessions, and give the money to the poor, and you will have treasure in heaven; then come, follow me."

MATTHEW 19:21

Clare wanted to give up her belongings and give Jesus her whole life. She wanted heavenly treasure. Her wealthy parents did not like the idea of their beautiful, golden-haired daughter owning nothing at all. When she was eighteen, she ran away in the middle of the night. When her parents found her, she was dressed in the simple clothes of a nun, not the lovely dress of a noblewoman. They told her to come home. Clare tore off her veil, and her parents gasped. Her hair had been cut off! Giving up her hair and clothes was Clare's way to say that she was totally devoted to Jesus.

SAINT CLARE OF ASSISI WAS A GREAT FRIEND OF SAINT FRANCIS OF ASSISI (OCT. 3). HE HELPED CLARE UNDERSTAND GOD'S VOICE. SHE DECIDED TO DEVOTE HER LIFE TO CHRIST AFTER A CONVERSATION WITH SAINT FRANCIS.

Jesus, help me value Your kingdom more than this world, just as Saint Clare of Assisi did.

SAINT JANE FRANCES DE CHANTAL

1572–1641 • FRANCE

FORGIVEN

"Forgive us our debts, as we also have forgiven our debtors."

MATTHEW 6:12

Jane mourned for her husband, the father of her four children. What was she going to do without him? And how could she forgive the man who killed him? Her husband, Cristophe, was killed in a hunting accident. The man who fired the shot that killed Cristophe lived in the same town as Jane and her family. Jane knew she would run into him all the time, and just seeing him would bring back the memory of her husband's death. But Jane was determined to forgive him. She started small. When she saw the man on the street, she offered a wave. After a few years, she invited the man into her house. She found she could even talk with him. God changed her heart through these acts. In fact, when the man asked Jane to be the godmother of his child, Jane said yes!

SAINT JANE FRANCES DE CHANTAL'S FRIENDS REMEMBERED HER AS VERY FUNNY. SHE WAS KNOWN FOR HER JOKES AND WITTY COMMENTS.

Jesus, help me forgive others, as You have forgiven me.

SAINTS PONTIAN AND HIPPOLYTUS

UNKNOWN–235 (PONTIAN), 170–235 (HIPPOLYTUS) • ROMAN EMPIRE (MODERN-DAY ITALY)

RECONCILED

[Christ] has made both groups into one and has broken down the dividing wall . . . that he might create in himself one new humanity in place of two, thus making peace, and might reconcile both groups to God in one body through the cross.

EPHESIANS 2:14–16

According to Hippolytus, Christians who fell away from God needed harsher punishments from the Church. Leaders like Pontian, who served as pope, were too forgiving. Hippolytus created a division within the Church, becoming the leader of his own group. Pontian tried to bring back Hippolytus, but he refused to reconcile, or come to an agreement with the Church leaders. The Roman emperor didn't care about the differences between Pontian and Hippolytus—he just knew they were both Christians, and that was bad enough for him. He sent both Pontian and Hippolytus to do hard labor in a salt mine. Chained together, Pontian and Hippolytus forgave each other.

> BOTH SAINTS WERE SENT TO THE MINES IN 235, ABOUT TWO HUNDRED YEARS AFTER JESUS DIED.

Jesus, when I disagree with others, help me focus more on loving others than being right.

AUGUST 14

SAINT MAXIMILIAN KOLBE

1894–1941 • POLAND

A FEARLESS WITNESS

For we cannot keep from speaking about what we have seen and heard.

ACTS 4:20

Maximilian spread the word about Jesus, even when conversation about Jesus became unpopular. As he studied for the priesthood and became a priest, he wrote frequently about the great love of God. He traveled around the world, returning to his home country of Poland, where the Nazis, a political group in Germany, were taking Jews and Christians from their homes and putting them into concentration camps. Maximilian hid Polish people from the Nazis. He even had an underground radio station to keep witnessing about Jesus. But Maximilian was found. He went willingly to the concentration camps where the Nazis were keeping their prisoners. In the spirit of Christ Himself, Maximilian agreed to die in place of another man in the concentration camp who was condemned to die of starvation.

> SAINT MAXIMILIAN KOLBE FOUNDED A MONASTERY IN NAGASAKI, JAPAN, THAT SURVIVED THE 1945 BOMBING OF NAGASAKI.

Jesus, help me speak about You fearlessly,
just as Saint Maximilian Kolbe did.

BLESSED VICENTA CHÁVEZ OROZCO

1867–1949 • MEXICO

CONSOLATION

Blessed be the God and Father of our Lord Jesus Christ . . .
who consoles us in all our affliction, so that we may be
able to console those who are in any affliction with the
consolation with which we ourselves are consoled by God.

2 CORINTHIANS 1:3–4

Vicenta came through the door of the tiny hospital, praying that she would find help. She had been sick for a long time, and she wanted to be better. The hospital had only six beds. As the hospital workers prayed for and cared for Vicenta, she started to heal. Vicenta dedicated the rest of her life to serving others in the tiny hospital, just as she had been served. God consoled, or comforted, Vicenta in her sickness. Vicenta would spend the rest of her life consoling others who were sick.

BLESSED VICENTA CHÁVEZ OROZCO ASKED OTHER CHILDREN TO PRAY WITH HER WHEN SHE WAS A LITTLE GIRL.

*Jesus, Blessed Vicenta Chávez Orozco helped others
because she was helped by You. Help me do the same.*

BLESSED VICENTA CHÁVEZ OROZCO IS ON
TRACK TO BECOME A SAINT.

AUGUST 16

SAINT STEPHEN OF HUNGARY

970-1038 · HUNGARY

KING'S HEART

The king's heart is a stream of water in the hand
of the LORD; he turns it wherever he will.

PROVERBS 21:1

S tephen had a big job on his hands. He was made king, and his country, Hungary, needed excellent organization. If the laws of the country weren't well thought out, then the people of Hungary would suffer. God guided Stephen, turning the king's heart toward worshipping God. Stephen knew that one of the best things for his people was worship, so he organized his country accordingly. He made sure churches were built throughout the land, and he started the practice of tithing, or giving 10 percent of your earnings to the church. He is also remembered for keeping his people safe from invading influences and sending missionaries from his country all over the world.

SAINT STEPHEN WAS CROWNED THE FIRST KING OF HUNGARY ON CHRISTMAS DAY IN THE YEAR 1000.

*Jesus, You can turn the hearts of leaders
all over the world toward You.*

SAINT JOAN OF THE CROSS

1666–1736 • FRANCE

GIVING BACK

"Give, and it will be given to you. . . . For the measure
you give will be the measure you get back."

LUKE 6:38

J oan crossed to the other side of the street, glancing away from the woman asking for money. Joan did her best to stay away from the beggars all over the street. She had a business to run, and she couldn't spare any change for them. All of Joan's money and actions were counted carefully, and she didn't think there was any room to be generous. One day Joan didn't cross the street fast enough, and one of the women asking for money touched her arm. Joan looked into the woman's eyes and truly saw her—she was a human in need. Suddenly, she wanted to pour out her life and her soul for God. She didn't need to count her money and her actions in such unforgiving ways anymore. Joan gave everything away.

AFTER SHE CLOSED HER BUSINESS, SAINT JOAN OF THE CROSS JOINED A RELIGIOUS ORDER AND FOUNDED HOSPICES AND SCHOOLS.

*Jesus, help me give freely to others, just
as Saint Joan of the Cross did.*

SAINT LOUIS OF TOULOUSE

1274–1297 • FRANCE

ANOTHER CROWN

You shall be a crown of beauty in the hand of the LORD,
and a royal diadem in the hand of your God.

ISAIAH 62:3

Louis didn't want any crown, except the crown of life that God gives to His followers. This was a problem because Louis was a prince who was expected to take a crown—whether he wanted it or not! But Louis had studied under monks who were inspired by Saint Francis of Assisi (Oct. 3), and he wanted the spiritual riches of the Franciscan order, who honored God by owning nothing. Louis didn't want the riches of any crown. He managed to convince his father to give the crown to his younger brother instead. A beautiful portrait of Louis shows him in both his royal robes and his humble Franciscan robes. He was a prince who understood the importance of the heavenly kingdom.

SAINT LOUIS OF TOULOUSE PRACTICED HUMILITY; HE ASKED ONE OF THE OTHER FRANCISCANS TO CORRECT HIM WHENEVER HE MADE A MISTAKE— EVEN IN PUBLIC.

Jesus, Your kingdom is the kingdom that matters the most.

AUGUST 19

SAINT JOHN EUDES

1601–1680 • FRANCE

FACING TEMPTATION

Blessed is anyone who endures temptation. Such a one
has stood the test and will receive the crown of life that
the Lord has promised to those who love him.

JAMES 1:12

John committed to the priesthood even though the Church was facing constant crises like plagues and divisions. Many priests were falling away from the Church at this time, but John inspired them to reconsider. God was forgiving, and they could always start fresh. John found that these priests needed so much of his time, he started focusing his efforts just on them. Many priests faced the temptation to quit, but John reminded these priests how much Jesus loved them and cared for them. He told the priests that crowns of life were waiting for them if they kept trusting in Jesus.

SAINT JOHN EUDES MINISTERED TO THE DYING DURING A TERRIBLE PLAGUE. TO KEEP FROM SPREADING THE PLAGUE TO OTHERS, HE LIVED BY HIMSELF IN THE MIDDLE OF A FIELD BETWEEN HIS VISITS TO THE SICK.

*Jesus, help me face the temptations of
this life and stay faithful to You.*

244

AUGUST 20

SAINT BERNARD OF CLAIRVAUX

1090–1153 · FRANCE

STORIES FOREVERMORE

You show me the path of life. In your presence there is fullness
of joy; in your right hand are pleasures forevermore.

PSALM 16:11

Even when he was just a boy, Bernard was captured by stories and writing. He loved literature because he understood that loving stories would help him understand and love God's story even more. When he was only nineteen, Bernard dedicated his life to God. After living with a group of monks and learning their way of life, Bernard founded a new monastery in a place called the Valley of Bitterness. Bernard and the other monks faced many trials there. The path of

SAINT BERNARD OF CLAIRVAUX'S FATHER AND ALL HIS BROTHERS JOINED HIS MONASTERY, WHICH WAS CALLED CLAIRVAUX.

life they were called to was difficult, but it had great results. Many new people joined their mission. Eventually, Bernard would use his love of literature to write beautiful letters and books that still inspire Christians today.

*Jesus, You gave Saint Bernard of Clairvaux the love
of Your great story. Give me the same love.*

245

SAINT PIUS X

1835–1914 · ITALY

GOOD WORKS

For we are what he has made us, created in Christ Jesus for good works, which God prepared beforehand to be our way of life.

EPHESIANS 2:10

P ius knew that *newer* didn't always mean *better*. Pius served the Catholic Church as pope at the beginning of the twentieth century. Nearly two thousand years had passed since Jesus had died and risen again, and many Christians were tempted to think that the new ideas and new technology of their modern times were superior to anything from the past. Some Christians started believing that Jesus wasn't really who He said He was. But Pius encouraged Christians everywhere to do what Jesus had always told them to do: to pray, to serve the poor, and to hope. He sent aid to earthquake victims and paid for refugees, or people who had to flee their own countries, to have shelter.

> SAINT PIUS X REMINDED THE CATHOLIC CHURCH OF ANCIENT SONGS, LIKE THE GREGORIAN CHANT, THAT HAD BEEN USED FOR CENTURIES TO HONOR GOD WITH BEAUTIFUL MUSIC.

*Jesus, help me always remember that
any good thing I do is for You.*

AUGUST 22*

SAINT MOSES THE BLACK

330–405 • EGYPT

FROM ALL UNRIGHTEOUSNESS

If we confess our sins, he who is faithful and just will forgive us our sins and cleanse us from all unrighteousness.

1 JOHN 1:9

Moses was a natural leader. When he joined a band of robbers, they chose him to be the leader because of his confidence and strength. Moses was an excellent robber too. He used his intelligence and his strength to take advantage of other people. But after several years of committing crimes, Moses went to a monastery, totally repentant and weeping over what he had done. The monks, who knew exactly who he was, didn't trust Moses' change of heart at first. But after a while, the monks believed him because they saw his life changed—he was cleansed from his unrighteousness. Moses then became a monk, and he was great at that as well. He could even pray the whole night through instead of sleeping.

AFTER MANY YEARS AS A MONK, SAINT MOSES THE BLACK DIED DEFENDING THE MONASTERY, HOLDING OFF AN ATTACK LONG ENOUGH FOR MOST OF THE OTHER MONKS TO ESCAPE.

Jesus, thank You for cleansing me from all unrighteousness.

SAINT ROSE OF LIMA

1586–1617 • PERU

ETERNAL BEAUTY

The grass withers, the flower fades; but the
word of our God will stand forever.

ISAIAH 40:8

Rose's parents loved her dearly. They had big plans for their daughter, whom they had named Isabel. One of their servants dreamed of the beautiful baby's face turning into a rose. Her parents were delighted because they thought the dream meant their daughter would marry well someday. What a wonderful bride their little "rose" would be! But the girl, who took the nickname, refused her parents' dreams for her. There are more important things to be than beautiful, and Rose wanted to be dedicated to God first and foremost. She prayed constantly, went to church to adore Jesus every day, and continually refused to be married, insisting that physical beauty wasn't as important as holiness. She devoted her whole life to prayer, knowing that beauty fades but God is eternal.

> SAINT ROSE OF LIMA WORE A HEAVY SILVER CROWN THAT REMINDED HER OF JESUS' CROWN OF THORNS.

*Jesus, thank You for the beauty You have created.
Help me understand that eternal beauty—a heart
devoted to You—is what matters most.*

VENERABLE FÉLIX VARELA

1788–1853 · CUBA AND THE UNITED STATES

RICH IN FAITH

Has not God chosen the poor in the world to be rich in faith and to be heirs of the kingdom that he has promised to those who love him?

JAMES 2:5

Félix became a priest when he was twenty-three years old. He studied and served in Havana, Cuba, the city where he was born, until he was moved to the United States. He became the first Cuban priest to serve in New York City. Félix knew that God had chosen the poor to be rich in faith and heirs of His kingdom, so Félix concentrated on serving the poorest people in the city, many of whom were immigrants from Ireland. Félix was so generous that he would give away his own coats to people who needed them.

> VENERABLE FÉLIX VARELA SERVED A POST IN THE SPANISH GOVERNMENT, REPRESENTING CUBA, UNTIL HE WAS EXILED BECAUSE SPANISH LEADERSHIP DID NOT LIKE HIS IDEAS.

Jesus, help me be rich in faith and to love the poor the way that Venerable Félix Varela did.

~~~~~~~~~~

VENERABLE FÉLIX VARELA IS ON TRACK TO BECOME A SAINT.

SAINT LOUIS OF FRANCE

1214–1270 • FRANCE

MOTHER AND SON

Honor your father and your mother, so that your days may
be long in the land that the LORD your God is giving you.

EXODUS 20:12

Louis wasn't ready to be a king. His father died when Louis was only eleven years old. Louis and his mother, Queen Blanche, grieved his death, but they relied on each other. Louis's mother wisely provided for Louis, helping him understand his role before he took on the power of his position. The nobles of France would gladly have taken advantage of the young king, but they were no match for his loving mother. She instructed Louis in the love and knowledge of God. Through her guidance and Louis's obedience, the kingdom was secured.

> SAINT LOUIS OF FRANCE WANTED TO HEAR THE CONCERNS OF HIS SUBJECTS. HE WOULD SIT UNDER AN OAK TREE AND INVITE ANYONE, RICH OR POOR, TO APPROACH HIM WITH THEIR PROBLEMS.

Louis eventually married and had eleven children of his own, all of whom he told about the wonderful love and guidance of God.

Jesus, help me love and honor my parents,
like Saint Louis of France.

SAINT JOSEPH CALASANZ

1556–1648 • SPAIN AND ITALY

THE BEGINNING OF KNOWLEDGE

The fear of the Lord is the beginning of knowledge;
fools despise wisdom and instruction.

PROVERBS 1:7

Joseph's heart went out to the poor boys he saw roaming the streets of his city. There was no school for them to attend, and they spent their days getting into trouble. Joseph, even though he was a very young priest, understood that it was more important to show them what it means to do good than to just prevent them from doing evil. Joseph and other kind priests like him could extend God's love toward these boys by inviting them to learn. They could help these boys start at the beginning of their education— the fear of God, that is, the understanding that

> SAINT JOSEPH CALASANZ WAS FROM A WEALTHY FAMILY WHO RESISTED HIS CALL TO BE A PRIEST.

God is good and does exist. Joseph opened the first free school for boys in Rome. The kinds of schools that he started are still around today.

Jesus, thank You for good teachers. Help me fear You and want knowledge.

SAINT MONICA

331–387 • NORTH AFRICA (MODERN-DAY ALGERIA)

HERITAGE

Sons are indeed a heritage from the LORD,
the fruit of the womb a reward.

PSALM 127:3

Monica cried. Her son Augustine (Aug. 28) refused to believe in God, so Monica wept and prayed for him diligently. Augustine lived foolishly, wasting money and treating people disrespectfully. But mothers don't give up, and Monica never gave up on her son. She kept praying for Augustine. She wanted him to share the faith that was so important to her, but he wanted no part of it. He wanted to go his own way.

SANTA MONICA, CALIFORNIA, IS NAMED AFTER THIS SAINT.

But finally, Augustine believed. Monica saw Augustine baptized, professing the faith in God that she had clung to throughout his disobedience. She died shortly after. Her son Augustine had been the source of her sorrow, but he became a rich heritage—that is, a legacy that would continue after her death—of faith. Augustine's writings are still read by Christians all over the world.

Jesus, help me keep praying for others with
hope and faith, just as Saint Monica did.

SAINT AUGUSTINE

354–430 • NORTH AFRICA (MODERN-DAY ALGERIA)

IN TIME

He has made everything suitable for its time; moreover he has
put a sense of past and future into their minds, yet they cannot
find out what God has done from the beginning to the end.

ECCLESIASTES 3:11

Augustine knew how to persuade people, and he fooled himself and many others about God. No matter what his mother said, Augustine thought that Jesus couldn't be God. But Augustine's time would come.

As he grew in knowledge, he finally had to admit that he had been wrong—God is the beginning and ending of everything, and Jesus is God's Son. When Augustine became a Christian, he used his training in philosophy to understand Christian ideas. Augustine combined Roman ways of speaking with Christian ideas. His work made the story of Jesus understandable to people living in the Roman Empire, which stretched throughout the world.

WE CAN READ SAINT AUGUSTINE'S WRITINGS! ALTOGETHER, MORE THAN FIVE MILLION OF HIS WORDS HAVE BEEN PRESERVED, OR KEPT, ALL THESE YEARS.

*Jesus, You changed Saint Augustine's heart
and mind. You can change anyone!*

AUGUST 29

SAINT JOHN THE BAPTIST

FIRST CENTURY • JUDEA (MODERN-DAY ISRAEL)

LOOK TO JESUS

The next day John again was standing with two of
his disciples, and as he watched Jesus walk by, he
exclaimed, "Look, here is the Lamb of God!"

JOHN 1:35–36

John was Jesus' cousin. His mother, Elizabeth (Nov. 5), told John a story about when he was just a baby inside her womb. When Mary (Jan. 1), Jesus' mother, walked into Elizabeth's house, John jumped inside of her. John was excited about Jesus before either of them was born! Later, John sent many of his own followers to follow Jesus instead. John knew he was just preparing them for Jesus and willingly let them go. Instead of saying that he knew the most and that he should have had the most followers, John always told people to look to Jesus, the Son of God.

> SAINT JOHN THE BAPTIST HAD A STRANGE DIET. HE ATE LOCUSTS (A BUG LIKE A GRASSHOPPER) AND HONEY.

*Jesus, Saint John the Baptist knew that You
were greater than he was. Help me know
that You are much greater than I am.*

SAINT JEANNE JUGAN

1792–1879 · FRANCE

REMEMBER THE POOR

They asked only one thing, that we remember the poor, which was actually what I was eager to do.

GALATIANS 2:10

Jeanne lost her father when she was only four years old, and life was hard for her and her family. But Jeanne didn't complain or blame God. Jeanne knew that God wanted to use her in a special way to help love the world, but she didn't know how He would use her yet. Then, on a wintery day when she was forty-seven years old, Jeanne brought a poor blind woman to her own house and laid her down in her own bed. She finally knew what call God was saving her for—she was going to be the hands and feet of Jesus to the poorest elderly people. Jeanne kept bringing people home, and more women joined her to help in this mission. They became the Little Sisters of the Poor.

> WHEN SAINT JEANNE JUGAN WAS YOUNG, A SAILOR PROPOSED TO HER TWICE, BUT SHE SAID NO BOTH TIMES.

Jesus, help me remember that I can serve You by serving the poor and respecting the elderly.

SAINT NICODEMUS

FIRST CENTURY • JUDEA (MODERN-DAY ISRAEL)

BORN AGAIN

You have been born anew, not of perishable but of imperishable
seed, through the living and enduring word of God.

1 PETER 1:23

Nicodemus was a Pharisee, which means he devoted his life to knowing about God. He studied and read the Scriptures, and he prayed and made sacrifices. When a young man named Jesus, whom some called the Messiah, started talking about God in new ways, Nicodemus was confused. Many of the other Pharisees called Jesus a liar and a troublemaker. But Nicodemus was curious. He met with Jesus at night so none of the other Pharisees would see him. There, Nicodemus asked many questions. Jesus told Nicodemus that He had come to save the world by dying for it and that all people must be born again. Nicodemus didn't understand what Jesus meant right away. Later, he would know that Jesus came to give new life.

SAINT NICODEMUS HELPED SAINT JOSEPH OF ARIMATHEA (MAR. 30) BURY JESUS' BODY IN THE TOMB.

*Jesus, You answered Saint Nicodemus when he
asked You questions. Please help me discover
the answers to my questions too.*

SEPTEMBER 1

SAINT GILES

650–710 · GREECE AND FRANCE

WISE COUNSEL

Without counsel, plans go wrong, but with
many advisers they succeed.

PROVERBS 15:22

Giles felt tired. The constant sounds of the city of Athens wore on him. He was a wise and faithful man, and his decision-making skills were constantly wanted by the citizens of Athens. Giles was a wise counselor, but after a while, the praise and attention was too much for him. Giles was wise enough to know that if he didn't get rest, he wouldn't be of much use as a counselor any-more! He wanted some peace and quiet and some time alone with God, so he left his city of Athens and moved far away from Greece. He eventually settled in France and made a community of monks there. Soon the leaders of France asked for Giles's counsel on many matters, and Giles helped bring peace to their country.

> ONE STORY ABOUT SAINT GILES SAYS THAT HE LIVED FOR MANY YEARS DEEP IN THE FOREST WITH ONLY A DEER FOR COMPANY.

Jesus, thank You for the wise people You've placed in
my life who can help me. Help me follow wise advice.

BLESSED LAURA VICUÑA

1891–1904 • CHILE

HE HEARS PRAYER

The LORD has heard my supplication; the LORD accepts my prayer.

PSALM 6:9

Laura loved her school. She attended school with her little sister, Julia, in the beautiful Andes Mountains. Nuns taught the girls about the love of Jesus and the importance of prayer. Laura spent many hours in a little chapel praying for her mother. Her mother, Mercedes, led a difficult life. After Laura's father died, Mercedes worked so hard to take care of the girls on her own and used her skill as a seamstress to make money. Unfortunately, her seamstress shop was destroyed one night. Mercedes turned to the nuns for help, and Laura and Julia were given a place at the school. Even so, Laura knew that her mother was struggling in her faith. So Laura asked Jesus to restore her mother's faith. "Help my mama know You!" Laura prayed. One day Mercedes would return to faith in Jesus.

> WHEN MERCEDES ASKED THE NUNS FOR HELP, BLESSED LAURA VICUÑA WAS NINE AND JULIA WAS SIX.

Jesus, You hear my prayers.

~~~~~~~~~~~~~~~~~~~~~~

BLESSED LAURA VICUÑA IS ON TRACK TO BECOME A SAINT.

SAINT GREGORY THE GREAT

540–604 • ITALY

ALL THE WORLD

He said to them, "Go into all the world and proclaim
the good news to the whole creation."

MARK 16:15

Gregory served the Church as pope, but he recognized the importance of every person in the Church. From the people living and working in the everyday world to the monks living in monasteries, from the priests serving churches to the bishops and cardinals serving the priests, Gregory knew that all people were called to love Jesus and their neighbors. Gregory wanted the Church to spread throughout all the world, so he worked hard to create stability and consistency in the Church. If everyone practiced their faith together and followed similar traditions, the Church was stronger. Not everyone could live by the strict rules that the monks did, but dedication to prayer and hard work could be a part of any person's life.

> SAINT GREGORY THE GREAT BELIEVED THAT THE CONVERSION OF THE COUNTRY OF ENGLAND WAS VERY IMPORTANT, AND HE SENT FORTY MONKS THERE.

Jesus, may Your Church spread into all the world!

SAINT ROSE OF VITERBO

1233–1251 • ITALY

HER WHOLE HEART

The word is near you, on your lips and in your heart.

ROMANS 10:8

Seventeen-year-old Rose pleaded with the people of Viterbo to love Jesus with their whole lives. The year before, Rose had almost died. While she was sick, Rose believed that she saw Mary, the mother of God, appear to her in a vision. Mary told Rose to travel around the churches in Viterbo. Shortly after, Rose was healed from her sickness, and she started her travels. Many people listened to Rose, inspired by the faith that was so dear to her heart. But many others were unimpressed that a seventeen-year-old thought she could tell them how to live their lives. She was thrown out of Viterbo for a time, but she was allowed to come back before she died the next year. Rose gave her whole heart to Jesus and inspired people to know and to love Him more.

EACH SEPTEMBER HUNDREDS OF PEOPLE FROM VITERBO DRESS UP IN COSTUMES FROM MANY DIFFERENT CENTURIES IN A PROCESSION AROUND SAINT ROSE OF VITERBO'S FEAST DAY.

Jesus, I want to give You my whole heart,
just as Saint Rose of Viterbo did.

SAINT ONESIPHORUS

FIRST CENTURY • EPHESUS (MODERN-DAY TURKEY)

NOT ASHAMED

May the Lord grant mercy to the household of Onesiphorus,
because he often refreshed me and was not ashamed of my chain.

2 TIMOTHY 1:16

Saint Paul (Jan. 24) often found himself in prison. He fearlessly preached about Jesus and His great love, and many people didn't want to hear it. In Rome, Paul was imprisoned yet again. Many of Paul's friends turned away from Paul during his time of need. It's possible that they were afraid that they would be thrown in prison too. But Onesiphorus was a loyal friend. Even though it was dangerous for him to help Paul, he helped him anyway. Onesiphorus, like Paul, was unashamed of Jesus and unafraid of what the Roman soldiers could do to him. He did good things to help spread the word about Jesus even when it was dangerous and difficult.

> SAINT ONESIPHORUS TRAVELED ALL THE WAY FROM HIS HOME IN EPHESUS (MODERN-DAY TURKEY) TO ROME TO HELP SAINT PAUL.

*Jesus, help me remember and pray for
people who are in chains for You.*

SAINT TERESA OF KOLKATA

1910–1997 • INDIA

HUNGRY AND THIRSTY

"Blessed are those who hunger and thirst for
righteousness, for they will be filled."

MATTHEW 5:6

Dressed in a blue and white habit, which is a type of religious clothing, Teresa walked the streets of the city of Kolkata, ready to meet the needs of the hungry people. Teresa knew that Jesus heard the cries of the poor, and she left her family at age 18 to become a missionary. Teresa served Jesus by helping the poorest of the poor, even when she was in need herself. Teresa struggled to feel the love of God. She chose to have faith that He loved her, even when she felt like He wasn't there. At the time of her death, four thousand other women had joined her organization, the Missionaries of Charity, and the world knew and loved her as "Mother Teresa."

SAINT TERESA OF KOLKATA RECEIVED THE NOBEL PEACE PRIZE, BUT SHE DONATED ALL THE MONEY THAT WOULD HAVE BEEN USED FOR AN EXPENSIVE DINNER TO HELP THE POOR.

Jesus, Saint Teresa of Kolkata served the poor
because You love them. Show me how I can
help those in need in my community.

SAINT REGINA

THIRD CENTURY • FRANCE

SHEPHERDESS

"I am the good shepherd. The
good shepherd lays down
his life for the sheep."

JOHN 10:11

Regina's Christian mother died shortly after she was born, but her father, who wasn't a Christian, gave Regina to a nurse who believed in Jesus. The nurse cared for Regina and taught her about the Christian faith. Regina grew up herding sheep in the beautiful hills and pastures of France. While she was herding, she often thought about the stories of the Saints that she had been taught. Regina wondered at their amazing sacrifices. She prayed that she would have the same kind of courage. When she was fifteen, she was engaged to a man who wasn't a Christian. This man wanted Regina to renounce, or deny, her beliefs, but Regina refused even though she knew she would be killed. Regina gave up her life for her faith because Jesus had given up His life for her.

THE PLACES IN FRANCE THAT ARE NAMED SAINTE-REINE ARE NAMED AFTER SAINT REGINA.

*Jesus, You are the Good Shepherd. You gave up
Your life for me. I want to give my life to You.*

SAINT GIUSEPPINA VANNINI

1859–1911 • ITALY

GOOD HEALTH

Beloved, I pray that all may go well with you and that you may be in good health, just as it is well with your soul.

3 JOHN V. 2

Giuseppina's childhood was lonely and challenging, and she often felt sick. She lost both of her parents when she was young and grew up in an orphanage. Maybe because of this, Giuseppina always wanted to care for the sick and forgotten. She founded an order that was inspired by Saint Camillus of Lellis (July 18), a Saint who cared for the sick. Since Giuseppina understood what it was like to be sick, she was an excellent caretaker of other sick people. With expertise, hard work, and prayer, she tried to restore the sick to good health, even when her task seemed impossible. She fulfilled Saint Camillus's hope that sick people would be cared for as tenderly as mothers care for their beloved sick children.

JUST LIKE SAINT CAMILLUS'S MINISTERS OF THE SICK, SAINT GIUSEPPINA VANNINI WORE A RED CROSS.

Jesus, You inspired Saint Giuseppina Vannini to care for the sick. Inspire me with a mission too.

SAINT PETER CLAVER

1581–1654 • SPAIN AND COLOMBIA

LOVE AND JUSTICE

*As for you, return to your God, hold fast to love and
justice, and wait continually for your God.*

HOSEA 12:6

Peter ran toward the docks to wait for the next ship. Peter was a priest and a missionary who lived in Colombia. During his life, full ships of slaves from African countries came to the docks in Colombia. The people on board the ships were treated with terrible injustice—animals would likely have been treated better. The people were tired, hungry, thirsty, and sick. They were so shocked by their horrible experiences that they often stared off into the distance, unable to respond. Peter offered food, water, and medicine to them. He didn't allow the horrific nature of their circumstances or the gigantic size of his task to stop him from loving them. After he had cared for them, he told them about the love of Jesus.

> SAINT PETER CLAVER SERVED THE PEOPLE FROM AFRICA EVEN THOUGH HE DIDN'T UNDERSTAND THEIR LANGUAGE.

*Jesus, You love justice. Help me bring Your love and Your
justice to the world, just as Saint Peter Claver did.*

SAINT THOMAS OF VILLANOVA

1488–1555 • SPAIN

EARLY MORNING

*But I, O LORD, cry out to you; in the morning
my prayer comes before you.*

PSALM 88:13

Thomas wanted to give the Christians in his church in Valencia, Spain, more opportunities to love and serve Jesus. Thomas was a priest and a bishop, and many bad practices had been taking place in Valencia before he arrived. The priests and the people didn't understand the point of marriage or of serving the poor. The churches were often empty. Thomas arranged for more church services to be held earlier in the morning so people could attend them before work. He helped rebuild a hospital that had burned down. He served hundreds of poor people at a time, using his own hands to show them generosity. Thomas showed the Christians in Valencia what being a Christian meant—constant prayer and dedicated service. Being a Christian meant having faith that lasted from morning until night.

> SAINT THOMAS OF VILLANOVA'S OWN PARENTS GAVE GENEROUSLY OF THEIR FOOD AND RESOURCES TO THE POOR.

Jesus, help me live for You from morning until night.

SAINT CYPRIAN

UNKNOWN—258 • CARTHAGE (MODERN-DAY TUNISIA)

NOT IN VAIN

We are . . . joint heirs with Christ—if, in fact, we suffer
with him so that we may also be glorified with him.

ROMANS 8:16–17

Before Cyprian became a Christian, everything was so meaning-less! Cyprian had seen the glories of the Roman Empire. Powerful politicians used other people to get whatever they wanted. Animals and people died in the gladiator arena, and the Romans watched for their entertainment. But compared to the riches of Cyprian's simple life in prayer with Christ, all of these glories were emptiness and nothingness. In Jesus, Cyprian had found glory that was not in vain. Cyprian became a bishop and gave his life for his faith in Jesus. When Cyprian was asked if he was a Christian, he responded that he was. He said he was a Christian who prayed all day and night for the emperor who wanted to kill him.

> WHEN SAINT CYPRIAN BECAME A CHRISTIAN, HE SOLD HIS MANY POSSESSIONS, INCLUDING A BEAUTIFUL GARDEN, AND GAVE UP HIS WEALTH.

*Jesus, You bring real meaning into my life.
Everything that isn't for You is in vain.*

SEPTEMBER 12

SAINT GUY OF ANDERLECHT

950–1012 • BELGIUM AND THE HOLY LAND (MODERN-DAY ISRAEL)

LOST TREASURE

"Store up for yourselves treasures in heaven, where neither moth
nor rust consumes and where thieves do not break in and steal."

MATTHEW 6:20

Guy felt devastated when he heard the news. The ship had sunk. The money was lost at the bottom of the ocean, just as if it had been stolen. Since he helped pay for the voyage, he would have received more money when the ship returned. Guy planned to share what he earned from the voyage with the poor, but now that chance was lost. Instead of despairing, Guy prayed. He knew that no matter how much earthly treasure was lost, there was spiritual treasure to be found. He traveled to Rome and to the Holy Land on a pilgrimage, visiting the places where Jesus and the apostles had lived. Guy never became rich, but he stored up spiritual treasure.

> SAINT GUY OF ANDERLECHT GREW UP SERVING IN CHURCH BY SWEEPING THE FLOORS AND RINGING THE BELLS.

*Jesus, You are the real treasure. Everything the
whole world offers can't compare with Your love.*

SAINT JOHN CHRYSOSTOM

344–407 • ANTIOCH (MODERN-DAY TURKEY)

GOLDEN WORDS

The ordinances of the Lord are true and righteous
altogether. More to be desired are they than gold.

PSALM 19:9–10

John's mother taught him about her Christian faith, and young John served his church by reading the Scriptures during services. When he grew up, he became a hermit and lived by very strict rules in order to hear God's voice. During his time as a hermit, John once stood up for two years straight and hardly slept the whole time; he was committing the entire Bible to memory. After his health failed, he returned to the city and put his knowledge into practice by preaching as a priest. He was well trained in the art of persuading people, and he knew the entire Bible in his head and in his heart. John was called Chrysostom, which meant "golden-mouthed." John's beautiful words led people to repentance.

FIFTEEN HUNDRED YEARS AFTER SAINT JOHN CHRYSOSTOM DIED, PYOTR TCHAIKOVSKY, WHO COMPOSED *THE NUTCRACKER*, ALSO COMPOSED A WORK OF MUSIC IN HONOR OF SAINT JOHN CHRYSOSTOM.

*Jesus, Saint John Chrysostom loved Your
Word. Help me love Your Word too.*

SAINT ALBERT OF JERUSALEM

1149–1215 • ITALY AND THE HOLY LAND (MODERN-DAY ISRAEL)

YOU, O LORD, ARE GOD

Answer me, O LORD, answer me, so that this people
may know that you, O LORD, are God.

1 KINGS 18:37

While Albert was working for the Church in the Holy Land, he met a group of monks. These monks lived in separate caves near Mount Carmel, the same mountain where the prophet Elijah had called down fire from heaven thousands of years before. In those days, Elijah the prophet told the Israelites to choose God over the false god Baal. In response to Elijah's prayers, God showed His power, and many Israelites returned to worshipping the real God. The monks who lived

> SAINT ALBERT SERVED AS THE PATRIARCH OF JERUSALEM, A ROLE HE TOOK ON EVEN THOUGH HE KNEW IT WOULD BE DANGEROUS.

by Mount Carmel wanted to say that God was God too, just like the Israelites had thousands of years before. Albert created a rule of life for them that was very strict. The monks, who would become known as the Carmelites, almost always kept silent, never ate meat, and spent long hours totally alone, all to remember and know that God was God.

Jesus, help me know and believe that You are God.

SAINT PETER CHRYSOLOGUS

380–450 • ROMAN EMPIRE (MODERN-DAY ITALY)

HEAR MY WORDS

Incline your ear and hear my words, and
apply your mind to my teaching.

PROVERBS 22:17

Peter wanted people to hear God's Word and take it to heart. He understood the power of repetition, and he believed that his church heard best if they heard it twice. That's why Peter, who was a priest, gave homilies, or sermons, that often quoted the Bible and offered the same message in slightly different words. Peter's messages were always easy to understand. Even if the subject of his homily was difficult to hear, Peter wasn't afraid to speak the truth in a simple way. He clearly told his church that they couldn't rejoice with both the devil and with God. Peter had a fail-proof way of getting his point across: he always kept his homilies very short so people didn't get too tired to concentrate on what he was saying.

> SAINT PETER CHRYSOLOGUS ONCE WROTE, "O MAN, WHY DO YOU THINK SO LITTLE OF YOURSELF WHEN GOD THINKS SO HIGHLY OF YOU?"

Jesus, I want to hear Your words and take them to heart.

SAINT CORNELIUS

UNKNOWN–253 • ROMAN EMPIRE (MODERN-DAY ITALY)

HIDDEN AWAY

Your life is hidden with Christ in God.

COLOSSIANS 3:3

Emperor Decius persecuted Christians relentlessly. He killed Christians who would not give up their faith, like Saint Fabian (Jan. 19), who had been the pope. Decius was convinced that the Christians would simply die out if they didn't have a strong leader. But what Decius didn't know was that the work of the Church was being carried out anyway, no matter how many Christians he managed to kill. Cornelius and several other brave Christians were in hiding, carrying on the faith in secret. Emperor Decius left for another war, and the Christians came out of hiding. They chose Cornelius to be their new pope. Cornelius led them bravely until his exile and death.

SAINT CORNELIUS SHOWED MERCY TO CHRISTIANS WHO WERE APOSTATES—THAT IS, CHRISTIANS WHO, WHEN FACING DEATH, DENIED THEIR FAITH AND WORSHIPPED IDOLS INSTEAD. SAINT CORNELIUS WELCOMED THEM BACK TO CHURCH.

Jesus, Your Church can withstand anything! Thank You for the strength You've given to Christians.

SAINT ROBERT BELLARMINE

1542–1621 • ITALY

HOPE IN HIM

"The LORD is my portion," says my soul, "therefore I will hope in him."

LAMENTATIONS 3:24

Anywhere Robert looked, people were divided against each other. Nations went to war, churches fell apart, and families argued endlessly. But Robert did not despair. He decided to hope, and he put his hope into practice by becoming a teacher, passing on his wisdom to the next generation. Robert was a priest as well, but he focused much of his time on teaching students, some of whom were young priests. His teaching was praised for being easy to understand. Robert published volumes—numerous books on a topic—that offered new understanding for difficult questions. His hope in God, shown through his many written works, was so admired that he became an advisor to the pope. Robert never took advantage of his high position. He was known to take the beautiful cloths hanging on the walls of his rooms and give them to the poor.

SAINT ROBERT BELLARMINE WAS THE NEPHEW OF POPE MARCELLUS II.

Jesus, Saint Robert Bellarmine hoped in You.
I want to put my hope in You too.

SAINT JOSEPH OF CUPERTINO

1603–1663 • ITALY

RAISED UP

We know that the one who raised the Lord Jesus will raise us also with Jesus, and will bring us with you into his presence.

2 CORINTHIANS 4:14

Not again, Joseph!" He had heard it a thousand times. Joseph tried to do the chores his mother asked, but he'd wander off in a different direction and forget what he was doing. He'd drop whatever he'd been asked to carry, often breaking the family's dishes. Sometimes Joseph didn't want to help at all, and he'd snap back at his mother angrily. Eventually, Joseph grew up and decided to become a monk. But his bumbling mistakes led the other monks to send him straight back to the house where he came from. When Joseph moved again to live with a different community of monks, he started working in a stable. Through the humbling work and a practice of prayer, Joseph settled into a routine and focused on God. He loved to spend time with the Lord alone and looked forward to the day he would rise with Christ.

> THE STORIES ABOUT SAINT JOSEPH OF CUPERTINO SAY THAT HE WOULD OFTEN LEVITATE—THAT IS, RISE UP IN THE AIR—WHEN HE PRAYED.

Jesus, help me focus my mind on You.

SAINT JANUARIUS

UNKNOWN–305 · ROMAN EMPIRE (MODERN-DAY ITALY)

THE BLOOD OF CHRIST

*Now in Christ Jesus you who once were far off have
been brought near by the blood of Christ.*

EPHESIANS 2:13

Januarius was unwilling to deny the truth about Jesus, that Jesus is the only Son of God and the Savior of the world. He was the bishop of Benevento, an Italian city, and he was killed during Roman Emperor Diocletian's persecution of Christians. Januarius was one of many martyrs killed by Diocletian, but he's remembered because of the relic that is still kept in a cathedral in Italy. A relic is something—a piece of clothing, a possession, or another object—that belonged to a Saint that is kept by the Church after the Saint's death. A small vial of Januarius's blood has been kept for almost two thousand years—a reminder of the blood that he was willing to shed for his faith.

> THE BLOOD IN THE VIAL IS TYPICALLY DRY AND POWDERY, BUT IT TURNS TO LIQUID SEVERAL TIMES EACH YEAR—AND NO ONE KNOWS WHY!

*Jesus, You shed Your blood for me so that
I could be brought near to You.*

SEPTEMBER 20

SAINT ANDREW KIM TAEGON

1821–1846 · SOUTH KOREA

WORTHY IS THE LAMB

Worthy is the Lamb that was slaughtered to receive power and
wealth and wisdom and might and honor and glory and blessing!

REVELATION 5:12

Many of Andrew's family members were martyred for their Christian
faith, including his father and his great-grandfather, because
Christianity was illegal in Korea. The Korean government wanted nothing to do with Christianity. They thought it would make their country
too much like Western countries, like England,
Italy, and France. In Korea, preaching about Jesus
was considered treason. But Andrew's mother whispered the truths of their faith to him, and thousands
of other Koreans were doing the same thing. They
passed their faith to each other, waiting for the day

> SAINT ANDREW
> KIM TAEGON
> WAS THE FIRST
> CATHOLIC
> PRIEST BORN IN
> SOUTH KOREA.

when the persecutions would end. Andrew grew up knowing that Jesus
was worthy of his faith, and Christianity was worth dying for. Andrew
became a martyr himself.

Jesus, You are worthy of all honor and glory and blessing!

279

SEPTEMBER 21

SAINT MATTHEW

FIRST CENTURY · GALILEE (MODERN-DAY ISRAEL)

FOLLOW ME

As Jesus was walking along, he saw a man called
Matthew sitting at the tax booth; and he said to him,
"Follow me." And he got up and followed him.

MATTHEW 9:9

Matthew collected taxes for a living. He was not very popular among his neighbors, and they grumbled when they saw him circle the neighborhood again, requiring them to give even more than last time. No one was happy to see him coming! Matthew kept some of that money for himself, and some of it he gave to the emperor. Matthew was used to being disliked, so when Jesus looked at him and said, "Follow me," he was shocked. Just two words from Jesus changed everything for Matthew. Matthew wasn't used to being wanted, but Jesus wanted him. Matthew would follow Jesus with everything he had.

SAINT MATTHEW IS ALSO CALLED LEVI IN THE NEW TESTAMENT GOSPELS.

*Jesus, I want to leave everything and follow
You, just as Saint Matthew did.*

SEPTEMBER 22*

SAINT PIO OF PIETRELCINA

1887–1968 • ITALY

DON'T WORRY

"Therefore I tell you, do not worry about your life."

MATTHEW 6:25

P io was a priest, called "Padre Pio" by those who loved him. He was adored around the world during his lifetime. This beloved priest encouraged people to pray, hope, and not worry about anything. He believed in choosing faith over worry, even though he could have worried about many things. He grew up in poverty and without much of an education, and he was turned away the first time he tried to become a priest. He was constantly battling some kind of health problem. From pains in his stomach to tumors in his ears, some part

OVER THREE MILLION PEOPLE AROUND THE WORLD PARTICIPATE IN PRAYER GROUPS STARTED BY SAINT PIO OF PIETRELCINA.

of his body could have caused him to worry, but he trusted God anyway. At one point, Padre Pio was asked to stop doing most of his priestly work, since too many people followed him. But through it all, Padre Pio followed his own advice. He didn't worry about his life.

Jesus, You tell me not to worry. Help me trust You with everything, just as Saint Pio of Pietrelcina trusted You.

SAINT LORENZO RUIZ

1600–1637 • PHILIPPINES

BY FAITH

For we walk by faith, not by sight.

2 CORINTHIANS 5:7

Lorenzo had always loved Jesus. He grew up in the island nation of the Philippines in a town called Binondo. He served in his church, helping the priest prepare the church for services. When he was an adult, he married and had three children. He worked as a calligrapher and faithfully provided for his family. Then Lorenzo was accused of a murder. He never committed the crime, but the authorities were convinced of Lorenzo's guilt. So he left, escaping from the Philippines on a boat to Japan. Lorenzo did not know that the Japanese emperor was killing all Catholic Christians he could find. Upon his arrival, Lorenzo was discovered by the emperor's guards and thrown in jail. They told Lorenzo to renounce his faith in Jesus. But Lorenzo wouldn't give up his faith, even when he couldn't find a way to escape. For his faith, Lorenzo became a martyr.

> MORE THAN 80 PERCENT OF PEOPLE LIVING IN THE PHILIPPINES ARE CATHOLIC.

Jesus, Saint Lorenzo Ruiz was faithful to You when life was at its worst. Help me be faithful to You in bad times too.

SAINT JOHN HENRY NEWMAN

1801–1890 · ENGLAND

LEAD ME

Lead me, O Lᴏʀᴅ, in your righteousness.

PSALM 5:8

John Henry Newman let God lead, no matter the cost. He often wrote poetry and hymns, and one hymn he wrote when he was a young man described the way he would face challenges in his life. John wrote "Lead, Kindly Light" while he was sick on a trip. He wrote, "The night is dark, and I am far from home, lead Thou me on." John meant that he would go wherever God led him, no matter how he felt. When John got back home, he read, he wrote, and he wrestled with the truths that he discovered. John eventually became a Catholic priest. John was criticized by people from many faith traditions for this choice, but he let God lead anyway. John's life and writings helped different groups of Christians understand each other better and have more compassion toward each other.

SAINT JOHN HENRY NEWMAN BECAME A SAINT IN 2019. POPE FRANCIS LED THE CEREMONY IN WHICH SAINT JOHN HENRY NEWMAN WAS CANONIZED, OR FIRST CALLED A "SAINT."

Jesus, I want to follow You. Lead me on!

SAINTS LOUIS AND ZÉLIE MARTIN

1823–1894 (LOUIS), 1831–1877 (ZÉLIE) • FRANCE

ALL THEIR HEARTS

Trust in the LORD with all your heart, and
do not rely on your own insight.

PROVERBS 3:5

Louis was a watchmaker, and Zélie was a lacemaker. When Louis asked to become a monk, he was turned away from the monastery. When Zélie tried to become a nun, she wasn't accepted either. God had a different plan for their lives—a plan that included their marriage. One day, in their small French town, Louis and Zélie walked over the same bridge in opposite directions. When Louis passed by, Zélie believed she heard God say, "This is him! This is the one whom you will marry." As a married couple, Louis and Zélie were devoted to their faith and dedicated to their children, whom they taught about Jesus. Louis and Zélie had nine children. Five of their daughters became nuns. Their youngest daughter was Thérèse of Lisieux (Oct. 1), who would write beautiful words about the love of Jesus—a love she had learned about from her faithful parents.

> SAINTS LOUIS AND ZÉLIE MARTIN ARE THE FIRST MARRIED COUPLE TO BE CANONIZED TOGETHER WITHOUT ANY COMPANIONS.

Jesus, Your plans for Saints Louis and Zélie Martin were better than their own plans! Help me trust Your plan always.

SAINT PAUL VI

1897–1978 • ITALY

BE ONE IN HIS NAME

"And now I am no longer in the world, but they are in the world, and I am coming to you. Holy Father, protect them in your name that you have given me, so that they may be one, as we are one."

JOHN 17:11

Paul knew it was difficult to live in the world but not be like the world. Christians believe that love and unity are more important than wealth and power. But during the twentieth century, Christians often heard that money and power would make them happy. Paul used his time as pope to speak against this lie. One of the ways he did this was by reconciling—or giving and receiving forgiveness—with Patriarch Athenagoras, the leader of the Eastern Church. The two Churches had been in conflict for over one thousand years! Paul spread the word about Jesus' desire for the Church to be one in His name.

ONCE, SAINT PAUL VI VISITED YANKEE STADIUM IN NEW YORK CITY.

Jesus, You were not of the world, but You love the whole world. Help me love the world like You do.

SAINT VINCENT DE PAUL

1581–1660 • FRANCE

CHRIST HAS SET US FREE

For freedom Christ has set us free.

GALATIANS 5:1

Vincent ran for his life, hardly daring to look back. He had spent the past two years as a slave, captured off a ship and taken to Africa. Before he was captured, Vincent studied, paying for his own education by working as a tutor for children. He had been ordained as a priest, but his plans were interrupted when he was captured and made a slave. When Vincent finally escaped and made it back to France, he made good use of his freedom. He was inspired to use his days in extremely productive ways, founding hospitals for the poor and for convicts. Vincent was so passionate about his mission that he gathered many more faithful men and women around him to help with all the ways he wanted to serve the poor. He's the patron Saint of all charitable causes.

SAINT VINCENT DE PAUL MAY HAVE WRITTEN AS MANY AS THIRTY THOUSAND LETTERS DURING HIS LIFETIME.

Jesus, help me make the most of my freedom by using my time to serve You, just as Saint Vincent de Paul did.

SAINT WENCESLAUS

907–935 • BOHEMIA (MODERN-DAY CZECHIA)

I SHALL AGAIN PRAISE HIM

Why are you cast down, O my soul, and why are you disquieted within me? Hope in God; for I shall again praise him, my help and my God.

PSALM 42:11

The young prince Wenceslaus praised God, even when it was difficult. Wenceslaus's faithful grandmother taught him about Jesus when he was young, and he was sent to study at a university. He trained to be a truly Christian prince. Even though Wenceslaus lost both his grandmother and his father when he was still young, he was determined to hope in God and serve as a faithful king and leader to his country, Bohemia. Many people who believed in false gods, including Wenceslaus's mother, wanted the country to be ruled by a different king. Even so, Wenceslaus modeled hope in God for his people, attending to the needs of the poor, finding time to pray in church, and choosing to worship Jesus only.

> SAINT WENCESLAUS IS THE SUBJECT OF THE CHRISTMAS CAROL "GOOD KING WENCESLAS," WHICH IS TRADITIONALLY SUNG THE DAY AFTER CHRISTMAS.

Jesus, help me praise You anyway, even when life is difficult.

SAINT OSWALD

UNKNOWN–992 • ENGLAND

MEET AND PRAY

Let us consider how to provoke one another to love
and good deeds, not neglecting to meet together, as is
the habit of some, but encouraging one another.

HEBREWS 10:24–25

The people living in England wondered, Why do monasteries matter? A monastery is a building that is used as a church and a school. Monks, who are men who dedicate their lives to the monastery, don't have families or other jobs—they pray, they learn, and they live in the monastery. During Oswald's life, some people thought monasteries were useless.

But Oswald didn't think so. Christians needed to pray all the time. They needed to pray alone and together. Monasteries offered space for people to pray together, so monasteries mattered. Oswald made sure the monasteries in England weren't closed. The monasteries stayed—Oswald even built a new one!

> SAINT OSWALD DIED AS HE LIVED—SERVING! HE DIED WHILE HE WAS WASHING THE FEET OF THE POOR.

*Jesus, thank You for the people gathered in places
like monasteries and churches. Thank You for the
people who are praying for the whole world.*

SAINT JEROME

347–420 • ROMAN EMPIRE (MODERN-DAY ITALY)

THEY MAY ALL BE ONE

"I ask . . . that they may all be one. As you, Father, are
in me and I am in you, may they also be in us, so that
the world may believe that you have sent me."

JOHN 17:20–21

Jerome mastered many languages and used this gift to give an amazing gift to the Church. Jerome studied Greek, Hebrew, and Latin, and because he studied so hard and for so long, he was able to translate the Bible, written in Hebrew and Greek, into Latin, a language that was understood throughout the continent of Europe. Jerome's work was so important because it helped the priests across many countries, who already knew Latin, understand what the Bible said. Regular people, those without higher education or training from the Church, could read and understand it. Jerome's translation of the Bible helped unify the Church.

> AS THE STORY GOES, SAINT JEROME REMOVED A THORN FROM A LION'S PAW, AND THE LION BECAME HIS PET!

Jesus, may we all be one through You and Your Word.

OCTOBER 1

SAINT THÉRÈSE OF LISIEUX

1873–1897 • FRANCE

NOT FORGOTTEN

"Are not five sparrows sold for two pennies? Yet
not one of them is forgotten in God's sight."

LUKE 12:6

Thérèse was the littlest sister in her family, the youngest of nine children. In school, she was often the smallest in her class. She wondered how she could do great things for God and longed to be remembered as a Saint someday. But the Saints accomplished great things and made huge sacrifices, and Thérèse was so *little*. But God helped Thérèse understand what He wanted. Even if she was little, she could surrender everything to God in a big way. Saints and souls were every shape and size. If the world was a garden of souls, God loved both the large roses and the tiny violets. Little Thérèse was not forgotten. And she took time to remember others too. She prayed for priests and people in need.

THE BOOK THAT SAINT THÉRÈSE OF LISIEUX WROTE ABOUT HER LIFE, *STORY OF A SOUL,* HAS BEEN READ AROUND THE WORLD.

*Jesus, You have never forgotten about me. Help
me remember the needs of those around me.*

VENERABLE NELSON BAKER

1842–1936 • THE UNITED STATES

FATHER OF ORPHANS

Father of orphans and protector of widows
is God in his holy habitation.

PSALM 68:5

Nelson opened a home for all of the orphan boys living in Buffalo, New York, the city where he lived and worked as a priest. But he also had a big problem—there was a large debt attached to the house, and he needed to pay thousands of dollars to keep it. If he couldn't pay, the bank would take the house. Nelson believed that God could give him what he needed to care for these boys. So, in faith, Nelson went to his bank and took out every bit of money he had. He used it all to start paying the debt. He asked others in his church to be generous too, and soon the boys' home was paid off. The boys grew up in that home, where they learned about loving and serving God.

> ONE OF THE FIRST THINGS VENERABLE NELSON BAKER DID TO MAKE THE BOYS' HOME MORE LIKE A HOUSE WAS TO TAKE THE BARS OFF THE WINDOWS.

Jesus, help me trust You. If I ask, You will
help me take care of others.

VENERABLE NELSON BAKER IS ON TRACK TO BECOME A SAINT.

SAINT FRANCIS OF ASSISI

1182–1226 • ITALY

FOLLOW IN HIS FOOTSTEPS

Whoever says, "I abide in him,"
ought to walk just as he walked.

1 JOHN 2:6

Francis, who had been a nobleman and a soldier, gave up his position and wealth to care for the poor and people suffering from disease. What did God want next for him? Well, one day, while he was listening to a sermon, Francis heard this story:

> Jesus sent out [the disciples] with the following instructions: . . . "Take no gold, or silver, or copper in your belts, no bag for your journey, or two tunics, or sandals, or a staff; for laborers deserve their food." (Matthew 10:5, 9–10)

Francis's heart leapt in his chest. God was calling him to give up everything and to live fully devoted to Jesus. Francis took off his shoes right there. He left the church barefoot and spent the rest of his days following in Jesus' footsteps.

Jesus, I want to hear Your words and do them, just like Saint Francis of Assisi.

SAINT FRANCIS OF ASSISI LOVED ALL OF GOD'S CREATURES, AND STORIES TELL THAT HE TALKED AND PREACHED TO ANIMALS, EVEN GIVING A SERMON TO BIRDS. BUT LIKE JESUS, SAINT FRANCIS OF ASSISI KNEW THAT PEOPLE WERE GOD'S MOST PRECIOUS CREATION.

SAINT THEODORA GUÉRIN

1798–1856 • FRANCE AND THE UNITED STATES

THROUGHOUT THE WORLD

"And this good news of the kingdom will be
proclaimed throughout the world."

MATTHEW 24:14

Theodora and five other women left France and crossed an ocean because they wanted to serve God throughout the world. But they weren't ready for what waited for them—or rather, what *wasn't* waiting for them! The women had gone to a small town in Indiana to teach in the school and serve in the church, but there were a few problems.

There wasn't a school or a church or really much of anything—just a small house surrounded by the woods. All six women lived in the two-room farmhouse with the family who was already living there. The women rolled up their sleeves and got to work, even though it wasn't what they expected. They were called the Sisters of Providence, and they trusted in God's ability to provide for them and work through them!

TODAY, A COLLEGE STANDS ON THE SAME PLOT OF LAND AS THE SISTERS' TWO-BEDROOM INDIANA FARMHOUSE.

Jesus, You give Your followers missions throughout the world. I want to go where You lead me!

OCTOBER 5

SAINT MARIA FAUSTINA KOWALSKA

1905–1938 • POLAND

MESSAGE OF MERCY

Let us therefore approach the throne of grace with boldness, so that we may receive mercy and find grace to help in time of need.

HEBREWS 4:16

Nothing about Maria was all that unusual. Maria's parents couldn't afford to pay much for her education, and she cleaned houses to help support her family. When she was able, she joined a religious order, or community. She spent time with the others in prayer, she served the poor, and she wrote her recollections in a diary. Her diary hid the unusual and incredible experiences of the seemingly ordinary woman. Maria believed that God spoke to her in a series of visions that she faithfully recorded in her diary. She believed He told her many beautiful things, but the most beautiful of all was His message of mercy—all could be forgiven, no matter what they had done. God wanted to tell her and the entire world about His longing for the world to return to Him.

SAINT MARIA FAUSTINA KOWALSKA'S DIARY HAS BEEN TRANSLATED INTO MORE THAN TWENTY LANGUAGES, INCLUDING ARABIC AND CHINESE.

Jesus, You are merciful. I want to share Your message of mercy with the world.

SAINT BRUNO

1030–1101 · GERMANY AND FRANCE

SHELTER

Truly, I would flee far away; I would lodge in the wilderness; I would hurry to find a shelter for myself from the raging wind and tempest.

PSALM 55:7–8

B runo gave his students the gifts of his prayers, wisdom, and humility. When another man became bishop for his own personal gain, not to serve Christ, Bruno refused to support him, even when he threatened Bruno's safety. Later, when the same position of bishop was offered to Bruno, he fled to the wilderness for the shelter of solitude, preferring to pray than to gain power. Bruno was so wise that the pope, who had once been a student of his, asked him to come out of his solitude to be one of his advisors. Bruno accepted, but he never wanted any of the power or glory—he left every bit of that to God. He knew God was his only hope for shelter from the temptations of the world.

> SAINT BRUNO AND THE OTHER HERMITS CONSTRUCTED SMALL CABINS IN THE WILDERNESS WHERE THEY LISTENED TO GOD.

Jesus, You are the only shelter from the temptations I face.

BLESSED CHIARA BADANO

1971–1990 · ITALY

UNDERSTANDING THE GOSPEL

For I am not ashamed of the gospel; it is the power of
God for salvation to everyone who has faith.

ROMANS 1:16

At the age of nine, while she was at a religious festival with her family, Chiara gained a new understanding of the gospel. She understood that speaking kindly to others was not the whole gospel, and she wanted to bring her faith to life by taking action. When Chiara returned to her town, she brought food to the homeless, visited sick classmates, and even cared for an elderly woman by washing her face and making her bed. At the age of seventeen, Chiara discovered that she had bone cancer. She had to go through painful treatments and even lost the use of her legs. But she praised Jesus through the pain and even as she was dying. Her friends and her family saw her faith and joy and were inspired to love Jesus even more.

> BLESSED CHIARA BADANO WAS CALLED "LUCE" BY HER PARENTS AND FRIENDS; THE NICKNAME MEANS "LIGHT."

Jesus, Blessed Chiara Badano loved Your gospel, the story of Your love. Help me understand the gospel at a deeper level.

BLESSED CHIARA BADANO IS ON TRACK TO BECOME A SAINT.

SAINT JOHN LEONARDI

1541–1609 • ITALY

THE SIGHT OF GOD

We refuse to practice cunning or to falsify God's word; but by the open statement of the truth we commend ourselves to the conscience of everyone in the sight of God.

2 CORINTHIANS 4:2

Other priests thought John was a great example and excellent teacher. John wanted to understand and promote the truths of the faith, but not everyone believed him. Some insisted that John only wanted personal gain and power. *He's dangerous!* they thought. The lies about John were widespread, so he spent much of his time in exile, away from his church, focusing on knowing and praising God. John waited patiently in exile, still reading and writing. Though not everyone believed him, John knew that he hadn't done anything wrong in the sight of God, and that's what mattered most.

WHILE SAINT JOHN LEONARDI WAS IN EXILE, ANOTHER PRIEST, SAINT PHILIP NERI (MAY 26), ENCOURAGED HIM BY GIVING HIM HIS CAT FOR COMPANY.

Jesus, I want to be righteous in Your sight, no matter what the world thinks of me.

SAINT DENIS

UNKNOWN–258 • ROMAN EMPIRE (MODERN-DAY ITALY AND FRANCE)

REAL LIFE IN CHRIST

We are treated as impostors, and yet are true; as unknown, and yet are well known; as dying, and see—we are alive.

2 CORINTHIANS 6:8–9

Denis was one of seven priests who was sent from Rome to Gaul to spread the good news about Jesus. The priests founded churches and saw many French people become Christians. But even though they were away from Rome, they couldn't hide from the persecution of the Roman emperors. Denis refused to give up his faith in Jesus, and he was beheaded. But even long after his death, people remembered his love for Jesus. A thousand years after he died, Saint Denis's legacy was important to people suffering from a terrible plague. Like Denis, these people looked to God, knowing that even though they were dying, their real life was in Christ.

SAINT DENIS IS SHOWN IN PAINTINGS AND STATUES AS A HEADLESS FIGURE CARRYING HIS OWN HEAD.

Jesus, You have defeated death! Even when I have nothing in this world, I have a real life in You.

OCTOBER 10

SAINT FRANCIS BORGIA

1510–1572 • SPAIN

CHOOSING TO BE LAST

"Many who are first will be last, and the last will be first."

MATTHEW 19:30

Francis was a duke, a wealthy man with land, servants, and power. But when his wife died, Francis surprised everyone by passing his title on to his son. He dedicated the rest of his life to Jesus by becoming a priest. When he entered the priesthood, he began at the very lowest position in the community. He had been "first" as a duke, but now he was "last." He was charged with gathering and washing the dishes of the other priests. But Francis, who had been served food by his servants for his whole life, was so clumsy with the dishes and trays of food that he often had to apologize to the other priests. But he never complained. For Francis, giving up his wealth and his title was the best gift he could think of to give to Jesus.

SO MANY PEOPLE ATTENDED SAINT FRANCIS BORGIA'S FIRST SERVICE, OR MASS, THAT HE HAD TO SAY THE MASS OUTSIDE.

Jesus, Saint Francis Borgia chose to be last. Help me do the same.

301

OCTOBER 11

SAINT JOHN XXIII

1881–1963 · ITALY

CALLED TO BE UNITED

Lead a life worthy of the calling to which you have
been called, . . . making every effort to maintain
the unity of the Spirit in the bond of peace.

EPHESIANS 4:1, 3

Twenty-two popes before him had chosen the name Pope John. John XXIII knew that his time as pope would likely be short, since he was seventy-six years old when he became pope. And he was right—he was the pope for only five years. During that short time, he gave the Catholic Church and the world a simple message—he wanted the world and the Church to be united. He invited many Christians who had left their churches to come back to the faith. Pope John XXIII also chose cardinals—that is, church officials—from many different countries, and he sent bishops to serve in Asia, Africa, and Oceania. His few short years as pope made a big difference for the Catholic Church. When he died, he was mourned by people all over the world.

> SAINT JOHN XXIII SERVED IN THE ITALIAN MILITARY AS A CHAPLAIN IN WORLD WAR I.

Jesus, please unify the Church in the spirit of peace.

BLESSED FRANCIS XAVIER SEELOS

1819–1867 • GERMANY AND THE UNITED STATES

NEVER ABANDONED

You have seen, O Lord; do not be silent! O Lord, do not be far from me!

PSALM 35:22

Even when he was a little boy, Xavier knew he wanted to be a priest. He grew up and studied in Germany, where he learned about the Redemptorists—a group of priests who wanted to serve the poorest and most abandoned people. These priests knew God had not abandoned these people in need, and the Redemptorists wouldn't either. Xavier knew this was his calling, and he was even willing to leave his home in Germany and cross an ocean to serve immigrants from Germany living in the United States. As a pastor, he worked with the poor and abandoned as well as with seminary students, and he paid particular attention to the religious education of children. He lived and worked in the United States for the rest of his life. God never abandoned Xavier, and Xavier never abandoned the people God put into his care.

> BLESSED FRANCIS XAVIER SEELOS MET ABRAHAM LINCOLN IN WASHINGTON TO ASK THAT HIS STUDENTS BE EXCUSED FROM SERVICE IN THE CIVIL WAR. THOUGH THEY WEREN'T OFFICIALLY EXCUSED, THE STUDENTS WERE NEVER DRAFTED.

Jesus, You are always with me, even when I feel abandoned.

BLESSED FRANCIS XAVIER SEELOS IS ON TRACK TO BECOME A SAINT.

BLESSED ALEXANDRINA MARIA DA COSTA

1904–1955 • PORTUGAL

SHARING CHRIST'S SUFFERINGS

Rejoice insofar as you are sharing Christ's sufferings, so that you may also be glad and shout for joy when his glory is revealed.

1 PETER 4:13

When Alexandrina was fourteen, she fell and became paralyzed. She couldn't walk. Somehow, she managed to get to church regularly to pray. Eventually her health worsened, and at twenty-one years old, Alexandrina was confined to her bed. But instead of despairing, Alexandrina totally devoted herself to Jesus. She believed that she actually experienced the pain of what Christ suffered on the cross. She prayed deeply during her experience of pain, dedicating all of her suffering and her prayers to the hope that young people would know and love Jesus.

> BLESSED ALEXANDRINA MARIA DA COSTA BEGAN DOING FARM WORK WHEN SHE WAS ONLY NINE YEARS OLD. SHE HAD UNUSUAL STRENGTH AND WAS ABLE TO WORK LONG HOURS.

Jesus, no one's pain is unknown to You. Help me pray to You when I am in pain, like Blessed Alexandrina Maria da Costa did.

BLESSED ALEXANDRINA MARIA DA COSTA IS
ON TRACK TO BECOME A SAINT.

SAINT CALLIXTUS I

UNKNOWN–222 • ROMAN EMPIRE (MODERN-DAY ITALY)

FACING TRIALS

My brothers and sisters, whenever you face trials of
any kind, consider it nothing but joy, because you know
that the testing of your faith produces endurance.

JAMES 1:2–3

Callixtus served the Catholic Church as the pope. He dealt with many of the same trials that popes have dealt with across the centuries: false teachings, divisions within the Church, and disagreements about how strict the Church should be in dealing with the sins of Christians. Callixtus dealt with other issues too. One Christian named Hippolytus disagreed with Callixtus so much that he started telling people that Callixtus wasn't really the pope at all! Many other Christians said that Callixtus was too soft on Christians who weren't faithful in their marriages. But Callixtus was able to deal with all of these trials because he followed Christ through every conflict.

HISTORIANS LEARNED MORE ABOUT SAINT CALLIXTUS I FROM THE WRITINGS OF HIPPOLYTUS.

Jesus, help me follow You through every difficult situation.

OCTOBER 15

SAINT TERESA OF ÁVILA

1515–1582 • SPAIN

ABIDE IN ME

"If you abide in me, and my words abide in you, ask for whatever you wish, and it will be done for you."

JOHN 15:7

Teresa knew that to abide in Jesus—that is, to accept Him as true and devote her life to Him—she would have to give up many things that mattered to her, like comfort and the good opinions of others. But Teresa struggled to abide in Jesus, even though she had already committed to life as a religious Sister. In fact, she struggled for fifteen years! Finally, Teresa gave Jesus everything she had. She gave up comforts, and she devoted herself to prayer. She started making changes within her own religious order, or community, that many people didn't like. Other churches, Sisters, and religious leaders said terrible things about Teresa. This would have bothered her before, but Teresa was abiding in Jesus. She encouraged other Sisters all around Spain to make sacrifices and pray for the redemption of the world.

> DURING HER LIFE, SAINT TERESA OF ÁVILA WAS ADMIRED BY THE KING OF SPAIN, PHILIP II.

Jesus, I want to abide in You.

SAINT MARGARET MARY ALACOQUE

1647–1690 • FRANCE

DO NOT FORGET

Take care that you do not forget the LORD your God.

DEUTERONOMY 8:11

Margaret promised to give her life to Jesus after she was healed from a four-year childhood illness. She longed to join a religious community and devote herself to prayer and service. Margaret's mother wanted her to get married and have a family. She sent Margaret to a dance in a beautiful dress in hopes that she would find a husband. But after the dance, Margaret believed she saw Jesus on the cross. He asked her, "Have you forgotten about Me?" From that moment, Margaret was completely dedicated to Jesus. She believed that He revealed to her many wonderful truths about His love. Even though many people didn't believe that Jesus had spoken to Margaret, she kept listening to Him.

SAINT MARGARET MARY ALACOQUE ENCOURAGED THE PRACTICE OF "HOLY HOURS," WHICH IN THIS CASE MEANT SPENDING TIME IN PRAYER AT CHURCH ON THURSDAYS, TO REMEMBER THAT THURSDAY NIGHT WAS WHEN JESUS SUFFERED IN THE GARDEN OF GETHSEMANE.

Jesus, Saint Margaret Mary Alacoque listened to You throughout her life. Help me remember to listen to You too.

OCTOBER 17

SAINT IGNATIUS OF ANTIOCH

50–110 • ROMAN EMPIRE (MODERN-DAY TURKEY AND ITALY)

GIVE THANKS

O give thanks to the God of gods, for his
steadfast love endures forever.

PSALM 136:2

Ignatius heard Emperor Trajan repeat the question, but he would never change his answer. "Will you sacrifice to the Roman gods?" Ignatius refused again. Ignatius heard Trajan announce that, because he wouldn't sacrifice to the Roman gods, Ignatius would be killed in the arena in Rome. Instead of recoiling in fear, Ignatius heard his sentence and reacted with joy, even thanking God for the news. Ignatius was honored to die for his faith. On his long journey from Antioch to Rome, Ignatius could have changed his mind. But he never did. He refused to honor any other god besides the God of the apostles, the God who had allowed His own Son to be put to death for the sake of all mankind.

> SAINT IGNATIUS OF ANTIOCH WROTE LETTERS ON HIS JOURNEY TO ROME, WHICH ENCOURAGED CHRISTIAN CHURCHES ACROSS THE LAND TO AVOID FALSE TEACHINGS AND KEEP THE FAITH.

*Jesus, Saint Ignatius of Antioch thanked You in the middle
of his trials. Help me be grateful through trials too.*

SAINT LUKE

FIRST CENTURY • ANTIOCH (MODERN-DAY TURKEY)

KNOW THE TRUTH

I too decided, after investigating everything carefully from the
very first, to write an orderly account for you, most excellent
Theophilus, so that you may know the truth concerning
the things about which you have been instructed.

LUKE 1:3–4

Once Luke learned the truth about Jesus, he dedicated his life to
sharing the truth with others. Luke told the story of Jesus and His
Church as it had been told to him, drawing on the testimonies of his
friend Paul, among others. Luke had a lot to catch up on—the stories
of Jesus' birth, death, and resurrection; the stories of the Holy Spirit
coming to the disciples; and of course, the stories that Jesus Himself
told. When he took up the task of writing to his friend
Theophilus to tell him these stories, Luke wanted, more
than anything, for Theophilus to know the truth about
Jesus—that Jesus is the just and merciful Son of God,
who came to save the world.

SAINT
LUKE WAS
TRAINED
AS A
PHYSICIAN.

*Jesus, Saint Luke told the truth about You
passionately. Help me do the same.*

OCTOBER 19

SAINT ISAAC JOGUES

**1607–1646 • FRANCE, CANADA, AND NEW
NETHERLANDS (MODERN-DAY UNITED STATES)**

WE ENDURE

When reviled, we bless; when persecuted, we endure.

1 CORINTHIANS 4:12

Isaac was a priest and missionary. After almost ten years of study, he was sent to live with some of the Native tribes in Canada. He taught the faith and helped those who needed it. After five years, he began helping a new tribe named the Ojibwa. In the midst of his new mission, the Iroquois tribe, who were warring against the Ojibwa, captured Isaac, another priest, and many people who had converted to the faith. They endured terrible persecution, but over a year later, Isaac was rescued and returned to France. Then Isaac did the most remarkable thing. When he was asked to return to his missions, he did—and was excited to return! He knew that with Christ's help, he could endure anything.

> AFTER HE WAS RESCUED, SAINT ISAAC JOGUES REACHED FRANCE ON CHRISTMAS IN 1643, COMING BACK TO A COMMUNITY THAT THOUGHT HE HAD DIED.

*Jesus, Saint Isaac Jogues endured so many difficulties for
the sake of Your work. Help me have faith that endures too.*

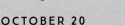

OCTOBER 20

SAINT PAUL OF THE CROSS

1694–1775 • ITALY

CHRIST CRUCIFIED

We proclaim Christ crucified.

1 CORINTHIANS 1:23

Paul believed that the story of Jesus' death held special importance for believers. Christians needed to remember His sacrifice to understand how much He loved them. The story about Jesus' death is often referred to as His "Passion." Since this story was so important to Paul, he and the others in his religious group were called "Passionists." Paul and the Passionists encouraged Christians to spend time in prayer to remember what happened when Jesus died—how He was crowned with thorns, was beaten with whips, and stumbled on His way to the top of the hill where He was killed. His Passion shows His love for us, as Paul taught all over Italy. Paul's teachings about the Passion spread around the world.

IN HIS TRAVELS, SAINT PAUL OF THE CROSS CARRIED WITH HIM A LARGE WOODEN CRUCIFIX, OR IMAGE OF JESUS ON THE CROSS.

*Jesus, You suffered and died for me. Help
me remember how You love me.*

SAINT HILARION

291–371 • ROMAN EMPIRE (MODERN-DAY GAZA)

GATHERING CROWD

Now more than ever the word about Jesus spread abroad; many crowds would gather to hear him and to be cured of their diseases.

LUKE 5:15

Just as Jesus would leave large crowds so that He could pray, so did Hilarion. Hilarion wanted to be alone to hear from God. His life inspired Saint Jerome (Sept. 30), who wrote about the many miracles that Hilarion prayed for. Even though people respected the hermit's practice of solitude and prayer, in their desperation, people would beg for his prayers. Saint Jerome records a story about a woman asking Hilarion to pray that she would be able to have a child. Hilarion prayed and within a year saw the same woman with her baby son. Hilarion prayed for people and their troubles throughout his life.

> ACCORDING TO THE STORIES ABOUT SAINT HILARION, HE ATE ONLY ONCE A DAY AND JUST A SMALL AMOUNT.

Jesus, Saint Hilarion didn't want to be admired by large crowds. He just wanted to be with You. Help me desire Your presence more than anything else.

OCTOBER 22

SAINT JOHN PAUL II

1920–2005 • POLAND AND ITALY

EXAMPLE OF LOVE

Let no one despise your youth, but set the believers an example in speech and conduct, in love, in faith, in purity.

1 TIMOTHY 4:12

When John Paul II became pope, it was the first time in four hundred years that the Catholic Church chose someone who wasn't from Italy. John Paul II grew up in Poland, and he lost his mother and his brother when he was very young. He pursued the priesthood early and studied at a seminary in Poland while World War II raged in Europe and around the world. Only three years into John Paul II's time as pope, an assassin shot him in Saint Peter's Square in Rome. He was rushed to a hospital. He forgave his attacker, sharing an example of true forgiveness with the Church and with the world. He also started World Youth Days to encourage the young to be bold in their faith.

> AS A YOUNG BOY, SAINT JOHN PAUL II ENJOYED SKIING AND SWIMMING.

Jesus, help me set an example of love in the world, just as Saint John Paul II did.

OCTOBER 23

SAINT JOHN OF CAPISTRANO

1386–1456 · ITALY

COME REPENT

The Lord is not slow about his promise, as some think
of slowness, but is patient with you, not wanting
any to perish, but all to come to repentance.

2 PETER 3:9

John woke up suddenly, finding himself in the same damp and dark prison that he had fallen asleep in. After his mission as an ambassador, or peacemaker, had failed, he'd been thrown into a prison. While he was there, he believed he saw Saint Francis in a dream. Saint Francis pointed John to a new life, a life as a priest. After John got out of prison, he became a priest right away and started preaching all over Europe about repentance. He wanted people everywhere to know that they could come back to God after falling away from him. Christians could renew their promises to God. John's words reached people whose hearts had become hard, and many repented!

> SAINT JOHN OF CAPISTRANO WAS ALSO CALLED THE "SOLDIER SAINT" BECAUSE HE LED A GROUP OF SOLDIERS INTO BATTLE.

Jesus, I can repent. I can turn back to You when
I fall away. You are patient with me.

SAINT ANTÔNIO DE SANT'ANNA GALVÃO

1739–1822 · BRAZIL

CARE FOR THE SICK

"Cure the sick who are there, and say to them, 'The kingdom of God has come near to you.'"

LUKE 10:9

Antônio's parents were known for their generosity as well as their wealth. His mother left many of her possessions to the poor after she died. Led by the example of his parents, Antônio resolved to live for the kingdom of God too. He gave up his wealth and social status and became a priest. Antônio was known and loved in São Paulo, his city, for his tender care for the sick. Antônio would often sit at the bedside of the sick, even when their cases seemed incurable. He comforted them with the truth that the kingdom of God was near to them. Antônio spent his life obeying the words of Jesus by caring for the sick.

SAINT ANTÔNIO DE SANT'ANNA GALVÃO SPENT TWENTY-EIGHT YEARS BUILDING A HERMITAGE AND CHURCH FOR THE MANY YOUNG PEOPLE HE HAD INSPIRED TO DEVOTE THEIR LIVES TO PRAYER.

Jesus, help me care for people like You cared for them.

OCTOBER 25*

SAINT ANTHONY MARY CLARET

1807–1870 • SPAIN

ETERNAL LIFE

"These will go away into eternal punishment,
but the righteous into eternal life."

MATTHEW 25:46

When he was just five years old, Anthony started thinking about eternity. *Forever and ever?* Anthony didn't want anyone to lose forever in heaven with God. But Anthony didn't do much more about it for many years. Then as an adult, as he was walking along the beach, he was swept away by a wave. Anthony begged to be saved, and he was returned to the shore. Ever after, he was a man on a mission. He became a priest and served as a missionary around Spain. He would walk through drifts of snow and terrible heat to visit churches all across the country. He would give sermons for hours and hear confessions for hours more. His energy was endless, as was his desire for people to hear the truth about Jesus and His promises about forever.

> SAINT ANTHONY MARY CLARET WORKED AS A WEAVER IN HIS FATHER'S TEXTILE SHOP WHILE HE WAS A TEENAGER.

Jesus, Saint Anthony Mary Claret understood Your promises about eternity. Help me understand them too.

SAINT PETER OF ALCÁNTARA

1499–1562 • SPAIN

COMPASSIONATE LORD

You have seen the purpose of the Lord, how the
Lord is compassionate and merciful.

JAMES 5:11

Even though Peter had been given a position of leadership, the other friars (the other religious men he lived with), who were supposed to be listening to him, refused. Peter's rules were much too difficult to follow. Why would God want people to follow difficult rules, anyway? Even though those friars could not accept the stricter rules, Peter knew that the purpose of the Lord was compassion, even when it looked like a list of rules. Peter found a place where his message stuck—with the poor. Peter then gave up his leadership role and began preaching to large crowds of people, many of them poor and hungry. He was a priest who was able to connect with the poor, since he was convinced that the Lord was compassionate toward them. Peter helped others believe that God was merciful. He loved them and wanted everyone to know Him.

> SAINT PETER OF ALCÁNTARA WOULDN'T ACCEPT A DRINK OF WATER WHILE HE WAS DYING BECAUSE JESUS HAD FELT THIRSTY ON THE CROSS.

*Jesus, You are compassionate. You care
for people who are hurting.*

SAINT FRUMENTIUS

FOURTH CENTURY • ETHIOPIA

THE LORD GOES BEFORE YOU

It is the LORD who goes before you. He will be with you; he will
not fail you or forsake you. Do not fear or be dismayed.

DEUTERONOMY 31:8

Frumentius set off for Ethiopia when he was a young Christian and
philosophy student. He was shipwrecked during a journey across
the Red Sea. But he kept looking to God for his next step. He was
rescued and taken to the Ethiopian court. Through
his hard work and diligence, Frumentius gained a high
position in the court. The Lord was with Frumentius,
and many people would come to know Jesus because
of Frumentius's courage. Frumentius even told the king
of Ethiopia about Jesus. The king believed, and after
the king's death, Frumentius served as the tutor of the
crown prince of Ethiopia, telling him the truths his father had believed.
After the prince became king, Frumentius baptized him. Christianity
became the official religion of Ethiopia.

SAINT FRUMENTIUS HELPED TRANSLATE SCRIPTURE INTO THE ETHIOPIAN LANGUAGE.

*Jesus, You know the whole plan. Help me remember
that when the plan seems to go awry.*

OCTOBER 28

SAINTS SIMON AND JUDE

FIRST CENTURY • JERUSALEM (MODERN-DAY ISRAEL)

DEVOTED TO THE KINGDOM

[Jesus] answered, "The kingdom of God is not coming with
things that can be observed; nor will they say, 'Look, here it is!'
or 'There it is!' For, in fact, the kingdom of God is among you."

LUKE 17:20–21

Simon and Jude were among the disciples who lived and prayed together after Jesus returned to heaven. Jesus had chosen His followers carefully, but He chose some pretty unlikely people! Simon was called "the zealot." He was passionate about his people, the Jews, having their own kingdom. But by the time Jesus returned to heaven, Simon understood which kingdom mattered most—the kingdom of God. At the Last Supper, Jude asked Jesus how He would reveal Himself (John 14:22). After three years of traveling with Jesus, Jude was still confused. But after His death, resurrection, and ascension, Jude would be one of the disciples spreading the word about Jesus throughout the world. Simon and Jude devoted themselves to Jesus and His kingdom.

> SAINTS SIMON AND JUDE ARE CELEBRATED ON THE SAME DAY. ACCORDING TO TRADITION, BOTH OF THEM GAVE UP THEIR LIVES INSTEAD OF THEIR FAITH ON THE SAME DAY.

Jesus, I want to be devoted to Your kingdom too.

SAINT NARCISSUS

99–216 • JERUSALEM (MODERN-DAY ISRAEL)

PURPOSES OF THE HEART

Do not pronounce judgment before the time, before the
Lord comes, who will bring to light the things now hidden
in darkness and will disclose the purposes of the heart.

1 CORINTHIANS 4:5

Three people who hated Bishop Narcissus told everyone that he had
committed a terrible crime. Each of the three men said that if they
weren't speaking the truth, they wished they would die. They didn't
believe that God really knew their hearts.
But Bishop Narcissus hadn't done it. After
the accusations of all three men were proven
false, all three of them died. Narcissus trusted
in the judgment of the Lord, and he knew that
the purposes of his own heart were good.
Narcissus continued in his good conduct in
Christ until he died at the age of 117.

A STORY ABOUT SAINT
NARCISSUS TELLS
THAT ONE EASTER,
WHEN THERE WAS
NO OIL TO LIGHT
THE LAMPS IN THE
CHURCH, HE PRAYED
OVER WATER, AND IT
WAS TURNED TO OIL.

Jesus, You will bring everything to light.
You see what's really in my heart.

SAINT ALPHONSUS RODRIGUEZ

1533–1617 • SPAIN

EXTRAORDINARY

We have this treasure in clay jars, so that it may be
made clear that this extraordinary power belongs
to God and does not come from us.

2 CORINTHIANS 4:7

Alphonsus was ordinary. When he interviewed to become a Jesuit priest at age thirty-five, he was told twice that he was too uneducated, old, and unhealthy to be a part of their mission. However, one of the priests with authority saw that Alphonsus had something else about him too—extraordinary holiness. Alphonsus was like a clay jar that was full of treasure. It was a very ordinary-looking object, but it could hold wonders inside. And Alphonsus held the wonders of charity, hope, and encouragement. He worked as a doorkeeper at a Jesuit college, running errands, welcoming guests, and comforting troubled students. One of these troubled students Alphonsus comforted would become Saint Peter Claver (Sept. 9), the missionary who ran to the aid of slaves in Colombia.

> BEFORE HE BECAME A PRIEST, SAINT ALPHONSUS RODRIGUEZ VIEWED HIMSELF AS A FAILED BUSINESSMAN.

Jesus, You use the ordinary to do the extraordinary.

OCTOBER 31

SAINT WOLFGANG OF REGENSBURG

934–994 • HUNGARY AND GERMANY

COMMITTED WORK

Commit your work to the LORD, and your plans will be established.

PROVERBS 16:3

Wolfgang learned about his faith from a tutor when he was only seven. He soon decided that he wanted to work for the Church. He studied hard and made good friends, learning about Church history and grammar, and even becoming a teacher. But the Lord had even more work for Wolfgang to do. Wolfgang was chosen by other priests to go and evangelize the Hungarians, a people who had just been conquered. Wolfgang went bravely. After that, he went to Bavaria, where he reorganized the roles of the abbots, or men living in an abbey. He helped them focus on worship. From teacher to missionary to reformer, finally Wolfgang withdrew to the woods to be a hermit. Throughout his life, all of his work was committed to God.

A STORY ABOUT SAINT WOLFGANG OF REGENSBURG TELLS THAT HE THREW AN AXE INTO THE WOODS, TRUSTING THAT IT WOULD LAND IN THE SPOT WHERE GOD WANTED HIM TO BUILD HIS HERMITAGE.

Jesus, I want to commit my work to You.

ALL SAINTS' DAY

CLOUD OF WITNESSES

Therefore, since we are surrounded by so great a cloud of witnesses,
let us also lay aside every weight and the sin that clings so closely,
and let us run with perseverance the race that is set before us.

HEBREWS 12:1

Each Saint is remembered and honored for his or her deep faith, commitment to Christ, and sacrifices made for God. Their stories can inspire those of us who are still running the race—that is, who have committed their lives to following Christ. The Saints ran this race, eager to meet the finish line, and their faithfulness reminds us to keep our eyes on the prize too—heaven with Christ forever! The wonderful stories of the Saints point to the love of Christ and encourage all to follow Him.

IN MEDIEVAL ENGLAND, THE DAY THAT CELEBRATED THE SAINTS WAS KNOWN AS ALL HALLOWS' DAY. THE DAY BEFORE WAS CALLED—AND STILL IS—ALL HALLOWS' EVE, OR HALLOWEEN.

Jesus, thank You for the witnesses who
are now with You in heaven.

NOVEMBER 2*

SAINT CHRISTOPHER

THIRD CENTURY • ROMAN EMPIRE (MODERN-DAY TURKEY)

ON YOUR WAY

Then you will walk on your way securely
and your foot will not stumble.

PROVERBS 3:23

Stories about Saint Christopher say that he was very tall—some even spoke of him as a giant! He used his great strength to serve kings. But he soon realized that the king he served was unworthy. After meeting a hermit who taught him about Christ, Christopher decided that the best way he could serve Christ was by carrying people across a river. The river was strong and dangerous, and there was no bridge across it. But Saint Christopher was tall enough and strong enough to walk through the river against the current. He'd wade across the river with people on his shoulders, remembering that whatever service he did to others was a service to Christ. Because of this legend, Saint Christopher is known as the patron Saint of travelers.

> THE NAME CHRISTOPHER MEANS "CHRIST-BEARER."

*Jesus, thank You for being with me on
the journeys I will take in my life.*

SAINT MARTIN DE PORRES

1579–1639 • PERU

DESPISED AND REJECTED

He was despised and rejected by others; a man of
suffering and acquainted with infirmity.

ISAIAH 53:3

Martin knew what it was like to be despised, or hated, by others. He knew what it was like to be rejected and left out. He had dark skin, like his mother, and his father wished that he looked different. When Martin was still a boy, his father left the family, and the family lived in poverty. After working to help his mother, Martin made a pledge to work for a group of priests living in Lima, his city. Martin vowed to accept others, even when they weren't accepted by society. Martin's life was marked by ordinary tasks—laundry, dishes, and routine care for the sick. But he was extraordinary in his dedication to God and to prayer, and many saw him as a strong spiritual leader.

SAINT MARTIN DE PORRES ONCE WORKED FOR A BARBER TO HELP TAKE CARE OF HIS FAMILY.

*Jesus, even though Saint Martin de Porres was rejected,
he accepted others generously, just as You did.*

SAINT CHARLES BORROMEO

1538–1584 • ITALY

REFUGE TO THE POOR

*You have been a refuge to the poor, a refuge
to the needy in their distress.*

ISAIAH 25:4

Charles started giving to the poor when he was young. His father, who was wealthy, wanted to give Charles a rich inheritance. But Charles told his father that he only wanted the money that was needed for his education. Everything else, Charles insisted, belonged to the poor.

Charles saw that many religious groups across Italy, especially in his home, Milan, were forgetting the poor and using money in ways that didn't honor God. Once, a famine struck Milan. There was nothing to eat, so the rich people of Milan fled, and the only one who could do anything to help the poor was Charles. He gave up his own fortune to feed people—as many as seventy thousand people in a day.

> SAINT CHARLES BORROMEO HAD A SPEECH IMPEDIMENT. WHEN HE WAS A BOY, UNLESS SOMEONE KNEW HIM WELL, IT WAS DIFFICULT TO UNDERSTAND HIM.

*Jesus, Saint Charles Borromeo was a refuge for the poor.
Help me use what I have to help the people that You love.*

SAINT ELIZABETH

FIRST CENTURY · JUDEA (MODERN-DAY ISRAEL)

MOTHER OF MY LORD

Why has this happened to me, that the mother of my Lord comes to me?

LUKE 1:43

Elizabeth waited for her whole life to have a child. She had longed for one, but she never became pregnant. After an angel named Gabriel appeared to her husband, Zechariah, Elizabeth was given what she wanted most—a child. When her cousin Mary came to see her, Elizabeth's son jumped up and down inside of her, and Elizabeth knew that Mary's Son would be the Savior of the world. Elizabeth was full of the Holy Spirit, and she called out to her cousin in a loud voice, "Blessed are you among women, and blessed is the fruit of your womb. And why has this happened to me, that the mother of my Lord comes to me?" (Luke 1: 42–43). Elizabeth was one of the very first people to call Jesus "Lord." She called Him "Lord" before He was even born!

AFTER HEARING THE ENCOURAGING WORDS FROM ELIZABETH, MARY SANG A BEAUTIFUL SONG THAT IS NOW KNOWN AS "THE MAGNIFICAT," WHICH IS FOUND IN CHAPTER 1 OF LUKE.

Jesus, Saint Elizabeth believed that You are the Lord and honored You. Help me honor You too.

NOVEMBER 6*

SAINT NICHOLAS TAVELIC

1340–1391 · CROATIA AND THE HOLY LAND

UNLESS YOU BELIEVE

"For you will die in your sins unless you believe that I am he."

JOHN 8:24

Nicholas traveled to the Holy Land, the place where Jesus had lived, died, and rose again while He was living on earth. Nicholas knew that unless the people in the Holy Land believed in Jesus and professed that He is God, they would be lost. So, out of love for these people who didn't believe, Nicholas spoke the truth plainly.

When he arrived in the Holy Land, he asked to see the person in charge—a person who didn't believe in Jesus. Nicholas told this official that all people must believe in Jesus. The official was shocked and said that Nicholas had to either take back his statement or die. Nicholas chose to die rather than give up his faith in Jesus.

SAINT NICHOLAS TAVELIC WAS A FRANCISCAN— HE AND THE OTHER PRIESTS WITH HIM WERE FOLLOWING THE RULES SET OUT BY SAINT FRANCIS.

Jesus, those who believe in You are saved and get to live in heaven with You one day! Help me tell others about You.

SAINT WILLIBRORD

658–739 · ENGLAND AND THE NETHERLANDS

IF THE LORD WILLS

I will come to you soon, if the Lord wills.

1 CORINTHIANS 4:19

Willibrord grew up in England. As a young man, he studied to become a priest and a missionary, and he learned about the faith and about the places he would travel. After he became a priest, Willibrord was sent to the Netherlands—a land that was then called Frisia. Willibrord boldly shared the gospel with the Frisians, and many believed in Jesus. Then, a cruel duke named Radbod conquered much of Frisia. All the work Willibrord had done, including building churches, was destroyed by Duke Radbod. But instead of losing hope, Willibrord trusted that he would be able to return to his work, as long as God willed it. After the cruel duke died, Willibrord started all over—building churches and sharing the news about Jesus in cities all over Frisia.

ON ONE OF HIS MISSIONARY JOURNEYS, SAINT WILLIBRORD DESTROYED AN IDOL. A MAN WHO SAW IT HAPPEN WAS SO MAD ABOUT IT THAT HE TRIED TO KILL HIM! THANKFULLY, HE WAS UNSUCCESSFUL.

Jesus, Saint Willibrord started all over because he wanted to do Your will. Help me be just as willing.

NOVEMBER 8

FOUR CROWNED MARTYRS

UNKNOWN–305 • ROMAN EMPIRE (MODERN-DAY HUNGARY AND ITALY)

TRUE LOYALTY

Those who worship vain idols forsake their true loyalty.

JONAH 2:8

Many Christians died because they refused to worship false gods. These Christians are remembered as martyrs, and some of their stories became confused over time. The title "Four Crowned Martyrs" actually refers to nine different men who died because they refused to give up their faith in Jesus. As the story goes, five of these men were stonemasons. They carved buildings and statues out of stone. Once, when Emperor Diocletian asked them to carve a statue of the god of medicine that he worshipped, the five stonemasons refused. They were loyal to Jesus, and they refused to make an idol of some other god. There was only one God, and He wasn't made out of stone. The emperor was furious and condemned the stonemasons to death.

THE OTHER FOUR MEN WHO ARE PART OF THE "FOUR CROWNED MARTYRS" WERE SOLDIERS WHO REFUSED TO SACRIFICE TO THE SAME GOD OF MEDICINE. THEY WERE ALSO KILLED BY DIOCLETIAN.

Jesus, You are the only true God, just like the Four Crowned Martyrs believed. I want to be loyal to You.

SAINT ANDREW AVELLINO

1521–1608 • ITALY

WORDS OF GRACE

Let no evil talk come out of your mouths, but only
what is useful for building up, as there is need, so that
your words may give grace to those who hear.

EPHESIANS 4:29

Andrew, an excellent lawyer, argued cases in front of the court, helping the bishop sort out right and wrong in many complicated situations. But something wasn't right in Andrew's heart—he was good at his job, but he realized that he would be willing to lie just to win a case. Andrew repented, but he knew that he needed to stay away from the courts. He didn't want any evil talk to come from his mouth, and he had enough wisdom to stay away from temptation. For the rest of his life, he preached and gave counsel to people. He helped set things right, and only spoke using kind words that encouraged others and gave them grace.

SAINT ANDREW AVELLINO WAS REPORTEDLY VERY HANDSOME, BUT HE CUT HIS HAIR TO DISCOURAGE ANYONE FROM ADMIRING HIS LOOKS.

Jesus, Saint Andrew Avellino wanted to speak
words of grace. Help me do the same.

NOVEMBER 10

SAINT LEO I

UNKNOWN–461 • ROMAN EMPIRE (MODERN-DAY ITALY)

THE CITY THAT IS TO COME

For here we have no lasting city, but we are
looking for the city that is to come.

HEBREWS 13:14

Even though some called the city of Rome "eternal," Leo knew that cities don't last forever. The only kingdom that would always last was the kingdom of God, which was unlike any kingdom on earth. During Leo's time as pope, the great city of Rome was crumbling. Invading armies came from everywhere, famine spread throughout the land, and politicians squabbled and forgot about taking care of the people. Leo built up the Church so it could survive the city's fall. Leo took on heresies, or false teachings, that said Jesus was not both God and man. And when the great empire of Rome fell apart, the Church kept on growing.

> SAINT LEO I MET WITH ATTILA THE HUN, A FEARED WARRIOR, AND ASKED HIM NOT TO ATTACK ROME. ATTILA AGREED AND TOOK AWAY HIS ARMY.

Jesus, Saint Leo I always looked for the city that is to come, the real kingdom of heaven. Help me keep my eyes on Your kingdom too.

SAINT MARTIN OF TOURS

316–397 • GAUL (MODERN-DAY FRANCE)

THE LEAST OF THESE

"The king will answer them, 'Truly I tell you, just as you did it to one of the least of these who are members of my family, you did it to me.'"

MATTHEW 25:40

Martin first heard about Christianity from other soldiers in the ranks. Their stories fascinated Martin. Who was this King they talked about who willingly died for their sins? Martin kept thinking about Jesus, even when he was sent far away from home to another part of the Roman Empire called Gaul. Once, when Martin was patrolling the streets of the city, he saw a man shivering in the cold. Martin thought of Jesus and what He said about taking care of the poor. Martin tore his own soldier's cloak in two and handed the other half to the man. Soon after, Martin became a Christian.

LATER, SAINT MARTIN OF TOURS BECAME A PRIEST BUT DIDN'T WANT TO BECOME A BISHOP. THE PEOPLE OF TOURS LOVED HIM SO MUCH THAT THEY TRICKED HIM INTO IT!

Jesus, help me remember that whenever I give to someone in need, I am giving to You too.

SAINT JOSAPHAT OF POLOTSK

1580–1623 • POLOTSK (MODERN-DAY BELARUS)

ONE BODY IN CHRIST

*We, who are many, are one body in Christ, and
individually we are members one of another.*

ROMANS 12:5

More than five hundred years before Josaphat was born, the Church split into two different groups. The two groups, the East and the West, disagreed on the best ways to worship and on who should be pope, among many other things. But Josaphat knew that the love of Jesus was greater than any divisions, even divisions that involved many countries and millions of people. No matter what, the Church should be one body—the body of Christ. Josaphat's teaching made other people so angry that they wanted to kill him. But Josaphat remained calm. He was completely at peace with the danger around him, and he willingly gave up his life to spread the message of unity in the Church.

AFTER SAINT JOSAPHAT OF POLOTSK DIED, MANY CHURCHES FROM THE EAST AND THE WEST BEGAN TO RECONCILE AND AGREE.

*Jesus, You want us to be united. Help churches
around the world reconcile with each other.*

SAINT FRANCES XAVIER CABRINI

1850–1917 • ITALY AND THE UNITED STATES

HIS STRENGTH

Seek the LORD and his strength, seek his presence continually.

1 CHRONICLES 16:11

As a little girl, Frances often felt sick and weak. But her heart was strong with God's love and with love for her neighbors in need. Ever since she was young, she wanted to be a missionary, serving others in new places for God's glory. But she wasn't considered healthy enough. That didn't stop Frances, though. She founded her own group of missionaries instead! She expected to be sent to China, but the pope told Frances to go the other way around the world—to New York in the United States. Frances went faithfully. As she served the Italian immigrants in the United States, she sought God's presence. In His strength, the woman who had been considered too weak to be a missionary traveled all over the world—back and forth across the Atlantic Ocean, to Europe, and all over the Americas.

SAINT FRANCES XAVIER CABRINI TRAVELED ON HORSEBACK THROUGH THE ANDES MOUNTAINS IN SOUTH AMERICA TO ESTABLISH A SCHOOL.

Jesus, when I am weak, You are strong.
Help me rely on Your strength.

SAINT GERTRUDE THE GREAT

1256–1302 · GERMANY

NOW I SEE

He answered, "I do not know whether he is a sinner. One
thing I do know, that though I was blind, now I see."

JOHN 9:25

Gertrude may have been an orphan—almost nothing is known about her parents, not even their names. As a very little girl, she was taken in at a religious school and was cared for by a woman named Mechtilde, who loved little Gertrude dearly. Gertrude did well in school, learning Latin and becoming a skilled writer. When she turned twenty-five, Gertrude believed she started having beautiful visions of Jesus, in which He taught her many wonderful things. Later she would write that before her visions, she was like a blind woman. But Jesus changed everything. Suddenly, she could see the truth about Him and His love for her. Over the years, Gertrude wrote down everything she learned about Jesus so her knowledge could be shared with everyone.

> SAINT GERTRUDE THE GREAT IS THE ONLY WOMAN SAINT WHO HAS THE TITLE "THE GREAT."

Jesus, You can help me see the truth about You and Your love.

SAINT ALBERT THE GREAT

1200–1280 • GERMANY

THE WORKS OF THE LORD

Great are the works of the LORD, studied by all who delight in them.

PSALM 111:2

Albert delighted in the world around him. There was nothing Albert didn't want to know. He wanted to know about the people who had lived long ago. He wanted to know about the stars in the heavens that could be seen at night. He wanted to know right from wrong and how to create the best kind of society. Albert learned new things, translated ancient works, and taught students to love the world around them. His most famous student was Saint Thomas Aquinas (Jan. 28). Albert loved science, and he loved it all the more because he loved the God who had created the universe. God had created such a beautiful world, and Albert loved learning all about it.

SAINT ALBERT THE GREAT TRANSLATED MANY WORKS OF ARISTOTLE, AN ANCIENT GREEK PHILOSOPHER, INTO LATIN SO THAT OTHER SCIENTISTS OF HIS TIME COULD UNDERSTAND THEM. THIS PROJECT TOOK HIM TWENTY YEARS!

Jesus, You've created an incredible world! Help me learn about it and cherish it, just as Saint Albert the Great did.

SAINT MARGARET OF SCOTLAND

1045–1093 · SCOTLAND

QUEEN'S HOPE

Rejoice in hope, be patient in suffering, persevere in prayer.

ROMANS 12:12

Even though she was a princess, Margaret had plenty of reasons to lose hope. Her father was known as Prince Edward the Exile, and he and his family had been thrown out of their home in England. They moved to Hungary, where Margaret was born. Her family did return to England, but her father died almost as soon as he arrived. Later, Margaret and her family had to flee England, away from a cruel conqueror. They arrived in Scotland and asked for protection. Malcolm, the king of Scotland, helped Margaret's family and soon fell in love with and married her.

> SAINT MARGARET OF SCOTLAND WAS SO BELOVED BY HER SCOTTISH SUBJECTS THAT SHE WAS KNOWN AS "THE PEARL OF SCOTLAND."

Queen Margaret cared deeply for the poor and for the faith of her subjects. She built churches and helped her husband become a gentler king. They had eight children together. Through everything, Margaret was hopeful, patient, and constant in her prayers.

Jesus, no matter what is happening in my life, I can hope in You, rejoice in You, and turn to You in prayer.

VENERABLE HENRIETTE DELILLE

1812–1862 • THE UNITED STATES

WE ARE THE LORD'S

If we live, we live to the Lord, and if we die, we die to the Lord;
so then, whether we live or whether we die, we are the Lord's.

ROMANS 14:8

Henriette's great-great-grandmother had been brought from Africa to live as a slave in Louisiana. Even though Henriette was free, many Black women like her had few options for work. It was difficult for women with any history of slavery in their family to live lives that were truly free. But Henriette devoted herself completely to God. She wrote that she wanted to live and die for God, in spite of everything else. She helped Black people enter the church and was a godmother to many babies, she worked in a school that educated young Black girls, and she cared for older women who had been freed from slavery.

VENERABLE HENRIETTE DELILLE LOVED TO READ AND SHARED A LIBRARY WITH OTHER WOMEN WHO SERVED THE CHURCH.

Jesus, Venerable Henriette Delille remembered that above all else, we are Yours. I want to give my all to You too.

VENERABLE HENRIETTE DELILLE IS ON TRACK TO BECOME A SAINT.

SAINT ELIZABETH OF HUNGARY

1207–1231 · HUNGARY

GIVE TO THE POOR

Whoever gives to the poor will lack nothing.

PROVERBS 28:27

Elizabeth lived most of her short life as a princess. She grew up in the court of the prince whom she would marry, and she went to church and gave to the poor and hungry. She would even walk out of the castle in simple clothing to spend time with the poor.

When the king died, Elizabeth married the prince, and they were happy together. Sadly, he died after they had been married for only six years. Elizabeth gave away everything and dedicated the rest of her life to prayer and to poverty. Even though she lost her husband and her many possessions, she was rich in Christ. Because she had God, she lacked nothing.

WHEN A TERRIBLE FLOOD AFFECTED THOUSANDS IN HER COUNTRY, SAINT ELIZABETH OF HUNGARY TOOK ROYAL CLOTHING FROM THE CASTLE TO GIVE TO PEOPLE WHO WERE LEFT WITH NOTHING.

Jesus, help me remember the poor, just as Saint Elizabeth of Hungary did. You are all that I need.

NOVEMBER 19*

SAINT AGNES OF ASSISI

1198–1253 • ITALY

UNMOVED

Those who trust in the LORD are like Mount Zion,
which cannot be moved, but abides forever.

PSALM 125:1

Agnes was the younger sister of Saint Clare of Assisi (Aug. 11). Agnes saw her parents' rage when Clare left their home, but Agnes wanted to follow Clare's example anyway. Only two weeks after Clare left for the convent, Agnes snuck away. This was too much for their father. He ran after Agnes and pleaded with her to come home. Agnes said no. She wanted to abandon everything for Jesus. As the story goes, her father grabbed her by the hair and was pulling her back home when suddenly he couldn't pull her along anymore. Agnes wouldn't move! She was stuck to the spot. It was as if the Lord were holding her there. Her father gave up, and Agnes ran back to the convent, thrilled that she would spend her days serving the Lord.

> SAINT FRANCIS OF ASSISI (OCT. 3) SAW SAINT AGNES OF ASSISI'S DEVOTION AND MATURITY, AND HE SET HER IN A POSITION OF AUTHORITY OVER OTHER NUNS WHEN SHE WAS STILL YOUNG— ONLY IN HER TWENTIES.

Jesus, I want my love for You to never move.

SAINT ROSE PHILIPPINE DUCHESNE

1769–1852 • FRANCE AND THE UNITED STATES

FOR EVERYONE

First of all, then, I urge that supplications, prayers, intercessions, and thanksgivings be made for everyone.

1 TIMOTHY 2:1

Rose took a group of women across the Atlantic Ocean to serve the tribes of Native Americans living in the American frontier. But when they arrived, the bishop—the man in charge of the churches in the area—said he had no place for them. He sent them to a small town in the territory of Missouri where no tribes lived. Rose couldn't serve the way she thought she would, but she could still pray for everyone she served and worked with. She worked hard and even built a school for girls in the area, but most of all, she prayed. Eventually, after she retired, she got a chance to serve the tribes. Though she couldn't learn their language, the Native Americans knew there was something special about her. They named her Woman-Who-Prays-Always.

SAINT ROSE PHILIPPINE DUCHESNE DEALT WITH MANY STRUGGLES, INCLUDING FOOD AND WATER SHORTAGES, FOREST FIRES, AND POOR LIVING CONDITIONS. BUT NONE OF THESE THINGS STOPPED HER FROM SERVING AND PRAYING.

Jesus, Saint Rose Philippine Duchesne prayed always, for everyone. Help me do the same.

NOVEMBER 21*

BLESSED FRANCES SIEDLISKA

1842–1902 · POLAND AND THE UNITED STATES

THE WILL OF THE LORD

Do not be foolish, but understand what the will of the Lord is.

EPHESIANS 5:17

As a girl, Frances didn't understand why God mattered. Her own governess, who taught her many different lessons and seemed to know a lot, hardly ever mentioned God. Then Frances met a priest who loved Jesus. The priest, Father Leander, was unlike anyone she had ever met. He knew what he wanted from life—he wanted to do the will of God! Father Leander's passion made Frances want to follow God's will for her life too. When she told her parents that she wanted to become a nun, they were shocked. But Frances followed God's will anyway. She became a nun and founded an order, or religious group, focused on praying and serving. She also traveled across the ocean as a missionary, living in the United States and traveling back to Europe to encourage other women of faith.

> BLESSED FRANCES SIEDLISKA OPENED SCHOOLS FOR CHILDREN IN ILLINOIS AND PENNSYLVANIA.

Jesus, help me understand Your will.

BLESSED FRANCES SIEDLISKA IS ON TRACK TO BECOME A SAINT.

NOVEMBER 22

SAINT CECILIA

THIRD CENTURY • ROMAN EMPIRE (MODERN-DAY ITALY)

SONG OF JOY

The LORD, your God, is in your midst, a warrior who gives
victory; he will rejoice over you with gladness, he will renew
you in his love; he will exult over you with loud singing.

ZEPHANIAH 3:17

Cecilia loved God, and as a child, she promised never to marry so that she could be totally devoted to Him. But when she was of age, her parents arranged her marriage anyway to a man named Valerianus. Still committed to God above all else, Cecilia spent her wedding ceremony focused on God, even singing to Him in her heart. As the story goes, Valerianus didn't believe in Jesus, but Cecilia made it a point to tell her new husband about God.

> PAINTINGS OF SAINT CECILIA OFTEN SHOW HER PLAYING THE ORGAN.

Because of Cecilia's courage and witness about Jesus, her husband became a Christian too. Eventually, they both died for their faith in Jesus, becoming martyrs.

Jesus, I have so many reasons to praise You!
I want to sing a song of joy to You.

BLESSED MIGUEL PRO

1891–1927 • MEXICO

CHRIST THE KING

The Lamb will conquer them, for he is Lord of lords and King of kings.

REVELATION 17:14

Miguel grew up in Mexico and studied to become a priest, but he lived on the run. The government in Mexico wanted to get rid of the Church, closing churches and passing laws that made it difficult to be a priest. While Miguel studied in Spain and taught in Nicaragua, the Church in Mexico went underground. When Miguel returned, he wore disguises to minister to the faithful people in Mexico. Miguel was discovered and falsely accused of assassinating a government official. Miguel was innocent, but he never became angry, even showing kindness to his executioners. His final words were "Long live Christ the King!"

THE PRESIDENT OF MEXICO HAD PICTURES TAKEN OF BLESSED MIGUEL PRO'S EXECUTION. HE WANTED TO SCARE PEOPLE. INSTEAD OF SCARING PEOPLE, THE PICTURES INSPIRED THEM. SIXTY THOUSAND PEOPLE CAME TO SEE THE BRAVE PRIEST BURIED.

Jesus, Blessed Miguel Pro worshipped You as the one true King. I want to do the same.

BLESSED MIGUEL PRO IS ON TRACK TO BECOME A SAINT.

SAINT ANDREW DŨNG-LẠC

1795–1839 • VIETNAM

NOTHING BUT THE CROSS

*May I never boast of anything except the cross
of our Lord Jesus Christ, by which the world has
been crucified to me, and I to the world.*

GALATIANS 6:14

A ndrew had nothing to boast about except for Jesus. He had grown up in poverty in Vietnam and learned about Christianity in secret. The emperor of Vietnam hated Christians, and he tried to get rid of Christianity in Vietnam. Even though he knew it was dangerous, Andrew became a priest. The emperor ordered his soldiers to drag anyone suspected to be Christians out of their homes and tell them to stomp on a crucifix. If any person refused to dishonor the cross, that person was guilty of being a Christian. The emperor was cruel to Andrew, but Andrew never gave up his faith in Jesus and His cross. Andrew is honored with 116 others who became martyrs in Vietnam between 1820 and 1862.

PORTUGUESE PRIESTS AND MISSIONARIES BROUGHT THE NEWS OF JESUS TO VIETNAM IN 1615.

*Jesus, Saint Andrew Dũng-Lạc boasted only
in Your cross. Help me do the same.*

SAINT COLUMBAN

543–615 • IRELAND AND FRANCE

BETTER THAN BEFORE

Today I declare that I will restore to you double.

ZECHARIAH 9:12

Columban fled from Ireland, away from distractions and toward a life as a monk. His mother, who didn't want him to leave, tried to block his way by lying down in front of their door, but Columban just stepped over her and began his journey. In England, he focused on his studies, then gathered many other monks to take to the sea and go to France.

There, God would use Columban to restore His Church. French churches and cities were in total disorganization. Columban worked to restore the Church in France, taking all kinds of people into their monasteries, or houses where people worked and worshipped. Soon, so many worshippers lived at a monastery that anyone walking by could always hear singing, no matter if it was day or night. The Church was even better than it had been before.

A LEGEND TELLS THAT SAINT COLUMBAN WAS ONCE SURROUNDED BY A PACK OF HUNGRY WOLVES. HE QUIETLY ASKED GOD FOR HELP. THE WOLVES SMELLED HIM AND WALKED AWAY WITHOUT ATTACKING.

Jesus, You can restore anything!

SAINT CATHERINE OF ALEXANDRIA

FOURTH CENTURY · EGYPT

DESTROYED ARGUMENTS

We destroy arguments and every proud obstacle
raised up against the knowledge of God.

2 CORINTHIANS 10:4–5

A s the story goes, Catherine was only eighteen when she marched into the court of Roman Emperor Maximinus II, but she was more than ready to stand up against injustice. The emperor, like many before him, ordered for Christians to be killed. Catherine dared to tell the emperor to put an end to the killings. She gave a brilliant defense of Christianity, which left the emperor dumbfounded. He called in many advisors who knew astronomy, history, and theology. Catherine took them on one by one, and none of them could stand against her. She destroyed every single one of their arguments. Catherine's faith and her knowledge of God gave her the courage to stand against the cruelty of the emperor.

> SAINT CATHERINE OF ALEXANDRIA WAS PUT IN PRISON, BUT EVEN THERE, SHE SHARED HER FAITH. BECAUSE OF HER MESSAGE, AT LEAST TWO HUNDRED PEOPLE BECAME CHRISTIANS.

*Jesus, help me defend my faith with courage,
just as Saint Catherine of Alexandria did.*

SAINT FRANCESCO ANTONIO FASANI

1681–1742 • ITALY

BY MY NAME

"If my people who are called by my name humble themselves,
pray, seek my face, and turn from their wicked ways, then I will
hear from heaven, and will forgive their sin and heal their land."

2 CHRONICLES 7:14

When he became a priest, Francesco promised that he would spend his life helping people draw close to God. He chose to follow the example of two priests who had lived before him: Saint Francis of Assisi (Oct. 3) and Saint Anthony (June 13). These great men led many of their followers to repentance, which means they were able to help people turn to God, follow Him, and know His love. Francesco knew that God didn't want people wallowing in sadness, putting themselves down, and feeling discouraged. God wanted people to know that He had called them by name. God wanted people to seek His face. Francesco gently encouraged people who had fallen away to come back to the God who loved them.

> SAINT FRANCESCO ANTONIO FASANI'S MISSION KEPT HIM CLOSE TO HIS HOME. HE EVEN BECAME THE PASTOR IN HIS HOMETOWN CHURCH.

*Jesus, You've called me by name, and I can
always repent and return to You.*

NOVEMBER 28

SAINT JAMES OF THE MARCHES

1391–1476 · ITALY

FALSE TEACHERS

False prophets also arose among the people, just
as there will be false teachers among you, who
will secretly bring in destructive opinions.

2 PETER 2:1

James's uncle, a priest, offered James the education that his family couldn't afford for him, and soon James became a priest too. Because he was so dedicated to his studies, James knew false teaching when he saw it. He traveled all over Europe, including Germany, Poland, Denmark, and beyond, helping Church leaders root out false teachers and discredit heresies, or lies about what Jesus really taught. James fought these false teachings with truth. But James didn't just tell these false teachers that they were wrong; he reached out to them with love. Fifty thousand heretics, or people who taught lies about Jesus, came back to the Church and the truth about Jesus because of James's preaching.

> SAINT JAMES OF THE MARCHES ONCE TOLD THE STORY OF SAINT MARY MAGDALENE (JULY 21) TO THIRTY-SIX WOMEN WHO HAD FALLEN AWAY FROM GOD, AND ALL OF THE WOMEN RETURNED TO THEIR FAITH.

*Jesus, help me recognize lies about You and
believe the truth about You instead.*

SAINT CLEMENT I

FIRST CENTURY · ROMAN EMPIRE (MODERN-DAY ITALY)

WE MUST OBEY

Peter and the apostles answered, "We must obey
God rather than any human authority."

ACTS 5:29

Clement knew many of the men and women who walked with Jesus, like the apostle Peter, and he wanted to follow Jesus the way they did, even unto death. Clement heard their stories about Jesus and admired their total dedication to God. About sixty years after Jesus died and rose, Clement became the pope. Even though Christians often died because they wouldn't give up their faith, Clement didn't fear death. He wanted to obey God. Clement heard the call to obedience clearer and stronger than the rules and laws of any emperor or king. When he wrote letters of encouragement to other Christians, Clement reminded them how important it was to obey God.

> ACCORDING TO LEGENDS, SAINT CLEMENT I WAS TIED TO AN ANCHOR AND CAST INTO THE OCEAN, WHICH IS WHY THE ART ABOUT HIM OFTEN SHOWS HIM WITH AN ANCHOR.

*Jesus, Saint Clement I obeyed Your
words. I want to obey You too.*

NOVEMBER 30

SAINT ANDREW

FIRST CENTURY · GALILEE (MODERN-DAY ISRAEL)

MESSIAH

He first found his brother Simon and said to
him, "We have found the Messiah."

JOHN 1:41

Andrew saw John the Baptist preaching and baptizing, and he wondered if John could be the Messiah. Was John the one who had been foretold in all of the books of the prophets, the one who would redeem Andrew's people? John told Andrew no—the Messiah was someone else. That someone else was Jesus. Andrew spent one day with Jesus, and he was convinced. This man was the Messiah! Filled with joy, Andrew knew he had to do something. He brought the wonderful news home. "Simon!" Andrew said. "It's Him! I know it is! Come and see!" Simon was Andrew's brother—the same Simon who was the first to call Jesus the Christ and whom Jesus would rename Peter. Both Peter and Andrew spent the next three years following the Messiah.

> SOME ANCIENT ACCOUNTS TELL THAT SAINT ANDREW TRAVELED AS FAR AS RUSSIA TO SPREAD THE GOSPEL.

*Jesus, Saint Andrew told his brother about You
joyfully. Help me share You with my family too.*

SAINT SIMON OF CYRENE

**FIRST CENTURY · CYRENE (MODERN-DAY LIBYA)
AND JERUSALEM (MODERN-DAY ISRAEL)**

CARRY THE CROSS

They compelled a passer-by, who was coming in
from the country, to carry his cross; it was Simon of
Cyrene, the father of Alexander and Rufus.

MARK 15:21

Simon traveled to Jerusalem to celebrate Passover with his sons. Simon wanted to honor God with his family, but he had no idea that he would meet God in person. On his way to Jerusalem, Simon saw Jesus. But Jesus wasn't preaching to crowds or healing anyone. Jesus was carrying His cross up a long road to be crucified. Most of His followers had abandoned Him. He was battered, bruised, and exhausted and looked nothing like a king. The soldiers with Jesus forced Simon to help Him carry the cross. Simon saw Jesus when He was suffering and in pain, and Simon helped Him. Simon is mentioned in the gospels of Saints Matthew, Mark, and Luke, which strongly suggests that Simon became a Christian soon after he helped Jesus carry the cross.

SAINT SIMON OF CYRENE'S SON, RUFUS, MIGHT BE THE SAME RUFUS MENTIONED IN SAINT PAUL'S LETTER TO THE ROMANS.

*Jesus, Saint Simon of Cyrene helped You when You were
suffering. I want to help those who are suffering too.*

SAINT EUTYCHIUS OF CONSTANTINOPLE

512–582 • BYZANTINE EMPIRE (MODERN-DAY TURKEY)

FULLY MAN

*Let the same mind be in you that was in Christ Jesus, who,
though he was in the form of God, . . . emptied himself,
taking the form of a slave, being born in human likeness. And
being found in human form, he humbled himself and became
obedient to the point of death—even death on a cross.*

PHILIPPIANS 2:5–8

Eutychius disagreed with the emperor, who was a dangerous person to disagree with. But he cared more about telling the truth than about how important Emperor Justinian was. Five hundred years after Jesus died and rose again, leaders like Justinian were spreading heresies, or lies, about Jesus. One of these lies was that Jesus never felt pain. Justinian and the others thought that if Jesus really was God, He wouldn't have felt any pain on the cross. Eutychius knew how wrong this was and defended the truth. Jesus was fully man, which meant he had real human flesh and felt real pain. Yet Jesus died for humankind anyway. Justinian exiled Eutychius for disagreeing with him, but Eutychius bravely stuck to the truth anyway.

SAINT EUTYCHIUS OF CONSTANTINOPLE'S FATHER WAS A GENERAL IN THE BYZANTINE ARMY.

Jesus, You suffered and died for us because You love us.

SAINT FRANCIS XAVIER

1506–1552 • SPAIN AND MALAYSIA

FORGIVENESS OF SINS

I, I am He who blots out your transgressions for my
own sake, and I will not remember your sins.

ISAIAH 43:25

Francis and Anjiro talked into the night, and Francis answered Anjiro's questions about Jesus. As a missionary, Francis had had these types of conversations before. He traveled the world, telling everyone the good news of God's forgiveness and Jesus' sacrifice. Maybe the easiest way to do this would have been to talk to the kings and important people of the countries he visited, but Francis always gave his message first to the children and the sick. He met Anjiro in Malaysia, and Anjiro followed Francis, desperate to know the truth about Jesus. Anjiro had been accused of a terrible crime and felt the brunt of unforgiveness. So he asked, "Can this God of yours really forgive sins?" And Francis gladly answered him, "Yes!"

BECAUSE SAINT FRANCIS XAVIER SHARED THE GOOD NEWS, ANJIRO WAS THE FIRST JAPANESE PERSON TO BECOME A CHRISTIAN.

*Jesus, I want to confess what I've done
wrong. I know You forgive sins!*

SAINT JOHN OF DAMASCUS

675–749 • SYRIA

PATIENT TEACHER

Proclaim the message; be persistent whether the time
is favorable or unfavorable; convince, rebuke, and
encourage, with the utmost patience in teaching.

2 TIMOTHY 4:2

John felt the disapproval of the other teachers and writers hanging over him like a cloud. He had an unpopular opinion—he claimed that pictures of Jesus and of Saints weren't idols. The other teachers disagreed and were so angry that they called for John to be thrown out of the city. Instead of becoming angry, John was patient. Instead of becoming discouraged, John got to work. He lived as a monk and wrote about the truth. Eventually, John and his teachings were restored. John listened to God first and others second. In obedience to God, John fought against the false teachings, convinced Christians of the truth, and encouraged other followers of Jesus to know Him and follow Him.

SAINT JOHN OF DAMASCUS WROTE OVER 150 BOOKS!

*Jesus, as I talk about my faith in You, help me be
patient with others just as Saint John of Damascus
was. Help me listen to others with kindness. Give me
courage to say convincing words about Your love.*

SAINT SABAS

439–532 • PALESTINE (MODERN-DAY ISRAEL)

PRAY ALWAYS

O Lord, God of my salvation, when, at night, I cry out in your presence, let my prayer come before you; incline your ear to my cry.

PSALM 88:1–2

Sabas prayed to God at all hours of the day, and at age eighteen, he decided to become a monk. The other monks were amazed that someone so young could spend so much time praying. Often, young men wanted adventures. But this young man seemed intent on giving himself to God. Sabas even asked to be a hermit to deepen his devotion to his prayers. He lived alone, gathering the food he could find in the wilderness and trusting God for everything. Many men saw Sabas's devotion to God, and they wanted to be like him. Even though they knew he preferred to be alone, many men gathered around him, asking him how to be more like Jesus. Part of Sabas's answer must have been this: pray always!

> DURING HIS TIME ALONE, SAINT SABAS WOULD WEAVE BASKETS.

Jesus, You hear my prayers. I want to pray to You always, day and night, just as Saint Sabas did.

BLESSED ADOLPH KOLPING

1813–1865 • GERMANY

SING TO THE LORD

Sing to him, sing praises to him; tell of all his wonderful works.

PSALM 105:2

Adolph heard the same story over and over, from many of the men in Cologne. They had come to the city from a small town, looking for work. Factories sprang up all over the city, and each one needed many workers. The factory workers were glad to have jobs, but they had suddenly been separated from their families and from the faith that they had known as boys. Many of them felt lonely and started slipping away from their faith. Adolph, who was a priest, knew he needed to do something for them. His solution was a creative one—he started a choir of these workmen. After their shifts were over, men would join together to sing about the Lord. They could share their faith and talk about ways to honor the Lord with their new jobs.

> BLESSED ADOLPH KOLPING LEARNED THE SKILL OF SHOEMAKING AS A BOY.

Jesus, I want to sing Your praises.

BLESSED ADOLPH KOLPING IS ON TRACK TO BECOME A SAINT.

SAINT AMBROSE

340–397 • ROMAN EMPIRE (MODERN-DAY ITALY)

RIGHT JUDGMENT

"Do not judge by appearances, but judge with right judgment."

JOHN 7:24

Bishop Ambrose saw a sea of people before him, all of whom wanted to speak with him. Some were rich, and some were poor. Some were men, and some were women. Some wanted his advice, and some wanted to tell him how to do his work! Ambrose prayed as he scanned the crowd. He knew that Jesus wanted him to see these people as He saw them, to be equally kind and caring to all, no matter how they looked, no matter if they liked him or not. Even though he had many demands on his time, he spent hours daily in prayer and writing personal responses to letters. He wanted to talk to people how Jesus would—to judge them not by their appearances but by God's heart for them.

WHEN SAINT AMBROSE GAVE A SERMON, HE DIDN'T USE NOTES! HE SPOKE WHATEVER WAS ON HIS HEART AND MIND.

Jesus, You can help me tell right from wrong and good from bad. Help me use right judgment.

SAINT THOMAS BECKET

1118–1170 • ENGLAND

FIRST KINGDOM

"Strive first for the kingdom of God and his righteousness,
and all these things will be given to you as well."

MATTHEW 6:33

Thomas rode to battle with King Henry. They were constant companions, even though Thomas was also a priest. Thomas gave the king important advice, and the king listened to him. They feasted together and traveled together. They disagreed with each other often but remained true friends. Then their friendship was tested. The king wanted Thomas to have a powerful position in the Church. Thomas knew that if he had this powerful job, he would likely have many reasons to disagree with the king. Thomas told the king his concern, but the king said he should have the position anyway. Everything happened like Thomas said it would. Thomas tried everything to restore their friendship after a big disagreement, but the king was furious. Still, every time, Thomas chose God's will over the king's happiness.

> SAINT THOMAS BECKET LOVED HUNTING WITH HAWKS. HE ONCE DOVE INTO A RIVER TO SAVE ONE OF HIS FAVORITE HAWKS.

*Jesus, help me do the right thing in Your eyes, even
when my friends think something else is best.*

SAINT JUAN DIEGO

1474–1548 • MEXICO

BLESSED BELIEVERS

Jesus said to him, "Have you believed because you have seen me?
Blessed are those who have not seen and yet have come to believe."

JOHN 20:29

Juan Diego carried a bouquet of roses to the bishop as proof of his vision. The bishop did not believe that Juan Diego had seen Mary, the mother of God, and Juan Diego hoped the roses would change his mind. He approached the bishop, offering the bouquet, and as he did, many more roses tumbled out of his cloak. As the story goes, the bishop believed he saw an image of Mary on the inside of Juan Diego's cloak. He was amazed. He had his proof, so he gave in to Juan Diego's request—he was allowed to build and care for a chapel, just as he wanted to do.

SAINT JUAN DIEGO BELIEVED HE HEARD FROM MARY IN HIS NATIVE LANGUAGE. HE WAS ONE OF THE CHICHIMECA PEOPLE, AND HIS NATIVE NAME WAS CUAUHTLATOATZIN, WHICH MEANS "TALKING EAGLE."

Jesus, I will listen to You, even when others do not hear You.

SAINT GREGORY III

690–741 • SYRIA AND ITALY

STRONGHOLD

The LORD is good, a stronghold in a day of trouble;
he protects those who take refuge in him.

NAHUM 1:7

Gregory, who served the Church as pope, lived in the city of Rome. Even though the city had strong walls and many soldiers, Gregory knew that his real refuge, his safest place, was God. Over many centuries, Rome had been attacked many times. While Gregory was pope, he handled disagreements and false teachings, but he also faced the threat of invasion and attack against his city. When it looked like trouble was going to overwhelm Gregory and the city of Rome, he turned to God for help. Because the Church had spread throughout the world, the Christians in Rome could ask the Church in other countries, like France, for help. God answered Gregory's prayers, and the Church in France helped defend Rome from attack.

SAINT GREGORY III WAS BORN IN SYRIA.

Jesus, You are my refuge when there is trouble. Help me call on You for help and accept help from others.

SAINT DAMASUS I

304–384 • ROMAN EMPIRE (MODERN-DAY ITALY)

GOD'S APPROVAL

*Am I now seeking human approval, or God's approval?
Or am I trying to please people? If I were still pleasing
people, I would not be a servant of Christ.*

GALATIANS 1:10

Damasus couldn't please both God and people, so he decided that he would focus on pleasing God. He served the Catholic Church as a pope, which wasn't ever an easy job, even during times of peace. But the times weren't peaceful. Many of the Church leaders, like the bishops and cardinals, disliked Damasus and wished that some-one else was the pope. They even spread lies about Damasus, telling everyone who would listen that the pope had committed a terrible crime. But Damasus wanted God's approval, not theirs. So he condemned the lies and spent his time making God's Word more available to people, even supporting those who were translating the Bible in other languages. Damasus served God to please Him, not to please people.

> DURING THE TIME THAT SAINT DAMASUS I WAS POPE, CHRISTIANITY BECAME THE OFFICIAL RELIGION OF ROME.

*Jesus, I want to please You. Help me want
Your approval above all others.*

DECEMBER 12*

BLESSEDS DAUDI OKELO AND JILDO IRWA

1902–1918 (OKELO), 1906– 1918 (IRWA) • UGANDA

FAITHFUL TEACHERS

What you have heard from me through many witnesses entrust to faithful people who will be able to teach others as well.

2 TIMOTHY 2:2

Daudi and Jildo became Christians when they were young. Inspired by the missionaries who had come to Uganda decades before, they became teachers of the faith when they were just teenagers. Both boys were sent to a town called Paimol to teach others what they had learned about Jesus. They began teaching the children there about what it means to know and follow God. However, Christianity was still seen as a terrible threat. When Daudi and Jildo refused to stop teaching about Jesus, they were killed for their faith and became martyrs.

> DAUDI AND JILDO'S TEACHING MINISTRY INCLUDED SONGS, GAMES, AND COMMUNITY PRAYER TIMES.

Jesus, help me faithfully teach others about You, just as Blesseds Daudi Okelo and Jildo Irwa did.

~~~~~~~~~~

BLESSEDS DAUDI OKELO AND JILDO IRWA ARE ON TRACK TO BECOME SAINTS.

368

DECEMBER 13

SAINT LUCY

283–304 • ROMAN EMPIRE (MODERN-DAY ITALY)

LIGHT OF THE WORLD

Jesus spoke to them, saying, "I am the light of the world. Whoever follows me will never walk in darkness but will have the light of life."

JOHN 8:12

Lucy followed Jesus' teachings, and she was inspired by the story of Saint Agatha. Like Agatha, Lucy's family was wealthy, and many men wanted to marry her because of it. But Lucy wanted Jesus more than she wanted wealth, and she wanted her life to shine in Jesus, the real Light of the World. Lucy convinced her mother to give part of her riches to the poor and also refused to marry a man who was greedy with his money. For refusing to marry him, Lucy was likely killed. Stories about Lucy's faith and her sacrifice spread far and wide, inspiring others to love Jesus and live in His light.

> SAINT LUCY IS HONORED IN SWEDEN AROUND CHRISTMASTIME WITH CANDLES TO SHOW THAT THE LIGHT OF CHRIST STILL SHINES.

Jesus, You are the light in the darkness of the world.

DECEMBER 14

SAINT JOHN OF THE CROSS

1542–1591 · SPAIN

LOOKING TO JESUS

Let us run with perseverance the race that is set before us,
looking to Jesus the pioneer and perfecter of our faith, who for
the sake of the joy that was set before him endured the cross.

HEBREWS 12:1–2

John grasped the scrap of paper, bending close to the lamp that lit his tiny cell. Stretching his sore fingers, he began writing, thinking of Jesus and the pain that He had endured for him. John had been kidnapped and thrown in prison. He believed that many monks in his order, or group that has taken religious vows, weren't focused on Jesus anymore. John argued that they should be more committed to prayer and to poverty. That is, they should live on what God gives them, not the beautiful things they buy for themselves. John used his time in prison to write beautiful poetry that would inspire others to look to Jesus and His incredible sacrifice.

> SAINT JOHN OF THE CROSS WAS A POET AND AN ARTIST. HE ALSO HAD THE TALENT OF SKETCHING.

Jesus, You endured the cross for me. I want
to spend my days looking to You.

BLESSED ANTHONY GRASSI

1592–1671 • ITALY

NEW MORNING

*His mercies never come to an end; they are new
every morning; great is your faithfulness.*

LAMENTATIONS 3:22–23

Anthony had become a priest as a young man, and with God's grace, he had overcome an overwhelming sense of guilt that he had felt since he was a child. What was next for him? Well, in Anthony's case, what was next was a bolt of lightning. A real one! While Anthony prayed peacefully in a chapel, he was struck by lightning. Everyone, including Anthony, thought he was going to die. He was paralyzed and burned. But miraculously, in a matter of days, he recovered. He could even walk again! Anthony gave the burned clothes to the chapel, called the Holy House at Loreto. He lived the rest of his life grateful for the new morning that God, in His great mercy, had gifted to him.

> BLESSED ANTHONY GRASSI WAS VERY CLEVER WITH LANGUAGE. HE WAS NICKNAMED THE "WALKING DICTIONARY" BY PROFESSORS.

*Jesus, You gave Blessed Anthony Grassi a second chance
at life. Thank You for the second chances You give to me!*

BLESSED ANTHONY GRASSI IS ON TRACK TO BECOME A SAINT.

SAINT ANASTASIUS I OF ANTIOCH

UNKNOWN–599 • ANTIOCH (MODERN-DAY TURKEY)

NO WORDS

*They sat with him on the ground seven days and
seven nights, and no one spoke a word to him, for
they saw that his suffering was very great.*

JOB 2:13

Anastasius came across people in trouble all the time. He met families who had lost children and husbands who had lost their wives. In his role as a priest and a bishop, Anastasius met with families whose loved ones had died. Some priests made the mistake of talking too much during these difficult times, but not Anastasius. Instead of trying to make people feel better by saying exactly the right thing, Anastasius simply sat with them while they were suffering. Anastasius knew that sometimes the very best thing to say was nothing at all. Just being with someone showed them how much God loved them.

SAINT ANASTASIUS I OF ANTIOCH DEFENDED THE CHRISTIAN FAITH AGAINST FALSE TEACHINGS, EVEN WHEN IT MEANT THE EMPEROR EXILED HIM.

*Jesus, help me know when to speak and when
to stay silent. I want to comfort my friends
and family when they are in trouble.*

SAINT HILDEGARD OF BINGEN

1098–1179 • HOLY ROMAN EMPIRE (MODERN-DAY GERMANY)

THE MYSTERIES OF GOD

For as the heavens are higher than the earth, so are my ways higher than your ways and my thoughts than your thoughts.

ISAIAH 55:9

Even as a little girl, Hildegard would sit and think about all the mysteries of God. She would wonder how He created the universe, and she would ponder the many ways He loved all people. She even believed that she received visions from God, which were lifelike dreams that told her more about all of His wonderful works and ways. The visions were powerful, and they gave her plenty to contemplate. Hildegard, in humility, didn't tell everyone about what she had seen. After talking with others who loved God, she wrote about the visions in a book, which is still read around the world. Her book helped others think about the mysteries of God and the perfect redemption He offers to all.

> SAINT HILDEGARD OF BINGEN LOVED READING, WRITING, AND LANGUAGE. SHE EVEN CAME UP WITH HER OWN LANGUAGE AS A KIND OF GAME.

Jesus, Your thoughts are higher than my thoughts. Teach me more about Your wonderful works.

SAINT DAVID THE KING

1040 BC–970 BC · ANCIENT ISRAEL

FROM BETHLEHEM

*Has not the scripture said that the Messiah is descended from
David and comes from Bethlehem, the village where David lived?*

JOHN 7:42

Jesus' disciples knew that He was the Messiah, the Son of God and the Savior of the world. After Jesus returned to heaven, many people refused to believe His disciples. The Messiah was supposed to be a great king, like King David, who lived about a thousand years before Jesus. King David lived in the small town where Jesus was born, and people overlooked him because he was the youngest in his family. But David believed in God, and God delivered giants into his hands. David once shouted at the giant named Goliath, "This very day the LORD will deliver you into my hand" (1 Samuel 17:46). David defeated that giant. Centuries later, David's descendant, Jesus, would defeat all the dark powers in the world.

> MANY OF THE PSALMS IN THE BOOK OF PSALMS WERE WRITTEN AND SUNG BY SAINT DAVID THE KING.

*Jesus, no matter who we are or where we come
from, we can do great things for You.*

SAINT EDMUND CAMPION

1540–1581 · ENGLAND AND IRELAND

THE WHOLE WORLD

*"For what will it profit them to gain the
whole world and forfeit their life?"*

MARK 8:36

Audiences hung on every word Edmund spoke. Even the queen respected Edmund. But the people who once respected him and loved his speeches turned on him when he sided with a different Church tradition. The Church in England and the Church in Rome had serious disagreements with one another, and Edmund decided to side with the Church in Rome. Then English soldiers captured him and paraded him through the streets, tying his feet and hands together and forcing him to ride backward. When he was condemned to die, people made fun of him and mocked him, even trying to get him to insult the queen, who had turned against him too. But Edmund declared that he was praying for her. Even at the end, Edmund still wanted the best for his enemies.

WHEN HE WAS YOUNG, SAINT EDMUND CAMPION WAS PRAISED FOR HIS GOOD LOOKS AND GREAT WIT.

*Jesus, I want to care more about following You
than about gaining praise from the world.*

SAINT DOMINIC OF SILOS

1000–1073 • SPAIN

LIFTED UP

*He has brought down the powerful from their
thrones, and lifted up the lowly.*

LUKE 1:52

Dominic's family wasn't wealthy or powerful. They didn't own large amounts of land, and they didn't have connections to the king. Dominic became a monk, which was a path taken by men who were rich and poor alike. But a king disagreed with the way that Dominic and some of the other monks were using their land, and he sent Dominic and a few other monks away, to a much worse plot of land. The king thought it was a fitting punishment—they wouldn't be able to do anything with it! But the monks took the little piece of land and thanked God for it. God blessed them, and the land became a famous monastery in Spain.

WHEN HE WAS A BOY, SAINT DOMINIC OF SILOS LOVED TO BE ALONE IN NATURE.

*Jesus, You bring down the powerful and lift up the
lowly. Help me find ways to lift up others too.*

DECEMBER 21

SAINT PETER CANISIUS

1521–1597 · GERMANY

ALL THINGS ARE POSSIBLE

Jesus looked at them and said, "For mortals it is impossible, but for God all things are possible."

MATTHEW 19:26

P eter ran up against the impossible on a regular basis. He was ordered to transport priceless documents called the Tridentine Tomes from Rome to Germany. Each document was more than two hundred pages long, and many people in Germany wanted to stop him and steal them. Peter was like a secret agent. He took the documents through Germany in a cart—it must have been difficult to hide those giant, encyclopedia-sized books in the cart, but Peter did it. He was respected in Germany, but he knew his good reputation wasn't enough to protect him. God protected him on his secret mission, and Peter delivered the documents to the right places.

SAINT PETER CANISIUS WROTE A BOOK FOR YOUNG CHILDREN THAT INCLUDED PRAYERS FOR MORNING, EVENING, AND MEALTIMES.

He was able to do this because he knew that anything that would have been impossible for him on his own was absolutely possible with the help of God.

Jesus, with You, anything is possible!

DECEMBER 22*

VENERABLE MARY ANGELINE TERESA MCCRORY

1893–1984 • FRANCE AND THE UNITED STATES

SPENT STRENGTH

Do not cast me off in the time of old age; do not
forsake me when my strength is spent.

PSALM 71:9

At the young age of nineteen, Angeline promised to spend her time serving the elderly poor. Angeline believed that Jesus cared deeply for them and that He had even crowned them with wisdom. She became a nun, and she lived with other women who had also promised to take care of older poor people who had no one else to care for them. She was soon sent to New York in the United States, where she saw that the elderly poor needed more care. Angeline brought the needs of the elderly to the attention of other believers. Because of her hard work, many people who would have been cast aside, or ignored, in their old age were instead shown the love of Christ.

> VENERABLE MARY ANGELINE TERESA MCCRORY WAS BORN IN IRELAND AND GREW UP IN SCOTLAND.

*Jesus, Venerable Mary Angeline Teresa McCrory
respected and loved the elderly. Help me do the same.*

**VENERABLE MARY ANGELINE TERESA MCCRORY
IS ON TRACK TO BECOME A SAINT.**

DECEMBER 23

SAINT JOHN OF KANTY

1390–1473 · POLAND

DENY YOURSELF

Then Jesus told his disciples, "If any want to become my followers,
let them deny themselves and take up their cross and follow me."

MATTHEW 16:24

John felt totally unprepared for his job as priest of the small church. He had spent several years learning and studying complicated books about God and the Scriptures. But the people at the small church didn't want a professor; they wanted a priest. From the blank stares he saw on the pews, John knew they didn't like him. John understood something important, though. Jesus always asked His followers to deny themselves, and He wasn't just talking about fasting. John knew that Jesus meant His followers needed to give up all kinds of comforts and desires, even the desire to be loved. Eventually the people grew fond of him as their priest, but John never put the desire to be liked over serving God.

> SAINT JOHN OF KANTY ALSO DENIED HIMSELF BY FASTING. HE NEVER ATE MEAT.

*Jesus, Saint John of Kanty didn't need other people
to love him to know that You loved him. Help me care
more about serving You than about being liked.*

SAINT NICHOLAS

FOURTH CENTURY • ROMAN EMPIRE (MODERN-DAY TURKEY)

GIFTS OF GRACE

Now I commend you to God and to the message of his
grace, a message that is able to build you up and to give
you the inheritance among all who are sanctified.

ACTS 20:32

Nicholas was the only child of his parents, and they had left him their wealth. Nicholas could have spent this inheritance any way he wanted, but he chose to spend it spreading the message of God's grace. Nicholas wanted to give the money away. He heard about a man living nearby who was too poor to provide for his three daughters. Nicholas brought the family three separate bags of gold, always taking care to hide himself so the family would not know it was him. He threw the gifts in through their window. When the family found them, they accepted the gifts gratefully.

THE STORY OF SAINT NICHOLAS AND HIS THREE GIFTS WAS TOLD AND RETOLD FOR CENTURIES. THE STORY BECAME PART OF THE INSPIRATION BEHIND THE TRADITION OF GIVING GIFTS AT CHRISTMAS.

*Jesus, Saint Nicholas used what You gave
him for good. Help me do the same.*

THE NATIVITY OF JESUS

FIRST CENTURY • GALILEE (MODERN-DAY ISRAEL)

IN THE MANGER

*So they went with haste and found Mary and
Joseph, and the child lying in the manger.*

LUKE 2:16

The shepherds left their flocks and ran to Bethlehem, the voices of the angels still ringing in their ears. They had never seen anything like it—heaven had opened before them, and an angel had shared the news that the Savior had been born! But why did the angel tell them? They weren't important! They weren't rich, and they weren't leaders. Yet they had witnessed a countless number of beautiful angels singing the praises of the King, who had just been born. The shepherds found the baby lying in a manger, just where the angels had said He would be. The shepherds beheld Him, the tiny King, the merciful Savior, the King who loved the entire world.

THIS STORY ABOUT THE SHEPHERDS HAS BEEN TOLD OVER AND OVER IN CHRISTMAS CAROLS LIKE "THE FIRST NOEL."

*Jesus, You want everyone to know about You.
Help me share the good news of Your birth.*

DECEMBER 26

SAINT STEPHEN

FIRST CENTURY · ROMAN EMPIRE (MODERN-DAY ISRAEL)

LOOK!

"Look," he said, "I see the heavens opened and the
Son of Man standing at the right hand of God!"

ACTS 7:56

"Look!" Stephen cried to the angry crowd. He pointed up toward the sky. The angry crowd didn't see anything, but Stephen saw Jesus. Stephen, who followed the leadership of the apostles after Jesus rose from the grave and ascended into heaven, had been chosen to serve the widows in the church. He had received the gift of the Holy Spirit and spoken about Jesus to large crowds often. But this time, his brave speech angered the crowd, who became violent. Right before the angry mob killed him for his faith, Stephen tried, one last time, to show them Jesus. As he died, he forgave his attackers, just like Jesus had.

SAINT PAUL (JAN. 24) WAS PART OF THE ANGRY CROWD THAT KILLED SAINT STEPHEN.

Jesus, Saint Stephen pointed toward You. Guide me as I help others really look at You and see You for who You are.

DECEMBER 27

SAINT JOHN THE APOSTLE

FIRST CENTURY • GALILEE (MODERN-DAY ISRAEL)

WHAT JESUS DID

There are also many other things that Jesus did; if every one of them were written down, I suppose that the world itself could not contain the books that would be written.

JOHN 21:25

John and his brother James started following Jesus as soon as He called them. They gave up their jobs as fishermen to "fish for people," as Jesus commanded (Matthew 4:19). John saw Jesus restore sight, multiply food, and raise the dead. John saw huge crowds follow Jesus and praise Him. John also saw the same crowds abandon Jesus when they didn't like what He said. John was the only disciple who saw Jesus die on the cross—all the others were too afraid to come. John loved Jesus, and he knew that Jesus loved him. He rejoiced with the other disciples when they saw Jesus had risen from the grave. After Jesus ascended into heaven, John wrote his own book about Jesus, His many miracles, and His amazing truths.

SAINT JOHN THE APOSTLE IS OFTEN REPRESENTED IN ART WITH AN EAGLE—THE SYMBOL ASSOCIATED WITH HIS GOSPEL.

Jesus, give me an opportunity to tell others about all the things You did.

SAINT ADELE

UNKNOWN–730 · GERMANY

PRESSING ON

I press on toward the goal for the prize of the
heavenly call of God in Christ Jesus.

PHILIPPIANS 3:14

Adele was born a German princess, the daughter of King Dagobert II. But she worked for God's kingdom, not just the kingdom of Germany. By the time she died, she had been a ruler, a wife, a mother, a nun, and an abbess—that is, a nun who was in charge of other nuns. Even though everything about her life kept changing, Adele kept following Christ. Whether she was taking care of her own child or a group of women dedicated to Christ, whether she was wearing royal robes or simple religious clothing, Jesus was her prize, and she kept moving toward Him.

SAINT ADELE WAS ONE OF THE DISCIPLES OF SAINT BONIFACE (JUNE 5).

*Jesus, for Saint Adele, You were the goal and
the prize. No matter what I do or who I become,
I want You to be my ultimate goal.*

DECEMBER 29*

BLESSED MARIE-CLÉMENTINE ANUARITE NENGAPETA

1939–1964 • DEMOCRATIC REPUBLIC OF THE CONGO

STEADFAST IN FAITH

Like a roaring lion your adversary the devil prowls around, looking
for someone to devour. Resist him, steadfast in your faith.

1 PETER 5:8–9

Anuarite resisted evil and remained steadfast in her faith, which means she chose to follow Jesus even when it was hard. She became a nun, even after she was once turned away for being too young. When terrible fighting broke out in her country, she and the other nuns were captured. A cruel colonel wanted to make Anuarite his wife, but she had already promised Jesus that she would never marry. Anuarite was killed for refusing to give up her faith, but as she died, she told her attackers that she forgave them. She believed in Jesus, loved her enemies, and remained true to her faith, even when it was dangerous.

TO CELEBRATE BLESSED MARIE-CLÉMENTINE ANUARITE NENGAPETA, PEOPLE COME TO AFRICA FROM ALL OVER THE WORLD TO SEE WHERE SHE WAS BURIED.

*Jesus, help me be steadfast even when
it is difficult and dangerous.*

**BLESSED MARIE-CLÉMENTINE ANUARITE NENGAPETA
IS ON TRACK TO BECOME A SAINT.**

DECEMBER 30

SAINT EGWIN

UNKNOWN–717 · ENGLAND

WATER FROM THE ROCK

"I will be standing there in front of you on the rock at Horeb.
Strike the rock, and water will come out of it, so that the people
may drink." Moses did so, in the sight of the elders of Israel.

EXODUS 17:6

A story about Saint Egwin tells that he traveled to Rome with some other pilgrims—that is, people who journeyed to see holy places. As they crossed a mountain range, they ran out of water. Egwin knew he had to do something, and he remembered the story from the Old Testament about Moses and the Israelites. God had given them water when they had none, and maybe He would do it again. Egwin struck a rock, just like Moses had, and water came out of it! The pilgrims drank gratefully and made the rest of their journey to Rome. God had provided everything they needed.

SAINT EGWIN WAS A NOBLEMAN. SOME MEMBERS OF HIS EXTENDED FAMILY WERE ENGLISH ROYALTY.

*Jesus, Saint Egwin asked You for what he needed.
I want to come to You with my needs too.*

DECEMBER 31

SAINT SYLVESTER I

UNKNOWN–335 • ROMAN EMPIRE (MODERN-DAY ITALY)

EVERLASTING AUTHORITY

For a child has been born for us, a son given to us; authority
rests upon his shoulders; and he is named Wonderful Counselor,
Mighty God, Everlasting Father, Prince of Peace.

ISAIAH 9:6

Powerful leaders have given answers to this question: Who is Jesus?
Some claimed that Jesus wasn't God's Son. Others said Jesus was a
criminal who never rose again after His death. But some
have called Jesus the Mighty God and Prince of Peace.
These leaders say that Jesus, the Son of God, has everlasting authority over the whole universe. Sylvester was
one of these leaders. During Sylvester's time as pope,
Emperor Constantine became a Christian. This was

AS THE
LEGEND
GOES, SAINT
SYLVESTER I
BAPTIZED
EMPEROR
CONSTANTINE.

important because Roman emperors had been killing Christians for a
long time. Christians had persevered in their faith, believing in Jesus
even though it was dangerous. Sylvester knew the truth and proclaimed
it to the world—Jesus is God, and He is more powerful than any ruler
on earth.

Jesus, You are the King of everything—
of the whole universe and all history.

SOURCES

aleteia.org

americamagazine.org

americaneedsfatima.org

angelusnews.com

archokc.org

ascensionpress.com

atonementfriars.org

beliefnet.com

biblegateway.com

biblehub.com

biography.com

biographyonline.net

britannica.com

brownpelicanla.com

cabriniworld.org

camilliani.org

capuchin.org

cardinaljohnhenrynewman
.com

carmelitesisters.org

catholic.edu

catholic.org

catholicculture.org

catholicdigest.com

catholicexchange.com

catholicinsight.com

catholicism.org

catholicnewsagency.com

catholicreadings.org

catholicsaints.info

catholicworldreport.com

christdesert.org

christianitytoday.com

cny.org

communio.stblogs.org

compellingtruth.org

dbpedia.org

donboscowest.org

ducksters.com

fatima.org

Flinders, Carol Lee.
    Enduring Grace. New
    York: HarperCollins,
    1993.

franciscanmedia.org

giveninstitute.com

goarch.org

henriettedelille.com

Hoever, Hugo. *Lives of
    the Saints.* Totowa,
    NJ: Catholic Book
    Publishing Corp, 1993.

ignatianspirituality.com

imagochrististudio.org

jesuits.global

juliagreeley.org

kofpc.org

kwomenonthespot.org

learnreligions.com

littleflower.org

littlesistersofthepoor.org

liturgies.net

loyolapress.com

miguelpro.org

mosestheblack.org

motherlange.org

motherteresa.org

mysticsofthechurch.com

nationalshrine.org

nbccongress.org

ncregister.com

newadvent.org

newworldencyclopedia.org

nobility.org

notablebiographies.com

osvnews.com

padrepiodapietrelcina.com

patheos.com

popehistory.com

roman-catholic-saints.com

saintagnes.org

sainthenrys.org

saintpaulofthecross.com

saintritashrine.org

sanctoral.com

sdow.org

secularfranciscansusa.org

seelos.org

self.gutenberg.org

sistertheabowman.com

smarthistory.org

solanuscenter.org

spiritanroma.org

spsmw.org

srcharitycinti.org

stapostle.org

stjeromeonline.org

stjohnneumann.org

stjosemaria.org

stlouiskingoffrance.org

stmarguerite.org

svfonline.org

the-american-catholic.com

thedivinemercy.org

traditioninaction.org

ugchristiannews.com

universalis.com

vaticannews.va

womenshistory.org

A Saint a Day

© 2021 Thomas Nelson

Tommy Nelson, PO Box 141000, Nashville, TN 37214

Published in Nashville, Tennessee, by Tommy Nelson. Tommy Nelson is an imprint of Thomas Nelson. Thomas Nelson is a registered trademark of HarperCollins Christian Publishing, Inc.

Tommy Nelson titles may be purchased in bulk for educational, business, fundraising, or sales promotional use. For information, please email SpecialMarkets@ThomasNelson.com.

Scripture quotations are taken from the New Revised Standard Version Bible. Copyright © 1989 National Council of the Churches of Christ in the United States of America. Used by permission. All rights reserved worldwide.

ISBN 978-1-4002-2856-0 (audiobook)
ISBN 978-1-4002-2855-3 (eBook)
ISBN 978-1-4002-2853-9 (HC)

Library of Congress Cataloging-in-Publication Data

Names: Hinds, Meredith, author. | Muñoz, Isabel, 1951- illustrator.
Title: A Saint a day : 365 true stories of faith and heroism / Meredith Hinds ; illustrated by Isabel Munoz.
Description: Nashville, Tennessee, USA : Thomas Nelson, [2021] | Includes bibliographical references. | Audience: Ages 8-12 | Summary: "Inspiring a child's faith with true stories of heroism and faithfully following God, A Saint A Day is an engaging daily devotional for kids ages 8 to 12 that shares some of the most significant and entertaining stories of the saints"-- Provided by publisher.
Identifiers: LCCN 2021019721 (print) | LCCN 2021019722 (ebook) | ISBN 9781400228539 (h/c) | ISBN 9781400228553 (ebook) | ISBN 9781400228560 (audiobook)
Subjects: LCSH: Christian saints--Biography--Juvenile literature. | Devotional calendars--Juvenile literature. | BISAC: JUVENILE NONFICTION / Religious / Christian / Devotional & Prayer | RELIGION / Christianity / Catholic
Classification: LCC BX4658 .H56 2021 (print) | LCC BX4658 (ebook) | DDC 242/.62--dc23
LC record available at https://lccn.loc.gov/2021019721
LC ebook record available at https://lccn.loc.gov/2021019722

Written by Meredith Hinds
Illustrated by Isabel Muñoz

Printed in Bosnia and Herzegovina

24 GPS 4

Mfr: GPS / BIH / February 2024 / PO # 12250257